GANDHI

A MEMOIR

William L. Shirer

Simon and Schuster
New York

Copyright © 1979 by William L. Shirer
All rights reserved
including the right of reproduction
in whole or in part in any form
Published by Simon and Schuster
A Division of Gulf & Western Corporation
Simon & Schuster Building
Rockefeller Center
1230 Avenue of the Americas
New York, New York 10020

Designed by Stanley S. Drate
Manufactured in the United States of America

1 2 3 4 5 6 7 8 9 10

Library of Congress Cataloging in Publication Data

Shirer, William Lawrence, 1904-
Gandhi, a memoir.

Includes index.
1. Gandhi, Mohandas Karamchand, 1869-1948.
2. Shirer, William Lawrence, 1904- 3. Statesmen—
India—Biography. 4. Journalists—United States—
Biography. I. Title.
DS481.G3S487   954.03'5'0924 [B]   79-17359
ISBN:978-1-4516-9605-9

To Mary

". . . Which can say more
Than this rich praise, that you alone are you?"

Generations to come, it may be, will scarce believe that such a one as this ever in flesh and blood walked upon this earth.

—EINSTEIN on Gandhi.

Mahatma Gandhi will go down in history on a par with Buddha and Jesus Christ.

—VISCOUNT LOUIS MOUNTBATTEN,
THE LAST BRITISH VICEROY OF INDIA.

We did not conquer India for the benefit of the Indians. We conquered India as the outlet for the goods of Great Britain. We conquered India by the sword, and by the sword we should hold it.

—LORD BRENTFORD, 1930.

Introduction

"Generations to come, it may be," Einstein once wrote of Gandhi, in words which stand at the head of this book, "will scarce believe that such a one as this ever in flesh and blood walked upon this earth."

I watched this man, a saintly, Christlike figure, walk upon this earth, in flesh and blood, at a moment when he had launched his great civil-disobedience movement that began to undermine the British hold on India and that, in the end, freed his country from two and a half centuries of British rule. It was one of the great accomplishments of history and for him a personal triumph such as our world has seldom seen.

But there were, in a deeper sense, even greater triumphs for this unique man who was unlike any great individual of our time, and perhaps of any time. He liberated India from a foreign yoke, but he also liberated the whole world from some of its encrusted prejudices and foolish ways of life. He was one of history's great teachers, not only by the example of his life but by what he preached and practiced. As such, he was, as Viscount Louis Mountbatten, the last British Viceroy of India, said of him on his martyred death, akin to Buddha and to Christ.

In a harsh, cynical, violent and materialist world he taught and showed that love and truth and non-violence, ideas and ideals, could be of tremendous force—greater sometimes than guns and bombs and bayonets—in achieving a little justice, decency, peace and freedom for the vast masses of suffering, downtrodden men and women who eke out an existence on this inhospitable planet.

Albert Szent-Györgyi, a Nobel laureate in medicine, took note of this in a jolting book, *The Crazy Ape*:

> Between the two world wars, at the heyday of Colonialism, force reigned supreme. It had a suggestive power, and it was natural for the weaker to lie down before the stronger.
>
> Then came Gandhi, chasing out of his country, almost single-handed, the greatest military power on earth. He taught the world that there are higher things than force, higher even than life itself; he proved that force had lost its suggestive power.

Gandhi, being a human being, was far from perfect, and was the first to admit it, publicly. Like all the great achievers in history, he was a man of many paradoxes and contradictions. He had his fads, peculiarities and prejudices, and some of them, when I observed them or listened to him explain and defend them, struck me as outlandish. I have not hesitated in this memoir, despite my immense admiration for him that at times bordered on adoration, to point them out.

Like other men, he quarreled with his wife, whom he had married when both were thirteen, and he was for a time a trial to her—we have his own word for it. I saw quite a bit of her in my time in India and liked and admired her. She was illiterate, lost in the world her dynamic husband was shaking, but she had her strengths.

The Mahatma was genuinely the humblest of men (though he was not unaware of his greatness), but I have seen him behave stubbornly and dictatorially to his co-workers, making what I felt were outrageous demands on some of them, as when he insisted that even those who were married, and happily, observe the celibacy he had imposed on himself in his late thirties after many years of what he called a lustful relationship with his own wife. But even after that act of self-discipline he could be, as Jawaharlal Nehru, his chief disciple and his successor, observed with puzzlement, obsessed with sex. In the evening of his long life, at the very moment of his crowning political triumph, though a dark one in his personal life, Gandhi shocked and offended many by his inexplicable practices with beautiful young Hindu women, which seemed to those who knew and loved and worshipped him contrary to all he had stood for and preached.

But against these human frailties there stood out the man of infinite goodness, a seeker all his life of Truth, which he equated with God, a pilgrim who believed that love was the greatest gift of man and that love and understanding and tolerance and compassion and non-violence, if they were only practiced, would liberate mankind from much of the burden, oppression and evil of life.

This was not to be, in his own country or in any other, and probably, given the cussedness of the human race, it will never be. But Gandhi gave his life and his genius to try to make it so, or at least more so than it had ever been—he was too wise to have many illusions but his hope was boundless.

To observe at first hand that mighty effort, to rub up against, if ever so briefly, the towering greatness, the goodness, the high spirits and humor, the humility, the subtlety of mind, the integrity and purity of purpose, and that indefinable thing, the genius, of this man was the greatest stroke of fortune that ever befell me.

I have tried in these pages to give a feeling of what it was like, and to indicate its impact on me, an ignorant young American foreign correspondent at the time. The mark it left on me has lasted to this day, through the subsequent half century of my life and work, helping me to bear the ups and downs of existence, to survive the strains of all the brutal man-made upheavals and the barbarism and the hypocrisy we have lived through in our time, and providing a certain light that helped to guide me toward an understanding, however incomplete, of the meaning of our brief sojourn on this perplexing planet.

The Indian revolution, like its leader, also was unique, the first non-violent revolution, I believe, in history, or at least the first that succeeded. It was Gandhi's genius that made it, led it, and saw it through, after incredible setbacks, to its moment of triumph. He never doubted its end nor, as he often insisted to me in some of the darkest moments, that it would come while he still lived. It was a difficult revolution to understand, even for Indians and especially for one like me who came to India loaded down with all the foolish prejudices and myths of the West, which had been dominated so long by force and violence. (So astute a statesman as Winston Churchill never faintly grasped it.) But I did my best to try to understand it, and perhaps a little light on it emerges from this memoir of the man who made it and won it, and who left so indelible an imprint on this world.

1

Mahatma Gandhi was out of jail again, and as soon as my ship docked at Bombay that February of 1931 I caught the Frontier Mail up to Delhi to see him.

There were reports that his negotiations with the Viceroy to call off the massive civil-disobedience movement in return for a British promise to begin serious talks about self-rule for India were breaking down. I was anxious to meet him before the British put him once more behind bars.

All through my first tour of duty in India during the hot, sultry summer, the autumn and early winter of 1930 the year before, Gandhi had been in Yeravda prison, held incommunicado, and I had been unable to see him. It had been a frustrating assignment. With his arrest and that of all the other leaders of the Indian National Congress, and of tens of thousands of his most active followers throughout the country, the momentum of his latest rebellion against British rule, which he had launched that spring, had slackened.

I had arrived in time to see some of it. Even with the prisons full to bursting there were still followers of his who gathered in the great cities to peacefully picket and demonstrate. I had watched them, men and women by the thousands, squatting on the pavement in Bombay, Calcutta, Delhi, Lahore and other places waiting for the inevitable lathi charge of British-led police or troops when they refused to disperse, and had seen them savagely beaten and then carted off to jail. It was a sickening sight, but I had marveled at their magnificent discipline of non-violence, which the genius of Gandhi had taught them. They had not struck back; they had not even defended themselves except to try to shield their faces and heads from the lathi blows.

At Peshawar, whose Moslems had not been converted to Gandhi's non-violence, the resistance had been different. Guns had gone off—on both sides. At one point, shortly before my arrival there, the wild Afridi and Pathan tribesmen had forcibly occupied most of this capital of the North-West Frontier and sprayed bullets into the British cantonment just outside the city. The front wall of my room in the rest house there was pockmarked with bullet holes.

But by early winter the British seemed to have just about put down the rebellion by force, though their ruthlessness, even toward the women agitators, thousands of whom had been brutally beaten and jailed, had left India seething with resentment from one end to the other. You could feel the tension in the fetid air of the bazaars, on the aroused campuses of the universities, in the stinking tenements of Bombay and Calcutta, in the littered streets everywhere, and wherever else Indians congregated.

What would Gandhi do now? I wondered. I needed to talk to him. Not only to learn something of how he would shape the tactics and the strategy of his strange revolution from now on, but also because he was, of all the world figures, the one I most wanted to get to know.

For years, ever since I had read of his first imprisonment in India in 1922 and had been overwhelmed by the eloquence of his words in his own defense at that famous trial, and then more recently read his autobiography and followed as best I could in the Western press his efforts to free India, I had had a feeling that perhaps he was the greatest living man on our planet.

Our time had never seen anyone like him: a charismatic leader who had aroused a whole continent and indeed the consciousness of the world; a shrewd, tough politician, but also a deeply religious man, a Christlike figure in a homespun loincloth, who lived humbly in poverty, practiced what he preached and who was regarded by tens of millions of his people as a saint. They had insisted, despite his protests, on calling him Mahatma, which meant Great Soul. They had got from him something so baffling to the Western mind and temperament—*darshan,* a sort of collective glow of suprapersonal happiness and assurance that comes from being in the presence of a manifestation of their collective consciousness. Gandhi had not liked that either. ". . . I was the victim of their craze for *darshan,"* he said. ". . . *the darshanvalas'* blind love has often made me angry, and more often sore at heart."* It also, he complained, impeded his work.

For ten years he had been leading the strangest revolution the world had ever seen. He had been trying to drive the British out of India and win independence for his country by a highly organized and disciplined campaign of non-violent civil disobedience. To British guns, bayonets and lathi sticks, he was opposing peaceful, unarmed, passive resistance. It was not the way we in the late 1770's had begun to drive the British out and win our own national freedom. We had opposed British violence with violence, used our guns against theirs, and it had worked.

I had not understood at first how you could wage a revolution any other way. What Gandhi was trying to do had not made much sense in the West, where violence was second nature to us and had dominated most of our history. He had tried at the outset to explain it—to his own people and to the world. "The British," he said, "want us to put the struggle on the plane of machine guns

*Mohandas K. Gandhi: *An Autobiography: The Story of My Experiments With Truth* (Boston: Beacon Press, 1957), p. 389.

where they have the weapons and we do not. Our only assurance of beating them is putting the struggle on a plane where we have the weapons and they have not." His logic was impeccable. This was the only strategy left to the unarmed Indians, but in the beginning, few in India or abroad understood this.

It was against that background that I had flown out to India from Vienna in August of 1930 to report for the *Chicago Tribune* on Gandhi's peculiar revolution. In the spring that year, by a symbolic act whose significance I myself did not grasp, a march through the stifling heat to the sea with a little band of followers to make illegal salt, Gandhi had aroused the Indian people from the lethargy into which they had long sunk after nearly three centuries of British rule, if you counted the incredible period when they were governed for two hundred years not by a foreign country but by a bizarre band of traders greedy for profit, the honorable members and agents of the East India Company. These hustlers had first come out from England early in the seventeenth century, found the pickings beyond their fondest dreams, and, by hook and by crook and by armed might, had stolen the country from the Indians.

It was the only instance in history, I believe, of a private commercial enterprise taking over a vast, heavily populated subcontinent, ruling it with an iron hand and exploiting it for private profit. Probably only the British, with their odd assortment of talents, their great entrepreneurial drive, their ingrained feeling of racial superiority, of which Rudyard Kipling would sing so shrilly, their guile in dividing the natives and turning them against one another, and their ruthlessness in putting down all who threatened their rule and their profits, could have done it, and got away with it for so long.

Perhaps only the Indians, divided as they were after the decay of the Mogul Empire into dozens of quarreling, warring states, great and small, could have succumbed so easily and so quickly to the aggression of a handful of determined merchants, backed by a small band of British troops in the service of the Company, and remained so long in abject subjection. As Radhakrishnan, the great Hindu philosopher, put it in our own time: "The day India lost her freedom a great curse fell on her and she became petrified."

Occasionally the Indians had risen in armed revolt against their white conquerors and there was savagery on both sides. "As early indeed as 1764," the *Encyclopaedia Britannica* ventures to inform us in a section on the history of India written with a typical British bias, "it had been necessary to quell mutiny by the usual oriental *{sic}* punishment of blowing away the offenders from the guns, when 30 sepoys were so disposed of"—a spectacle I myself would witness in Kabul, where the Afghan executioners, about to dispatch a wretched rebel from the mouth of a cannon, would explain that there was nothing "oriental" about it; they had learned the trick, they said, from the British during the Afghan wars.

Every British schoolboy knew the story of the Black Hole of Calcutta and believed it to be an example of Indian cruelty, though the Indians saw it somewhat differently. In 1756 an Indian nawab had captured the English trading settlement of Calcutta, imprisoning 146 Englishmen in their own military prison, which measured eighteen by fifteen feet. The heat was sweltering and the next day only 23 prisoners emerged alive; the rest had suffocated. How many Indian prisoners had died previously in that hole is not known. By this time the English were writing the history of India.

There had to be a turning point. In the changing world of the mid-nineteenth century the rule by a trading company of a continent of a quarter of a billion people, possessed as they were of a rich culture much older than that of their conquerors, and deeply influenced by two great religions, Hinduism and Mohammedanism, was an anachronism. It could not last much longer.

The explosion that did away with it came in 1857 when the sepoys of the Bengal Native Army, commanded by British officers, revolted and set off a rebellion that spread through most of northern and central India. The slaughter on both sides in the suffocating heat of an Indian summer was terrible; no quarter was given. In the end the Company's British troops put it down.

But it was a close thing. There were moments that long, hot

summer during a score of crucial battles when it seemed that the East India Company, with all its British officials, officers and troops, would be thrown out of the country and India restored to the Indians. In London the government concluded that a trading company was no longer fit to rule over so vast a territory with such a large slice of the human race. On August 12, 1858, the thirty-nine-year-old Queen Victoria signed an Act transferring the Indian subcontinent from the hands of the Company to the Royal Crown. Some 258 years had passed since another English queen, Elizabeth, had granted on December 31, 1599, a charter to the East India Company to open up trade with the East Indies. At that time the British had been mainly concerned with breaking the Dutch monopoly on pepper and other spices from the Indies and reducing the price—from such a trivial matter had come the conquest of a rich continent. The span of two and a half centuries of the Company's occupation, rule and exploitation of India constitutes one of the oddest chapters in history. For the Indians it was, as Radhakrishnan said, a curse, though the British, with that insensitivity common to all imperialists, never seemed to be aware of this.

Queen Victoria was crowned Empress of India, which became a British colony, the jewel of the Empire, its largest, most populous, most profitable imperial holding.

There now began for India another episode in its experience of British domination, the Victorian era, celebrated by the Indian-born jingoistic poet and storyteller Rudyard Kipling, from whom the West, principally England but also to a large extent America, got its British-biased, colorful but superficial view of India. To Kipling and to his immense following, the English were the Master Race, destined to rule over the "lesser breeds." The governing of hundreds of millions of Indians, Kipling was sure, had been "placed by the inscrutable design of providence upon the shoulders of the British race." And though Kipling knew India well, he, like his fellow countrymen who spent their lives in the service of the

Crown there, seemed to be unaware that the "lesser breeds" were still living in a civilization not only more ancient but in many ways much richer and maturer than his own. There is no hint in his prolific writings of the deep Hindu religious and philosophical consciousness that had knit the vast majority of Indians together for more than two millenniums through all the foreign conquests and preserved one of the great heritages of the human race.

Still, as Radhakrishnan had said, and as Gandhi would reiterate to me after I came to know him, British rule, especially beginning with the Victorian era when the Empire reached its zenith, left India petrified, its people without hope that they would ever regain their freedom. In my first few months in India many of the older generation had given me an inkling of the despair they had felt as they began to grow up under the British yoke. Some, like Gandhi, had gone to England for their university and professional education, learned English and English ways and conceptions, absorbed the Englishman's passion for political freedom, and returned to their native land only to be considered by the English little better than outcasts, made aware constantly of their inferior status by the white sahibs.

Indeed they told me that around the turn of the century, when the British had consolidated their hold on the country, built roads, railroads and telegraph lines to knit the huge country together, and make it more profitable and easier to govern, the imperial mastery of the subcontinent had seemed so complete that they reluctantly were forced to conclude that the white foreigner would rule them forever. He would milk them to the last rupee and emasculate them as human beings by depriving them of any say in the way their country was run, or even in the way their own lives could develop.

So far as I could see, the Englishmen who governed India were completely insensate to the fact that they were masters in someone else's country, were unwanted and unloved there, and that their very presence, their arbitrary rule, their condescending attitude toward an ancient and highly civilized people whom they regarded as racially, socially, culturally and even intellectually inferior and not fit to govern themselves, was a constant humiliation to the Indian people.

The necessity for an Indian to bow and scrape to the white sahib if he wanted to get ahead, or even to decently survive, was a ceaseless mortification. The activities of the legion of Christian missionaries was another. I did not realize until I got to India the depth of the resentment of Hindus and Moslems to the zealous endeavors of these good people to convert the "heathen" to Christ. Even Gandhi, the most tolerant of men toward all religions and who often would tell me of how much he had found in the New Testament that was uplifting (he took a grim view of the Old), expressed unusual resentment at the proselytizing of the Christian missionaries in his hometown as he grew up. A devout but liberal-minded Hindu, he found it insulting to his religion and to him.

Until Gandhi's appearance on the scene, it had been easy enough for the British to lord it over the Indians. Since the end of the Company's reign, they had ruled a quarter of a billion people with a handful of Englishmen: some 2,000 members of the Indian Civil Service and 10,000 officers and 60,000 regular troops who kept the 200,000 "native" soldiers of the Indian Army in line and often used them to keep down their fellow countrymen.

Over all was the Viceroy, with the power of an absolute monarch, with no responsibility at all to the Indian people and subject only to the British government in London. There were, of course, thousands of English, and especially Scottish, traders, shopkeepers, lawyers and doctors, journalists who manned the dozen or so major English-language newspapers (English was the official language of the country, though only a small minority of Indians understood it), clergymen and missionaries.

The Hindus had their rigid caste system, but so did the British. The English "in trade" were scarcely accepted socially by British officials and Army officers. Indeed they were snubbed by them, but at least they had the satisfaction of being regarded as a cut above the "natives," even the highest of the Brahmans. The British did not mix socially with those they governed, no matter how highly cultivated the latter might be. This was taboo. A few days after arriving in Bombay, a high official who took me to lunch at the Bombay Yacht Club boasted as we were leaving that no Indian had ever crossed its portal. And once when I invited a distinguished Moslem couple and their daughter, one of the first woman students (and possibly the first Moslem woman) to be enrolled in the Medical College to study medicine, to dinner with me at the Taj Mahal Hotel, where I was staying, and afterward danced with the young lady, who I thought looked very beautiful in her crimson sari, I was set upon the next day by some English acquaintances who told me "it was never done" and that I must mend my ways.

This I had no intention of doing. I had come out to cover the struggle of the Indians for independence. It would be necessary, of course, for a correspondent to get to know the British officials, who, in line with their government at home, were determined to deny the Indians their political freedom. What was in their minds and hearts? Why were they and their government in London so set against the Indians obtaining what they themselves, what every Englishman, would die to preserve—the right to govern themselves.

But more important for me was to penetrate, if I could, the Indian mind and soul—of the Moslem minority as well as the Hindu majority, between whom there was a hatred and gulf of misunderstanding of a magnitude and ugliness that only quarreling religions can generate. Europe had seen that in the devastating Hundred Years' War between fanatical Catholics and Protestants, and Northern Ireland would experience it in our own time, though in these senseless, bloody wars both sides were Christian.

That the British, with their cunning policy of divide and rule, had often encouraged Hindu-Moslem animosity and sometimes fomented it was no excuse for the Indians to give in to it. But they had. It was one of the problems that Gandhi, I knew, had been striving to solve all his life. As long as Hindus and Moslems were at one another's throats there was no hope of uniting the two religious groups in the struggle for independence. Gandhi at first did have some success. He had brought prominent Moslems into the Indian National Congress and maneuvered them even into the presidency of it, but there had been many failures and they would pile up as the years of revolt went by. This would be his greatest frustration, except for one: the determination of the British to hold on to India. It was against this that he now was devoting most of his considerable energies, his subtle political mind and his genius.

The story of how Mahatma Gandhi had reached this point in history has been told in many books, and best of all by himself in his autobiography* and in his prolific writings in his weekly publication, *Young India.*

I had mulled over it for ten days on the boat coming out from Trieste and now, before meeting Gandhi for the first time, I tried to review it briefly in my mind on the train going up to Delhi. But it was too vast a subject, terribly complicated, interwoven with many strands of history, Indian and British, affected by the accidents of life and thought and personality and their impact on men, masses and human development, affected too by the clash of two widely different cultures, European and Asian, and I could not get it very straight. It would be best to see Gandhi first, to try to grasp the nature of his genius and its tremendous hold on the Indian masses, to get from the master himself an understanding of his unique contribution to the revolutionary politics of the twentieth century, *Satyagraha,* a word he had coined from his native Gujarati and which, I suspected, meant much more, at least in the Hindu consciousness, than civil disobedience, passive resistance, non-cooperation and non-violence, though it encompassed all of these. It seemed to me, from the experience in India I had gained the previous year, that it had to do also with something

---

*Gandhi, op. cit. The book takes him only to 1921, but his numerous articles in his weekly magazine—he usually filled more than half the space himself, for he was a superb journalist—kept the account of himself and his strivings up to date.

more subtle—and fundamental: the search for truth, for the essence of the spirit, for some way of decency in human intercourse, and—all in all—offering to man something very new, something that so far had eluded him, a moral and indeed a practical alternative to oppression, violence, war. Perhaps Gandhi would tell me if I had understood *Satyagraha* rightly, since he had invented it and had over the years welded it into an instrument of considerable power as well as a guide to revolutionary action.

Perhaps I could get from him too some idea of what he thought lay ahead in his struggle to overthrow British rule, and by what means he thought the British, who still had all the guns, all the police power and all the crammed prisons, would oppose it.

One thing seemed fairly certain to me, from what I had seen and felt of the Indian revolution in the past months: Gandhi and India and the British had converged at a crossroads of their destinies. Such conjunctions happened rarely in history and then only at the crucial moments when the future of nations and peoples was decided. At this one, the fate of 350 million Indians and of the British Empire was at stake.

The outcome rested largely on the bony shoulders of one frail little Hindu, whom the unpredictable forces of time and circumstance had placed in the unique position where his genius might determine the course of Anglo-Indian history. The world had seen examples of the immense impact of one solitary figure on great events. In our own time in Europe there had been Lenin, and there would shortly be Hitler. Like Gandhi they appeared at the propitious moment when only they had the mind and the character, the imagination and the understanding, to shape deep historical currents to their own ends and to those of the masses that followed them. Without Lenin and Hitler the Bolshevik and the Nazi revolutions most probably would not have succeeded. Without Gandhi there would have been no serious threat to British rule as the 1930's began. In India I began to see that Gandhi, as Friedrich Meinecke would say of Hitler, was already one of the examples of the singular and incalculable power of the personality in historical life. In India it was the only such personality there was.

In Delhi, when I arrived, Gandhi and Lord Irwin, the devoutly Christian Viceroy, were negotiating daily and sometimes far into the night over the terms by which the civil-disobedience movement might be called off in return for the release from prison of fifty thousand Indian nationalists and a British promise at last, after so many years of stalling, to negotiate seriously about giving back India to the Indians. Busy as he was, Gandhi agreed to see me immediately. It was the first instance in his case, but far from the last, of this special capacity I have found in many great men: no matter how preoccupied by matters of the utmost importance, they somehow contrive to find time for less pressing business with the likes of me.

I did not know then—I found out only later—that Gandhi, who was a shrewd appraiser of the means and the value of getting his message out to the world, attached more importance to my dispatches than I realized. I was the only American sent out by an American newspaper to cover his struggle on the scene. My daily cables, which cost nearly a dollar a word to transmit, were published not only in the *Chicago Tribune* but in scores of other major newspapers in the United States which subscribed to our syndicated news service. They were giving the American people for the first time, I believe, an unbiased account (not only the British but the Indian side) of the Indian revolution.

The Paris edition of the *Tribune,* which also published my cables daily, was giving Europe a similar picture, for none of the journals on the Continent had correspondents of their own in India, and many, especially in Paris, lifted my pieces at will. Even the august *New York Times* had no correspondent of its own in India. It depended on the dispatches of *The Times* of London man in Delhi, an able, hard-drinking English journalist, who labored daily to put across an exclusive British view, the only one he understood.

2

It happened the day before my twenty-seventh birthday, on February 22, 1931.

Gandhi sent word he would see me an hour before his daily prayer meeting and invited me to stay on for prayers if I felt inclined. This was a birthday present I much appreciated. When I arrived at the home of Dr. Mukhtar Ahmad Ansari, an eminent physician and a Moslem, which overlooked the river Jumna, a sluggish stream sacred to the Hindus, Gandhi was squatting on the floor in the corner of the verandah, spinning. He greeted me warmly, with a smile that lit up his face and made his lively eyes twinkle. The welcome was so disarming, his manner so friendly and radiant, that my nervousness evaporated before I could say a word. He turned to a tall, pale, white-skinned woman, whose sari, pulled partly back from above her gaunt eyes, revealed a shaved head, and asked her to bring up a chair for me. This woman must be, I conjectured, Mirabai, the former Madeleine Slade, who had shocked her parents, Admiral Sir Edmund Slade and Lady Slade, by forsaking London society to join Gandhi's ashram, taking the vows of chastity and poverty, and throwing herself into the struggle for Indian independence. I sensed at once a strong empathy between Gandhi and her—there will be more to say about this. Kasturbai, Mrs. Gandhi, sat nearby. She had a rather wizened face, but one could see that she must have been a spirited and attractive woman in her younger days. Her large, round eyes were very bright.

"Please don't bother," I said as Miss Slade started to pull up a chair. "I would prefer to sit on the floor."

"If you like," Gandhi said as I squatted down. There was almost an impish humor in his eyes as he watched me awkwardly sinking to the floor. "But if it becomes uncomfortable, please tell me."

As our talk began I tried to take in not only what Gandhi was saying but how he looked. I had seen many photographs of him but I was nevertheless somewhat surprised at his actual appearance. His face at first glance did not convey at all the stature of the man, his obvious greatness. It was not one you would have especially noticed in a crowd. It struck me as not ugly, as some had said—indeed it radiated a certain beauty—but it was not uncommon either. Age—he was sixty-one—and fasting, an Indian sun and the strain of years in prison, of long, hard, nervous work, had obviously taken their toll, turned the nose down, widened it at the nostrils, sunk in his mouth just a little so that the lower lip protruded, and teeth were missing—I could see only two. His hair was closely cropped, giving an effect of baldness. His large ears spread out, rabbitlike. His gray eyes lit up and sharpened when they peered at you through his steel-rimmed spectacles and then they softened when he lapsed, as he frequently did, into a mood of almost puckish humor. I was almost taken back by the gaiety in them. This was a man inwardly secure, who, despite the burdens he carried, the hardships he had endured, could chuckle at man's foibles, including his own.

He seemed terribly frail, all skin and bones, though I knew that this appearance was deceptive, for he kept to a frugal but carefully planned diet that kept him fit, and for exercise he walked four or five miles each morning at a pace so brisk, as I would learn later when he invited me to accompany him, that I, at twenty-seven and in fair shape from skiing and hiking in the Alps below Vienna, could scarcely keep up. Over his skin and bones was a loosely wrapped *dhoti,* and in the chilliness of a north Indian winter he draped a coarsely spun white shawl over his bony shoulders. His skinny legs were bare, his feet in wooden sandals.

As he began to talk, his voice seemed high-pitched, but his words were spoken slowly and deliberately and with emphasis when he seemed intent on stressing a point, and gradually, as he warmed up, the tone lowered. His slightly accented English flowed rhythmically, like a poet's at times, and always, except for an occasional homespun cliché, it was concise, homely, forceful.

For so towering a figure, his humble manner at first almost disconcerted me. Most of the political greats I had brushed up against in Europe and at home had seemed intent on impressing you with the forcefulness of their personalities and the boldness of their minds, not being bashful at all in hiding their immense egos. But here was the most gentle and unassuming of men, speaking softly and kindly, without egotism, without the slightest pretense of trying to impress his rather awed listener.

How could so humble a man, I wondered, spinning away with his nimble fingers on a crude wheel as he talked, have begun almost single-handedly to rock the foundations of the British Empire, aroused a third of a billion people to rebellion against foreign rule, and taught them the technique of a new revolutionary method—non-violent civil disobedience—against which Western guns and Eastern lathis were proving of not much worth. That was what I had come to India to find out. So I simply said:

"How have you done it?"

"By love and truth," he smiled. "In the long run no force can prevail against them."

That was all very well, I did not doubt it, but I did not want to be pinned down by such highfalutin generalities. There was more to the Indian revolution than that, with all the cracked skulls, the fifty thousand of his followers in prison, and he only just released from one, with the government faltering and British trade with India already nearly ruined by Gandhi's boycott of British goods, and Gandhi's Indian National Congress, the only political party in India that counted, demanding complete independence now.

"I understand," I said. "But could you be more specific?"

Gandhi, of necessity, had put certain restrictions on this first interview. He had informed me at the very beginning that he and the Viceroy had agreed not to say anything publicly which might prejudice their present negotiatons.

"Ask me any questions you like except about that," he had said, "and I'll answer them if I can. After my talks with Lord Irwin are finished, regardless of how they come out, we can have further talks and delve more deeply into our problems, if you like."

"I would like it very much," I said.

There was one thing he wanted to add, he remarked, to what he had said about love and truth being the main elements of his non-violent movement.

"I know it is difficult for you from the West to understand. But I was quite serious. You cannot comprehend what we are trying to do and the way we are trying to do it unless you realize that we are fighting with soul-force."

"With what?" I asked.

"Soul-force," he said emphatically and then paused to see if it would sink in. I had begun to see that he was a man of infinite patience. "We call it *Satyagraha,*" he continued. "Whatever results we have so far attained in our struggle for *Swaraj . . .*"

"*Swaraj?*" I interrupted. "Meaning complete independence?"

"That is right. The Congress laid down that goal at Lahore December before last.* We will take nothing less. As I was saying, we intend to get it by *Satyagraha.*"

---

*In a ringing declaration that began (and no one but Gandhi could have written it): "We hold it to be a sin before man and God to submit any longer to a rule that has caused a fourfold disaster to our country." It specified the four areas of disaster: the economic, political, cultural and spiritual life of the nation.

Satyagraha, or soul-force, sounded very religious and spiritual to me—a fine thing for the human race to embrace, but not a very effective or even practical way to fight a revolution against an alien ruler who depended upon old-fashioned brute force.

My face must have betrayed my disbelief, for Gandhi immediately added: "Believe me, *Satyagraha* is a very practical weapon."

I realized, and I thought Gandhi saw, that I was too ignorant to pursue the subject further for the moment.

"We will go into it further at another time," he said. "Is there anything else on your mind today?"

"A great deal," I said. "Supposing that your negotiations with the Viceroy are successful and you reach an agreement. Do you still have faith in British promises?"

"I had faith in them—until 1919," he said. "But the Amritsar Massacre and the other atrocities in the Punjab changed my heart. And nothing has happened since to make me regain my faith. Certainly nothing in the last ten months."

Gandhi was confirming what I had long suspected: that for him, and for India, the cold-blooded slaughter by the British of unarmed Indians gathered for a peaceful meeting at the holy Sikh city of Amritsar on April 13, 1919, had been the turning point in the relations of the Indian people to their British rulers. It had blasted, at last, Gandhi's loyalty to the British Empire, which he had maintained in two wars, and it had forced him to the bitter conclusion that the British would stoop to any barbarity and to the enforcing of the most lawless oppression in order to hang on to India and to thwart the right of Indians to govern themselves. After the Amritsar killings Gandhi had turned in his two British war decorations and taken over the leadership of the Indian nationalist movement.

During my first assignment in India the autumn before, when Gandhi was still in jail, I had journeyed up to Amritsar to see the place of massacre and to try to get clear in my mind what had happened there. It had been difficult for me to believe that the British had deliberately perpetrated such a killing of innocent people, and I could not understand why the bloody act had received the approbation of most of the English in India and a large body of them at home, including the House of Lords, which had passed a motion condoning the British general who had ordered his troops to open fire at point-blank range at the defenseless Indians.* The English in India had expressed their approval of the general by raising a purse for him of £26,000 ($125,000 at the time); in England an even larger sum was raised by popular subscription. Probably no general in British history had been so handsomely rewarded in cash for so foul a deed.

For foul it was, though there had been some provocation, which in turn had been caused by an orgy of what Gandhi called "lawless repression" by the British authorities. As the Mahatma spoke calmly and without bitterness—in all the time I would know him he never showed the slightest trace of bitterness, not even at having been imprisoned without trial, nor at any other outrage the British had practiced on him and his people—I recalled my own visit to Amritsar and the shock of piecing together on the spot what had happened there. One had to see the physical layout of the Jallianwalla Bagh, the small public meeting place into which several thousand peaceful, unarmed Sikhs, Hindus and Moslems had jammed that spring day of 1919; and one had to know why they had gathered there.

They had assembled to protest the savage repression of the Punjab so soon after the war, in which India had furnished the British Empire 1.3 million troops, suffered 106,000 casualties and had not only borne the expense of its vast overseas force but contributed nearly a billion dollars to the British cause. Indians had expected something in return: a promise of self-government, but

---

*It ill becomes an American, I realize, to take a holier-than-thou attitude toward the British. What American soldiers did at My-Lai in Vietnam, half a century later, was just as barbarous as what British troops did at Amritsar, and the reaction of many Americans was just as callous. The American atrocities, it is true, were committed in a war (though an unjustified war, in my opinion) and the British ones in peacetime by a colonial power, but this does not make our killings any more justified than the British.

they had received only a vague promise in 1917, the year when British fortunes in the war were at their lowest ebb, of "a gradual development of self-governing institutions." When they realized that they had been deceived they reacted with some violence from one end of the country to the other. To repress the outbreak the British passed the celebrated Rowlatt Act in 1919, which instituted virtual martial law in much of India and deprived the people of the most elementary civil rights. Gandhi, who had been gradually assuming the lead of the nationalist movement, countered by calling a *hartal,* an Indian version of a one-day general strike, but something more than that. Not only would all the factories and shops close down, but everything else: schools, newspapers,restaurants, offices, courts. Indians would simply stay at home, and for one day paralyze the country. The *hartal* was called for April 6. It was not as peaceful as Gandhi had urged. All over the country there were acts of violence. They were perhaps worst in Amritsar, where five Englishmen were killed, a lady missionary was assaulted, and British banks, schools and churches were attacked. Gandhi tried to reach Amritsar and quiet the mobs, but was arrested on his way and turned back. Brigadier General Reginald E. Dyer, the commanding officer at Amritsar, decided to teach the "natives" a lesson.

He later claimed to have posted martial-law orders forbidding public meetings, but in the chaos few citizens of Amritsar had seen them. Some ten thousand gathered on April 13 in the Jallianwalla Bagh to protest not only the savagery of government oppression under martial law but also the excesses of their own mobs. The place, you could see when you visited it, was obviously not the ideal spot to hold a large public meeting. A tract of two or three acres in the center of the city, it was entirely surrounded by the walls of three- and four-story buildings. The only entrance to it was a narrow alley about ten feet wide and a hundred feet long, like the neck of a bottle.

It was into this enclosed park, jammed with Sikhs, Hindus and Mohammedans, that General Dyer marched with fifty troops on the afternoon of April 13, 1919, set up his machine guns, and without a word of warning opened fire on the densely packed crowd. The soldiers fired 1,600 rounds in ten minutes and nearly every bullet found its mark. For though the Punjab government at first hushed up the story and then reluctantly admitted that there had been a few casualties, the officially appointed Hunter Commission later found that 379 persons were killed and 1,137 wounded, a total of 1,516 casualties. Fifteen out of sixteen bullets had struck home. There had been no way of dodging them, no place to flee. A few dived down an old well and were drowned. The rest stayed where they were and were mowed down. According to a study of the Indian National Congress, at least the lives of some of the wounded might have been saved had medical services been available. But the general refused to allow Indian medics into the compound to succor the wounded. He insisted that they respect his curfew order and stay off the streets.

There is a simple plaque in the Jallianwalla Bagh at the spot where General Dyer's machine guns started firing. I copied the words down in my notebook: "To the martyrdom of fifteen hundred Sikhs, Hindus and Moslems, killed and wounded by British bullets."

Something else occurred at Amritsar, Gandhi said, that to him was even worse than the cold-blooded killings. That was General Dyer's "Crawling Order." It was a humiliation Gandhi and most Indians never forgot—or forgave. As punishment for the mob's assault of the English missionary woman, the general issued a command ordering all Indians who had to proceed up or down the street where she lived to crawl along it on their bellies. Hundreds of venerable old Indians, who had had nothing to do with the mob, who deplored its violence, lived in the street. General Dyer posted soldiers with fixed bayonets to see that they and all other Indians who had to use that street crawled with their bellies in the dust.*

---

*Though General Dyer became a hero to the English in India and to the Tory English at home and his action at Amritsar was approved by the Punjab government, he was eventually reprimanded and forced to retire from the Army—with a full pension. He

"Like worms," Gandhi said quietly, and I recalled the words in his memoirs. "Before this outrage," he had written, the Jalianwala {sic} Bagh tragedy paled into insignificance in my eyes . . ." *

"Have you read the unofficial report I made on behalf of the Congress on the lawless repression and the atrocities committed by the government in the Punjab?" Gandhi asked.

I said I had read it—the year before.

"It gives you an idea," he said, "of the atrocities perpetrated on the people of the Punjab. It shows you to what length the British government is capable of going, and what inhumanities and barbarities it is capable of perpetrating in order to maintain its power."

For Gandhi it was the last straw. From that spring of 1919 in the Punjab until the present moment he had dedicated his life to overthrowing British rule. This had already cost him two long sojourns in prison and seriously affected his health, though not his spirit, nor his determination to achieve his goal before he died. This was plain, as he talked on and on in answer to my questions. Though I feared he must be exhausted from his long daily talks with Lord Irwin, which were followed each evening by several hours of discussion with the Working Committee of the Indian National Congress, he fairly bubbled with good humor. There was no sign of fatigue.

I suddenly realized it was getting late. In a few minutes we would have to break off so that Gandhi could go out to the lawn for his daily evening prayer meeting. There was not much time left to go into anything very deeply. So as he spun away at his wheel I probed here and there with the idea of opening up subjects that he could return to in some detail and depth later.

I had been surprised, I said, at the role Indian women had played in the civil disobedience movement, considering their subordinate

---

believed he had saved the country from another Indian mutiny and vigorously defended his action, reportedly saying that he felt he had "done a jolly good thing" and that under similar circumstances he would do it again.

* Gandhi, op. cit. p. 471.

relation to men in Hindu and especially in Moslem society, where millions of Mohammedan women were still kept in *purdah*. The previous year I had seen them by the thousands squatting on the pavement at the side of their men, braving the lathi sticks, getting hurt and getting jailed.

"I'm glad you've seen the part played by our women in our movement," Gandhi beamed. "The world has never seen such a magnificent spectacle. They were as brave as our men. You have no idea how what they did and suffered increased my faith in our people. The awakening of our women has helped mightily to awaken India. We cannot achieve freedom without them."

"How do you account for it?" I asked.

"It can only be the work of God," he smiled. "Certainly God is with us in this struggle!"

It was the kind of answer I would often get from Gandhi, and I was not satisfied with it, not this first time nor later. It was his way of mixing religion with politics that so baffled not only the British and American correspondents such as I, but his own people and especially his closest aides. Jawaharlal Nehru, his brilliant young associate, a Brahman Hindu but a non-believer, could sometimes scarcely hide his irritation at it.* Or with another aspect of Gandhi's philosophy when I told Nehru of the Mahatma's answer to the next question of mine at this first interview.

"Some twenty years ago, Mr. Gandhi," I said, "you wrote a book, *Indian Home Rule,* which I believe stunned India—it certainly stunned the rest of the world—with its onslaught on modern Western civilization. You called it 'satanic' and you said Hindus called it a dark age. And, as I recall, you said your idea of an ideal state would be one without factories, railways, armies or navies and

* "What a problem and a puzzle he has been," Nehru exclaims in his autobiography when writing about these weeks in Delhi during the Gandhi-Irwin talks, "not only to the British Government but to his own people and his closest associates! . . . Often the unknown stared at us through his eyes."—Jawaharlal Nehru: *Toward Freedom: The Autobiography of Jawaharlal Nehru* (New York: The John Day Co., 1941), p. 190.

with as few hospitals, doctors and lawyers as possible. Now, in the third decade of the twentieth century, have you changed your mind about these things?"

Gandhi sat patiently through the long question, a smile growing on his face. I must say I appreciated his patience—it must be infinite, I thought. Still, it was a serious question. If he gained independence for India, would he set it back a couple of centuries to a preindustrial stage?

"Have I changed my mind?" Gandhi said, almost with a laugh. "Not a bit! My ideas about the evils of modern Western civilization still stand. If I republished my book tomorrow I would scarcely change a word, except for a few changes in the setting."

I couldn't believe it. I didn't question Gandhi's sincerity, but I couldn't believe he meant what he was saying. Young Nehru, either, when I told him about it a few days later.

"Gandhiji says a lot of things like that," Nehru said. "Perhaps he thinks they are necessary to arouse the people. But I can't believe he really means them. He is much too intelligent and experienced not to know that if a free India lapsed back to the simpler times, it couldn't survive in the modern world. I try to tell him that we will have to adopt Western technology to make an independent India function in the twentieth century. Gandhiji listens—and then he tells you stuff like that!"

But consistency, I remembered Gandhi repeating in his autobiography, was the refuge of fools. And now he seemed to give an example. For when I asked him if he really believed that most of India's many ills would be cured by self-government he became unrealistically optimistic. They would indeed, he said.

"But naturally not without trouble and difficulty," he added.

"But the great social and economic problems," I asked, "such as the relations of capital and labor, landlord and tenant, your own communal problems beween Hindus and Moslems and those of the depressed classes, especially the millions of Untouchables—do you think self-government can necessarily solve them?"

"Yes, I do," he said quietly. "All these problems will be fairly easy to settle when we are our own masters. I know there will be difficulties, but I have faith in our ultimate capacity to solve them—and not by following your Western models but by evolving along the lines of non-violence and truth, on which our movement is based and which must constitute the bedrock of our future constitution."

A society of a third of a billion people based on the solid rock of non-violence and truth seemed a fine ideal, much to be desired, but dreadfully unrealistic to me. Gandhi went on to assert, with that quiet confidence I was beginning to see was an important part of his being, that the "inequalities and injustices" of the capitalist system, of which he said he was fully aware, would be solved "quickly and successfully." The problems of education too, he added.

"It is not true," he said, "as some Englishmen have asserted, that I would abolish our schools. I am as anxious as anyone to maintain our great culture by education. But in our schools today we learn only what our masters want us to learn. We do not get the training we most need. When we are free people, standing on our own feet, we shall see to that. But perhaps we can discuss that further. I have given considerable thought to it."

During our talk we had been occasionally interrupted by visitors. Once a group of schoolchildren tiptoed in, the youngsters bowing. They were obviously in awe of the great man. Gandhi smiled at them and gave them his blessing in Hindu fashion, clasping his hands together under his chin.

"There is so much we can do for them," he said, turning to me as they left.

A few moments later an Indian who, Gandhi explained to me, represented the Christians in the Legislative Assembly, slipped in and bowed, and I was fascinated at the good-natured banter with which Gandhi greeted him.

"Ah, my friend," he said. "I'm told you've given up smoking as a commemorative act of self-purification on Pandit Motilal's death.* I congratulate you!" And the Christian politician, after mumbling his thanks, went away beaming.

I could see from the verandah that it was getting dark outside and that it was time for the evening prayer meeting.

"I am rather busy with these talks with the Viceroy," Gandhi said. "But if you like, I shall find time to continue *our* talks."

I thanked him and followed him out to the lawn for the prayers. There were some five hundred persons in all kinds of garb, obviously of all kinds of religion, gathered there as Gandhi strode toward the small raised platform. Many, I was told, had walked for days from their villages to Delhi to get a glimpse of the holy man and to receive his *darshan*. They stood there in the dusk, bowing as Gandhi passed, and a few bent down and tried to kiss his feet, but he brushed them aside. Gandhi mounted the platform, turned and grasped his hands to give his *darshan*, and the throng squatted down on the grass. Mirabai (Miss Slade) began to chant a prayer from the *Bhagavad Gita* and Gandhi and the worshipers joined in. It sounded rather mournful to me, as Hindu chants usually did to a Westerner, but I could catch the flowing cadences of the Sanskrit words, without of course understanding them, and grasp a little of the beauty of this sublime poem, a work of genius whose religious and philosophical teachings, Gandhi had remarked to me in passing, were the foundations of his own religion and of his way of life.

In thirty minutes the prayer meeting was over and the worshipers, obviously carried away by this brief communion with the great man, began to disperse, most of them as if in a daze.

---

*Pandit Motilal Nehru, father of Jawaharlal and a leader of the Indian National Congress, had died two weeks before. A Kashmiri Brahman and a highly successful lawyer, he was long a moderate in politics until 1919 when the Punjab oppression and the Amritsar Massacre awakened him and he threw himself into Gandhi's nationalist movement. Despite his age and precarious health, he had been imprisoned by the British during the recent civil-disobedience struggle. Released from prison shortly before his death, he said to Gandhi as he lay dying: "I am going soon, Mahatmaji, and I shall not be here to see *Swaraj*. But I know that you have won it and will soon have it." Jawaharlal Nehru recalled the words in his autobiography, op. cit. p. 185.

Gandhi trudged past them, smiling, offering a greeting here and there, and made his way to his room, followed by a dozen members of the Working Committee, a sort of shadow cabinet of the Congress. He would probably keep them up until midnight, he had remarked half laughingly to me as he passed, for the next day was a Monday, and at the stroke of midnight he would begin to observe his weekly twenty-four hours of silence, and there was much to thresh out beforehand with his aides before he resumed his talks on Tuesday with Lord Irwin in the Golden Hall of the great viceregal palace in New Delhi.*

As I watched him disappear into the house, as I recalled his friendly, simple, relaxed manner during our long interview, I found it difficult to grasp that this humble little man in his loincloth was in the midst of negotiations on which so much hung—the hopes of the Indian people and the fears of the British Empire. The load was great, but he carried it lightly!

* The spectacle "nauseated" Winston Churchill. In a speech in the Commons the week before, he expressed his revulsion at "the nauseating and humiliating spectacle of this onetime Inner Temple lawyer, now a seditious fakir, striding half naked up the steps of the Viceroy's palace, there to negotiate and parley on equal terms with the representative of the King-Emperor."

3

For the next eleven days, except on his day of silence, Gandhi continued his talks with the Viceroy, their sessions often lasting far into the night. It was some four miles from Dr. Ansari's residence in old Delhi, where he was staying, to the viceregal palace in New Delhi, but the frail Indian leader usually walked it except when there was a heavy downpour of rain. It was a sight—for me, at least, however "nauseating" to Churchill—to see the Mahatma, clad in his loincloth and an old blanket wrapped over his shoulders, trudging in his clumsy wooden sandals up the marble steps of the great palace past the scarlet-coated guards standing stiffly at attention. He hardly looked like a statesman or a revolutionary.

It was obvious that the negotiations had become extremely complicated, with dozens of problems to be worked out in detail, such as safeguards during the transitional period when power would be transferred to the Indians, how much of the national debt should be borne by the British, the relations of the princely states to an Indian government, the Moslem-Hindu issue, the rights of the 70 million untouchables, terms for calling off the boycott of British goods, for restoring the property of tens of thousands of Indians seized by the government, for releasing fifty thousand men and women not guilty of violence, and so on. Gandhi must have carried the facts and figures on these matters in his head, for all he carried to and from these meetings was a small, tattered manila envelope, tucked under his arm, which could not have held much material.

From day to day the negotiations had their ups and downs. My daily cables from Delhi, which form the basis for these pages, tell the story of those crucial days.

Monday, February 23, my birthday, was Gandhi's day of silence, and though he conferred for several hours with the Congress Working Committee, listening to its views and conveying his own by signs and scribbled notes, he did not of course see the Viceroy. I spent most of the day at government headquarters trying to find out how far Lord Irwin would—or could—go in meeting Gandhi's demands. I was told the Viceroy was in constant touch with London, which had the final say. One snag was Gandhi's insistence on an investigation of the excessive brutality of the British-led police at Borsad, where hundreds of Indian women had been savagely beaten before their arrest. Irwin, a compassionate man, was said to be inclined to give in on this, but his cabinet of British officials was firmly opposed. Toward evening I dropped by Gandhi's place to talk to some of the members of the Working Committee. They had spent most of the day, they said, working out plans for a nationwide no-tax campaign in case the Gandhi-Irwin negotiations failed. They were encouraged by a violent attack on Gandhi in *The Statesman* of Calcutta, the leading organ of British opinion in India. It accused the revolutionary movement of costing tens of millions of pounds and disclosed that state revenues were falling off disastrously. This pleased the men around Gandhi and revolted *The Statesman. It* called for putting Gandhi in his place.

The talks between Gandhi and Irwin resumed on Tuesday and continued throughout the week. It was difficult for a reporter to find out what was holding up an agreement. Actually, I was getting most of my news from British officials and this troubled me. They were too much the gentlemen, I thought, to lie to me, but it was natural that they would slant to their own advantage what they gave out. Gandhi, whom I spoke with briefly each day, would not say much. He had an exaggerated idea, I thought, of his agreement with the Viceroy not to divulge anything that might harm the negotiations.

One day I complained to Jawaharlal Nehru, Mrs. Sarojini Naidu and Mahadev Desai that a foreign correspondent was getting most of his news from the British because Gandhi and his aides were not talking.* Didn't they want to get their side of the story reported in the world press? I taunted them. My grumbling had some effect, for after discussing this with the Mahatma, all three began confiding in me. Desai, a tall, pleasant-looking, scholarly man, was especially valuable. As Gandhi's principal secretary, his "alter ego," as Gandhi described him to me during our first interview, Desai not only had a better grasp than any other of what was going on in his chief's mind but, as he often accompanied Gandhi to the talks with Irwin, he also knew at first hand how the negotiations were going. I think I won his trust for good that week. From then on, right through to the days of the Round Table Conference in London in the fall of 1931, which was my last assignment to cover Gandhi, Desai kept me well informed and in dozens of ways facilitated my work and my understanding.

Mrs. Naidu too. To a good many people in India Sarojini Naidu was the "Indian nightingale." Her lyric poetry had for years been widely read and had given her a renown as a poet perhaps second to Tagore. Now in 1931 she was better known as the greatest of the women nationalists, one of Gandhi's chief aides and the only woman member of the Congress Working Committee. She had met

*Years later in his autobiography Nehru remembered this. ". . . many foreign journalists, especially Americans, . . . were somewhat annoyed with us for our reticence. They would tell us that they got much more news about the Gandhiji-Irwin conversations from the New Delhi Secretariat than from us, which was a fact."—Nehru, op. cit. pp. 187–88.

the Mahatma in London in 1914 when she was already celebrated as a poet and over the years a close friendship and collaboration had grown. No two Indians could have been more unlike—and perhaps that added to the attraction. In contrast to Gandhi's ascetic life in poverty, Mrs. Naidu enjoyed the good life. She was rich and fashionable and wore—except for a period when in loyalty to Gandhi, she reluctantly put on the coarse homespun clothes of all good nationalists—richly embroidered, brightly colored saris with sparkling jewels. Not for her was the ascetic life the Mahatma led, the filthy third-class accommodations in the trains, the peasant huts or the ashrams one slept in while traveling. She went first-class and put up at the best hotels and liked good food. She was not ostentatious about this; it came naturally to her.

We soon became good friends. I enjoyed her company, her humor, her wit, her ebullience, her frankness, her knack of deflating the pompous, be they British or Indian. She loved Gandhi, admired him immensely, followed him loyally, but she could tease him about his eccentricities and wittingly comment, without a touch of malice, on them to others. She liked to tell of their first meeting in London in the early months of the Great War. Gandhi, already famous for his civil-disobedience campaigns in South Africa, was staying, she said, in a rather run-down rooming house in Bloomsbury. When she arrived to meet him, she found him in his decrepit room squatting on an old blanket surrounded by dishes and pots, and eating his lunch.

"Will you share my meal?" he asked her, after greeting her. Mrs. Naidu took one glance at what seemed to her rather grisly food.

"Certainly not!" she said.

Like Jawaharlal Nehru, Sarojini Naidu respected but could not share Gandhi's simple life. Sometimes she would say that he was overdoing it, and indeed I heard her during those weeks in Delhi, and not infrequently thereafter, jokingly taunt him for it. She would suggest, for instance, that if he traveled first-class he could get some work done or at least find time for contemplation, whereas in the filthy, jammed third-class compartments one was taken up with sheer survival. She thought he took valuable time from his work in spinning, though she realized the symbolic value of it to the masses. Her favorite crack in those days was: "You will never know how much it costs us to keep that saint, that wonderful old man, in poverty!"

Her pleasantries notwithstanding, Mrs. Naidu was a dedicated worker and a dynamic leader. On the platform, she was an eloquent, moving speaker. In dealings with British officials and with the Moslem leaders, she was a tough, shrewd negotiator. Gandhi often delegated such assignments to her. And it was Sarojini Naidu whom he appointed as his successor, as the leader of Congress, when he was arrested shortly after the Salt March the year before. In that capacity she led the assault on the Dharasana Salt Works north of Bombay, the most bloody encounter of the campaign, in which several hundred Gandhi volunteers were brutally beaten into unconsciousness and half a dozen to death, and Mrs. Naidu herself was arrested and jailed.

We saw each other a good deal in India and later in London during the Round Table Conference, and beginning in Delhi she became one of my chief sources of information of what Gandhi and the Congress (and sometimes, the British) were up to. In appearance, I thought, she resembled a North American Indian, with a strong aquiline nose, high cheekbones and expressive eyes that could be one moment mischievous or laughing and the next moment sad. She was wholly and seriously involved in the struggle for independence, but she could look at life too with amused detachment and get a great deal of enjoyment and pleasure from it. Like Gandhi, she knew the value of relaxing. Sometimes, when she was out of jail, but deeply involved in some negotiation, she would call and say: "Let's forget the troubles of the universe today. I'm going to take you to a Hindu wedding. It will be fun."

I think Nehru was relieved to get Gandhi's approval that week for frank talks with me. It had become clear to me that he was far from pleased with the way the Gandhi-Irwin talks were going. He felt his leader was giving away too much. But what could he do? He struck me in our talks as a somewhat sad and disillusioned young man, in continual battle with himself to suppress not only his doubts about himself but about his disagreements with Gandhi, to whom he was utterly loyal. He realized, he would say, that Gandhi was the only man who could lead the struggle for independence. No other figure had anywhere near Gandhi's hold on the masses nor his political acumen in dealing with the British. But he was sometimes difficult to follow and even to understand, and there were occasions, Nehru said, when he found the Mahatma "almost incomprehensible." He had his "fads and peculiarities" that often confounded one.

Nehru was forty-one at this time, but he looked much younger. There was something boyish about his handsome, sensitive look and manner, a jauntiness even, that in a flash could give way to the impatience of youth and then an expression of sadness and finally sorrow. He was impatient that after so long a time the Indians were still ruled by the British, and so callously and autocratically and insensitively, and the more he contemplated it—and there had been much time for contemplation in British prisons*—his impatience would give way to a sadness and a disillusionment. There was in him also, I felt, something that Gandhi, so utterly different, had not a trace of: a bitterness—not so much for the British personally, for whom he had rather a deep contempt, but for the fact that they held his people in bondage. The bitterness, I think, was felt also for his own people, who had taken their subjugation for so long lying down and especially for those— wealthy Indian merchants and industrialists and Indians who served in the British government of India and in its courts—who had not joined, as he and his illustrious father had done, in Gandhi's nationalist movement.

Jawaharlal Nehru, like Gandhi, had studied in England, first at Harrow and then at Cambridge, from which he took his degree in

---

* And there would be more—a total of nine years behind bars.

1910, and then, as Gandhi had done, studied law and was admitted to the bar. Like Gandhi too, he at first, but for a longer time, had aped English ways, outfitting himself in clothes tailored in Bond Street, and generally, as he later joked, acting the part of a prosperous, somewhat empty-headed English man about town.

His English education and the seven years he had spent in England (Gandhi had stayed only three years to study law and qualify for the bar) had a much greater impact on Nehru than on Gandhi. They made him much more Westernized and modern in his outlook, awakening his interest in a world rapidly industrializing and arming, and in the economic, social and political problems that arose from it. His Westernization cut him adrift from much in his native India that was dear to Gandhi, especially their Hindu religion and the more ancient and primitive way of life that still prevailed in most of the country. Returning to India in 1912 at the age of twenty-two, to practice law, like his father, he found it difficult and sometimes impossible to adjust to the old way. This would become the basis for his frequent differences with Gandhi. He could not share, he told me during those days in Delhi when he felt sore at heart over his disagreements with the Mahatma, Gandhi's deep religious feelings.

"Many of us had cut adrift from this peasant outlook," he wrote later in his autobiography of his feelings during the Gandhi-Irwin talks in Delhi, "and the old ways of thought and custom and religion had become alien to us. We called ourselves moderns and thought in terms of 'progress,' and industrialization and a higher standard of living . . ."*

For Gandhi, as he had told me in our first talk, modern civilization, at least in its Western, industrialized aspect, was satanic, a dark age, and it was no wonder that in this he and Nehru could find no common meeting ground. Nor could they on the value and importance of the *Bhagavad Gita,* which to Gandhi, more than any other sacred work, showed the path to a more

*Nehru, op. cit. p. 190.

meaningful life and to man's eventual salvation. I often went out to the garden with Nehru to Gandhi's evening prayer meeting, where I noticed he joined in the chanting of the *Gita* verses. He said he liked the poetry of them and their general message that in this life a man ought to try to do his duty, as he saw it, without regard to the consequences, good or bad. Beyond that, he did not care much for the metaphysical part of the *Gita*. In fact, he said he did not understand it, and I gathered he did not intend to try to, despite Gandhi's urging.

Nehru spoke English with almost an Oxford accent, slightly tinted with his native Hindi and its rolling cadences. His voice was soft, his manner at first rather guarded, as though there was an inner part of his being he did not want an intrusion upon. But his personality, his mind, his ideas, attracted me. I judged from what Gandhi said that he already regarded Nehru, relatively young as he was, as his successor. He was a man to watch.

By February 25 Gandhi sensed, I think, a revolt in the Congress Working Committee, some of whose members, led by Nehru, felt that he was making too many concessions to the Viceroy. Late that evening he called the committee into session and persuaded it to agree to abide by whatever terms he got in the end.

"What else could we do?" Nehru told me afterward. You could see how torn he was between his loyalty to the Mahatma, his belief in his genius, and his fear of a sellout. "We have to go along with him, whatever our doubts—and I have several," he said. "If we disavowed him, the whole nationalist movement would collapse." Nevertheless, I got an impression from Gandhi himself that the stiff attitude of his colleagues actually encouraged him to hold out for all he could possibly get.

This became evident three days later, on the twenty-eighth. My cable that night began: "There is to be no peace in India." The Working Committee, with Nehru, as the Congress president, in the chair, but with Gandhi of course dominating the discussions, met all day and finally decided to reject outright the Viceroy's peace proposals, which Irwin, after consultation with London, had handed Gandhi the evening before after the two had talked for four hours. Gandhi tried his best not to divulge the news when he invited me to sit down with him for a brief talk after the prayer meeting. But he pretty much gave himself away.

"I cannot break my pledge to the Viceroy. I cannot divulge the results of the negotiations," he pleaded in his gentle way. "But tomorrow I'll probably be able to give you the whole story."

That meant the parleys had foundered, and the Mahatma seemed to confirm this when I asked him if he was at all hopeful.

"Even if the negotiations failed, I would remain hopeful of the future," he smiled. He was not spinning that evening, as he usually did.

That the talks had broken down, some of Gandhi's lieutenants soon made clear to me. The Viceroy's proposals, they said, were not half enough. These had made it clear that the road to self-government would be a long one, over many years. The British had proposed many "stages," they said, before even Dominion status could be considered. "Stages" and "safeguards." The Viceroy had rejected even discussion of the goal the Congress had laid down at Lahore the year before: *Purna Swaraj,* complete independence. Gandhi, Lord Irwin told the Indian leader, could bring the subject up at the next Round Table Conference if he wished. But Gandhi, no less than the Viceroy, knew that no government in London would consider it in any future they could foresee. At least, the Mahatma also knew, not until it was forced to by the Indian revolution.

Still, it was obvious that both sides feared a final breakdown. All day long on March 1 and far into the night there was a great deal of activity at the viceregal palace. Gandhi conferred alone with Irwin for nearly four hours—until 6 P.M., when he asked to be excused so he could return home to lead the evening prayers. The Viceroy then held an emergency meeting with his executive council that lasted until Gandhi arrived back at 9 P.M. One of Irwin's aides told me Irwin was having almost as much difficulty with his British Civil

Service bureaucrats as he was having with Gandhi. Predictably, they were holding out against any further concessions to the nationalists. They wanted to clamp Gandhi back in jail. Obviously they didn't like what I cabled that evening, for the government censors killed my dispatch. It never got through to Paris or Chicago.

Sensing that the Viceroy and Gandhi were not talking all afternoon and evening for nothing—and on a Sunday, at that—I went over to the palace toward midnight in the hope of getting some late news—perhaps, at last, definite word whether there would be a settlement. Gandhi emerged a little after midnight, an unusually late hour for him to be about, and trudged back most of the four miles to Dr. Ansari's home before allowing someone to pack him into a dilapidated car for the last mile or so. I walked along with him for part of the route, amazed at his vitality at this late hour after so strenuous a day. He was in fine spirits, and though he would tell me nothing of substance, his bubbling optimism, I thought, told a lot. He was also in a hurry, he said, as he strode along, because his day of silence was supposed to begin at midnight, which had already come, and he must talk to the Working Committee immediately. He would simply have to postpone by a couple of hours, he explained, the beginning of his silence—something he had almost never done. To gain time, he reluctantly crawled into the waiting car.

Back at his home he explained the results of the day's negotiations to the members of the Working Committee. That meeting, like all the others, was closed, and broke up at 2 A.M.* I had decided to make a night of it; it was a good opportunity to see how Gandhi worked under pressure. He emerged from the meeting smiling and serene, with no sign of fatigue, as though nearly eleven hours of continuous talking with the Viceroy and his own people

---

*Nehru explained to me once during the days in Delhi that if the sessions of the Congress Working Committee had been open to the public, as some zealous "democrats" wished, British informers among the journalists would have reported to the government every move the Congress secretly planned.

had been just another day for him. If he was sleepy, it did not appear on his face. Instead of going to bed—it was now after 2 A.M.—he decided to spin for an hour, announcing half jokingly before he began his silence that he had to meet his daily quota of two hundred yards of yarn, and that he had not found time to do it before now.

I watched him spin for a few minutes and then, tired and sleepy myself, left. There was still a dispatch to write on the night's happenings—one could file from Delhi until dawn because of the eleven- or twelve-hour time difference with Chicago. Next morning Desai told me that Gandhi had spun for an hour, turned out his two hundred yards of yarn, slept for an hour, got up at four for morning prayers and then set off on his matinal four-mile walk. I began to see that it was all wrong of us to write of Gandhi as being a frail old man. By exercise and diet and self-discipline he kept himself at sixty-one as trim as an athlete. There was iron in him too—I was beginning to see that.

On Tuesday, March 3, Gandhi made up for his previous day of silence by spending all day at the viceregal palace conferring with Lord Irwin and key members of the government. After a break for supper and prayers he returned at nine in the evening, driving through a blinding rain and remaining at the palace again until midnight.

A side of Gandhi that few but his closest associates knew was emerging and it astounded not only the correspondents who were covering him but the Viceroy and the hard-bitten British members of his council. This was the Mahatma's amazing grasp of detail. He was not only negotiating a general settlement but insisting on bargaining over a multitude of details. This was too much for the Viceroy, who twice during the day arranged for Gandhi to make his points with the Home Secretary, in charge of the nation's police, and then with the Finance Secretary. From the first Gandhi demanded restitution of property confiscated by the government from those convicted of civil disobedience and also the remission of their fines. The return of property was all the more complicated because much of it had already been resold by the government. Gandhi insisted it be turned back.

For two hours Gandhi hammered out a compromise agreement with Sir George Schuster, the Finance Secretary, over the salt tax, the very issue on which Gandhi had launched his civil-disobedience movement the spring before. Though the government refused to abolish the tax, it agreed to allow the millions of poor living along India's long coastline to manufacture and sell salt they gathered from the sea—despite the law. By midnight the Mahatma believed he had reached agreement on all but two points: restitution of property and remission of fines. He agreed to make one more effort to solve the problem by further talks with the Viceroy and the Home Secretary the next day.

But a hitch arose. When he returned from the viceregal palace shortly after midnight Tuesday, Gandhi had told me he hoped to finish the negotiations Wednesday. But after conferring with the Viceroy and his Home Secretary from noon until 7 P.M., he still could not reach an agreement on what seemed to him important points: restitution of property the government had seized from those convicted of civil disobedience and remission of their fines, many of which had been punitive. The first matter was somewhat embarrassing to Lord Irwin because the British governor of Bombay province had authorized the auctioning off of the seized property with a guarantee to the purchasers that they would not have to give it back. But Gandhi stuck to his demand that it be given back.

He returned from the palace at seven o'clock for his prayer meeting and then called in the members of the Working Committee. At 10 P.M. the committee dispatched a letter to the Viceroy stating that the Congress could not further compromise on the two issues. It felt that Gandhi had gone to the extreme limit in making concessions.* It asked Lord Irwin to reply in writing that

---

*Nehru, who was not happy about them, had confided to me the nature of the concessions. If a truce were reached, Gandhi had agreed to attend a second Round Table Conference to discuss a new constitution for a self-governing India. Since a conference without Gandhi's participation would be meaningless, the government in London had

evening. The implication was that unless he accepted the Congress' view on this, there was no further point in discussions between the two sides. The truce seemed imperiled at the last moment.

Once more gloom settled over Dr. Ansari's home as the meeting of the Working Committee broke up shortly before 10 P.M. Gandhi did not seem to share it, however, He was his usual bubbling self when he came out of the meeting and stopped to have a few words with me.

"There is no settlement yet," he said. "There will be none tonight." Then, breaking into a laugh and patting me on the shoulder, he added: "So, my dear Mr. Shirer, you can go home and get some sleep. I do not plan to see the Viceroy until tomorrow."

When I returned to my room at the Hotel Cecil to write my dispatch, there was a cable from Chicago that took the wind out of my sails. It said the Associated Press was scooping me. It was announcing that the Gandhi-Irwin truce had been signed and that "peace had settled over India."

Like many "scoops" in my profession, this was not true, or to say the least, it was, as it turned out, premature by twenty-four hours. But the A.P., with its invented but colorful story, got the headlines in America and I got hell from my editors in Chicago for having been scooped. It hurt, but what did it matter?

The next morning at the viceregal palace Gandhi and Lord Irwin ironed out their last differences and signed the agreement they had been hammering out in nearly a month of negotiations. That was the important thing. Of what import, I kept asking myself, was it

---

insisted on this, and the Mahatma had reluctantly consented. He had made further concessions, which troubled Nehru. These were about "safeguards" during the transitional period to self-government. Gandhi had won a point by insisting that the safeguards be only those "in the interests of India" and that this condition be included in the text of the truce agreement. Nehru found them more in the interests of the British Empire than in those of India. The safeguards provided for the British to handle India's military defense (i.e., by the British Army and the British-officered Indian Army), foreign affairs, government finances, the public debt and relations with minorities. Not much was left for the Indians to deal with.

that in Chicago the *Tribune* did not publish my dispatch, the most important one I had yet cabled from Delhi. It had printed the "news" the day before, the editors cabled me, reprimanding me for wasting cable tolls.

I did my best to swallow my wounded pride. Gandhi's agreeing to call off his massive civil-disobedience movement was what counted. What I needed to do was to try to assess its historical significance.

4

The Gandhi-Irwin truce, signed in New Delhi on March 5, 1931, marked a turning point in the Indian revolution and in the affairs of the British Empire. Not that Gandhi won much. I was surprised that he conceded so much, and Nehru was bitter. The Mahatma seemed to have given in on almost every issue. Not even his eloquent defense of what he believed he had achieved, which he imparted to me in long talks on the succeeding days, convinced me that he had not, to an amazing extent, surrendered. It would take some time for me to realize that Gandhi, with his subtle feeling for the course of history, had actually achieved a great deal. For the first time since the British took away India from the Indians, they had been forced, as Churchill bitterly complained, to deal with an Indian leader as an equal. For the first time the British acknowledged that Gandhi represented the aspirations and indeed the demands of most of the Indians for self-government. And that from then on, he, and the Indian National Congress he dominated, would have to be dealt with seriously. The Congress might be outlawed again and Gandhi jailed—this would happen. But they could no longer be permanently suppressed, nor their goals of Indian independence for very much longer denied. From now on it was a question not of whether the British were willing to grant independence to India, but of *how* and *when*.

I think Gandhi understood this very clearly that first week of March in 1931 in Delhi. I realize that in the long talks we had then he tried to tell me as much. I admit I was slow to comprehend what seemed so evident to him. I was not alone. Even the Indian leaders around him, Nehru above all, were terribly disillusioned. They went along with Gandhi and publicly praised him for what he had "won" because, as Nehru explained, there was nothing else to do. In private, and sometimes to me, they spoke of Gandhi's "surrender."

By the main provisions of the truce Gandhi agreed to call off the civil-disobedience movement, participate as the representative of the Congress in the Round Table Conference to discuss the new constitution, relax the boycott of British goods and drop his demand for an investigation of police brutality. In return, the government agreed to release all political prisoners convicted of non-violent offenses, withdraw pending prosecutions and all the special ordinances promulgated to put down civil disobedience, restore seized property which the government still held (but not property it had sold), and allow the poor along the seacoasts to make and sell salt locally despite the Salt Act, which would not be repealed.

What troubled the men around Gandhi most was his agreement to British terms for the new constitution to be hammered out at the Round Table Conference. "It comes as a tremendous shock to me," Nehru told me. He was concerned mostly about the safeguards Gandhi had agreed to "in the interests of India," which remained exactly as Nehru had outlined to me a few evenings before.* They left the running of the new "constitutional" government of India

* See footnote, pages 52–53.

almost exclusively in British hands. There was no mention of the declared goal of the Congress: complete independence. I must say I sympathized with Nehru's distress.*

There was no distress discernible in Gandhi when he called in a half dozen of us correspondents for a long talk before his evening prayer meeting. He seemed not only relieved at having called off the first non-violent revolution in history but pleased at the prospect of peace.

"I am a man of peace, after all," he began, "and now we have peace." As if he anticipated one of us breaking in to ask if it was not a "peace at any price," he added: "But it is only peace that comes with a truce. And the continuation of that truce depends upon the granting of self-government."

"I do not find that in the agreement you have just signed," I blurted out.

Gandhi was used to me by now, and merely beamed. He had begun to munch his supper of dates and oranges and goat's milk, which the barefooted Miss Slade brought in on a tray and placed at one side of him on the floor. He paused for a moment to masticate his food and to take a drink of milk from a battered jug he had taken along with him from prison.

"I must confess," he said, as if to answer my remark, "that what seems to have been yielded by the English at the first Round Table Conference in London is not half enough. If the Congress succeeds in making its position acceptable at the next conference, then I claim that the fruit of it will be complete independence for India."

This was rather astounding, I thought. The provision of the pact that he had just signed, and which had so troubled young Nehru, called for Gandhi (on behalf of the Congress) to participate in a Round Table Conference which in advance accepted enough "safeguards" to preclude India from having any semblance of independence.

* "For a day or two I wobbled," Nehru recalled in his autobiography. Then, ". . . not without great mental conflict and physical distress," he says, he decided "to accept the agreement and work for it wholeheartedly."—Nehru, op. cit. p. 194.

"The goal of the Congress," Gandhi went on, "remains complete independence. It is India's birthright, as it is of any nation worthy of the name. India cannot be satisfied with anything less."

That was all very good—who could deny that complete independence was India's birthright, as it was that of Great Britain, and of every other nation?—but Gandhi had not even obtained mention of it in the truce agreement, in which there was not a line that the British had the slightest intention of granting it. I asked him about the safeguards—"in the interests of India"—to which he had agreed in the pact.

"Safeguards in the interests of India," he said, "may be purely illusory and constitute so many ropes tying the country hand and foot, and strangling her by the neck."

"That's what some of your closest aides in the Congress think," I said.

"But safeguards could also be helpful to a young country which has been deprived of the experience of governing itself," he answered. He seemed to me to be indulging in one of those contradictions which so baffled his associates, not to mention us correspondents.

"Let me try to make our position clear," he said, after he had bitten at an orange and had another swallow of milk. "Congress does not consider India a sickly child requiring outside help and props. The implication in the government's inviting the Congress to join the Round Table Conference is that the Congress will not be deterred from any consideration, save that of incapacity, from pressing for the fullest freedom."

Then, as he so often did in the midst of a political discussion, Gandhi digressed to religion and talked briefly about the peace having been achieved "by the will of God." A question brought him back to the realities of politics.

"In view of what you told me a few days ago," I asked, "about your inability to trust the British since the days of the Amritsar Massacre, may I ask if you now trust them to carry out scrupulously the terms of the truce you have just signed?"

I called his attention to a rather ominous sentence with which the government of India's communiqué on the truce had ended.

In the event of Congress failing to give full effect to the obligations of this settlement, Government will take such action as may become necessary for the protection of the public and individuals and the due observance of law and order.

Nothing was said in the communiqué about the consequences of the government failing to live up to the pact, and indeed his signature was hardly dry on the document before Gandhi would reproach the government for one breach after another. However, Gandhi's answer was to throw out a new olive branch to his English tormentors.

"If India," he said, "is to come into her own through conference and consultation, the good will and active help of Englishmen is necessary. Only, they must dare to give the Indians the freedom to err and sin. For it passes human comprehension how human beings, be they ever so experienced and able, can delight in depriving other human beings of that precious right."

Gandhi's logic about the necessity of freedom was impeccable, but did he really expect "good will" and "active help" from the English? It seemed to me, as Gandhi was making the point, that there was precious little good will or even understanding on the part of the British toward the Indians' aspirations for political freedom, and that it was naïve to count on their "active help" in abandoning so valuable a holding as India, which, after all, constituted most of the Empire. And anyway, there was not much logic in history, or if there was, no one understood it.

One of the correspondents asked Gandhi if he thought he had won "a victory." He obviously was ready for that one.

"It is not possible nor wise to say which side has won a victory by this truce. If there is any victory I should say it belongs to both. The Indian National Congress did not bid for victory. Congress has a definite goal—self-government—and there can be no question of victory until that goal has been achieved."

There was much more to the interview. Gandhi spoke to us for two hours, touching on many other subjects. For the first time in years he broke his silence about the so-called Indian States and the medieval rule maintained, with British support, by their autocratic princes.* The Congress, with its superb political organization in every province of British India, had steered clear of trying to organize the subjects of the princely tyrants since it feared its organizers would be clapped into jail, tortured and even murdered. Gandhi had explained briefly to me one day another, and perhaps more important, reason. His struggle had to be directed against the British, since they ruled India. When that rule was broken and India became self-governing, the pampered princes would have to fall in line. They would no longer have the British around to prop up their shaky thrones. In the meantime the Congress had supported a separate States Peoples' Movement for democracy within the autocratic princely states. Now, suprisingly, Gandhi turned to the subject. I think he knew already that the British would try to turn the maharajas and nawabs against the Indian nationalists at the Round Table Conference. The divide and rule

---

*Some 80 million Indians lived in 562 states, which had a combined territory of 575,000 square miles. Most of them were small and petty principalities. Only forty states were large enough to have much political significance. In them most of the 80 million Indians lived "in a state of things which no civilized government should countenance or tolerate," to quote the president of the Indian States Peoples' Conference in 1927. An eminent Indian, Sir Albion Bannerji, had found that these hapless people were "treated like dumb, driven cattle" by their tyrannical maharajas, many of whom were cruel, corrupt, depraved and debauched. The government of India and the British government in London knew all about the state of things in these princely states.

One of the worst despots in my time in India was the Maharaja of Patiala. When a group of distinguished Indians once charged him with everything from rape to murder, Lord Irwin ordered an investigation—by a British official chosen by the Maharaja. The investigation was secret, and cleared the ruler. Shortly afterward the Maharaja withdrew his support for a self-governing India, and was immediately promoted by the King-Emperor to be an honorary lieutenant general in His Majesty's armed forces. Though honorary, that was quite a high rank.

policy of successive Viceroys had favored the princes against the Indians of British India.

Explaining that an independent India would be a democracy, Gandhi said: "Undiluted autocracy, however benevolent it may be, and undiluted democracy are an incompatible mixture which is bound to result in an explosion. It is only with the greatest restraint that the Congress has refrained from mixing in the affairs of these states. I hope the princes will not now shut their ears to the pleas of their people, who also want to be free."

What Gandhi said in a number of frank talks with me on the days immediately following the truce formed the basis of a new and unswerving stand to which he would adhere through many setbacks until in the end—in a very few years—it brought him what he sought. The last stretch of the road to India's independence began that first week of March in Delhi in 1931. Gandhi tried to tell me this in one talk after another that week and in ensuing weeks. But I was too skeptical, too ignorant, too much impressed by British power to fully believe him.

The next day, March 6, I had a long conversation with Gandhi. I came prepared in my mind with a number of definite questions, and I told him I would appreciate it if he would answer them as concisely as he could. It became obvious from his first words that he was having second thoughts about the truce. The pact with Lord Irwin, which he had praised so highly the day before because it brought peace to the country, was actually, he now stressed to me, a very provisional thing. Unless it brought India self-government very quickly, it would fall apart. I tried to pin him down on this, since his position the day before, I thought, had been so contradictory. He on his part denied any contradictions. At the coming conference in London, he would, he said, insist on "complete independence—with but the shadow of safeguards the British were talking about."

"I am willing," he explained, "to reconcile complete independence with remaining in the British Empire, provided it is as an equal partner, with the right to secede from the Empire if and when India wishes."

Gandhi must have been giving this aspect considerable thought, for he launched into a long explanation of his views.

"My idea of *Purna Swaraj*, complete independence, does not exclude association with the Empire to the mutual advantage of both parties. But the right to secede is certainly there. Complete independence may mean separation, but if we remain a part of the Commonwealth, instead of Downing Street being the center of India, Delhi would become the center. I admit that the popular imagination cannot conceive of the British rising to the height to grant this. The British are said to love liberty for themselves and for others. But they have a faculty for self-delusion that no other nation has."

I pressed Gandhi to define the safeguards which he would accept at the coming conference.

"You agree to some safeguards—that's in the agreement you signed."

"Certainly. But not the present ones."

"What safeguards would you accept?"

"Minority safeguards, for one thing," Gandhi said. "We must safeguard the rights of minorities. That is a legitimate safeguard. I would accept also a safeguard in the matter of finance. As much of the debt as falls to our lot would have to be secured, and to that extent I would be bound to entertain safeguards for the country's credit and its consequent expansion."

It was interesting to hear this most unworldly man talking about a nation's finances and credit. One of his advisers on such questions, Professor K. T. Shah, of Bombay University, had told me he was constantly astonished at the Mahatma's grasp of them.

"Would you repudiate the national debt?" I asked Gandhi. The British-owned newspapers in India had been saying he would.

"I would not repudiate one single farthing that can be legitimately credited to us. The Congress never sought to repudiate a single rupee of the national debt. What it has insisted on is the justice of the obligations that might be imposed on the incoming government." And he went into some detail to explain that he opposed shouldering those parts of the debt that had been incurred in fighting Britain's wars in which India was not involved, or in keeping up an excessive British military establishment in India merely to keep the Indians down. This led to another question.

"What about the Army?" I asked. "The safeguard that leaves India's so-called defense solely in the hands of the British."

"As far as the Army is concerned," Gandhi said, "I cannot think of any safeguard except that we should guarantee the pay and the fulfillment of any other conditions in respect to British officers and soldiers whose services may be necessary to India."

Nehru had told me he reluctantly agreed that an independent India would have to pay the rather affluent pensions of the British soldiers, but he was for packing the whole lot of them home as soon as independence came.

I then asked Gandhi if he could clear up the dispute that already was breaking out between the government and the Congress about the calling off of the boycott of British goods. The truce agreement stated that the boycott of *British* goods *as a political weapon* would be discontinued. But Jawaharlal Nehru, as president of the Congress, had issued a statement immediately saying the boycott of *foreign* goods would continue as before. This had brought charges of bad faith from the government.

"I don't see why there is so much misunderstanding of the boycott," Gandhi said, a smile breaking over his face. "The boycott will not be relaxed, as it is not a political weapon. It is indispensable for our national existence."

There was a great deal of concern, not only in India but abroad, I said, about a much more important problem: the inability of the Hindus and the Moslems to settle their differences as a prelude to joining together to seek independence for India.

"Do you really expect," I asked, "to settle the Hindu-Moslem quarrel before the next Round Table Conference, which you are pledged to attend? I know you've been working on it for years, sometimes with success, but a final settlement has always eluded you. Do you really expect to achieve one now?"

"I hope to," he responded. "And if we don't settle it, there's not much use of holding another Round Table Conference." He paused a moment, and then looked me straight in the eye. "I think you've seen yourself since you came out to India that there's no enmity between the masses of Hindus and Moslems. For the most part they live peacefully side by side—all over India.

"The problem is not the enmity between the masses, but between their Hindu and Moslem leaders. They are the ones who stir up the trouble. And by doing so they play right into the hands of the British. However, I've not given up. In the next weeks and months before the conference I shall spend most of my time and energies on this problem. It has to be solved."

Gandhi was as good as his word. I would watch him during the rest of my stay in India laboring week after week to reach an agreement with the Moslem leaders before he went to London. Sometimes, as in previous years, he seemed very near to success, but in the end he could not quite achieve it. Perhaps, I thought at the summer's end, it was, like so many problems in history, insoluble for the moment. In India it would prove so right up to the end.

When the solution finally came, on the eve of India's independence and as a condition for achieving it, Gandhi would refuse to accept it. It would break his heart.

Late on the following evening, after his supper and prayer meeting, Gandhi called me in and asked if I would take down on my portable typewriter a statement he wanted to make first of all to his fellow countrymen and, secondly perhaps, to the world. There had been many misunderstandings of the truce, he said, which he wanted to clear up, especially with his own people.

"What I have in mind to say," he mused, "probably is of little or no interest to you as an American journalist. But if there is anything you can use, feel free to do so."

I was a little surprised, but certainly delighted, at his request.

Surely there must be a typewriter around the house, I thought, though I had never seen one. However, Gandhi already had done me so many personal kindnesses, had been so generous of his time with me, that I was glad to do this little chore. Every moment in his luminous presence, despite my moments of skepticism, was precious to me.

That evening, as he dictated his statement to me, Gandhi seemed more eloquent than I had ever heard him before. He was both relaxed and rather somber, his voice low and beautifully modulated, the words coming out slowly but distinctly in a sort of rhythm that at times approached poetry. A good deal of what he said was a repetition, in different and more flowing words, of what he already had told me, and in omitting them here I lose some of the poetic effect they had on me. But some of Gandhi's philosophy, especially about violence, freedom and suffering, comes through.

First, the Mahatma addressed his fellow countrymen.

"I know," he said, "that there will be many Indians disappointed with this settlement. Heroic suffering is like the breath of their nostrils . . . But suffering has its well-defined limits. Suffering can be both wise and unwise. And when the limit is reached, to prolong it would not only be unwise but the height of folly . . . I am therefore thankful to the Almighty that the settlement was reached, and the country was spared, at least for the time being, and I hope for all time, the suffering which in the event of a breakdown would have been intensified a hundredfold."

I wanted to interrupt and ask him why and how it would have been so greatly intensified, but this was not an interview. He went on to assure the Indian people that the goal of the Congress remained complete independence, repeating much of what he had told us earlier but enlarging a little on what he expected from the English and expressing it with growing and, for him, unusual passion. I thought for a moment of how eloquent it would sound and how moving to the Indian masses if they could hear it over the newfangled radio, which had not yet come to India.

"If the English really want to help us," Gandhi said, "they must be prepared to let India feel the same glow of freedom for which they themselves would die in order to possess. In our new freedom we may make mistakes. Freedom is not worth having if it does not connote freedom to err and even to sin. If God has given the humblest of His creatures the freedom to err, it passes my comprehension how human beings, be they ever so experienced and able, can delight in depriving other human beings of that precious right."

He next appealed to the small band of terrorists in the country to give him a chance to finish the revolution in his own non-violent way. I had got the impression that Gandhi did not like to talk of, or even think of, the terrorists, small in number though they were, since it so offended his lifelong dedication to non-violence as the only means of achieving independence. But now he plunged into the subject. He had his reasons.

"There is, no doubt," he said, "a small but active organization in India which would secure India's liberty through violent action. I appeal to it, as I have done before, to desist from its activities, if not yet out of conviction, then out of experience. They will not deny that the almost miraculous mass awakening in India was possible only because of the mysterious but unfailing effect of non-violence.

"After all," he went on, "it is hardly a few months since my march to the sea. A few months in the life of an experiment affecting three hundred million souls are but a second in the cycle of time. Let them wait for a while. Let them preserve their precious lives for the service of the Motherland, to which all presently will be called. And let them give the Congress an opportunity of securing the release of all the other political prisoners who were convicted of acts of violence, and maybe, even, rescuing from the gallows those who are condemned to them as guilty of murder—though I want to raise no false hopes."

This last was a reference to Bhagat Singh, a fiery young Sikh revolutionary and his two companions, who had been convicted on extremely circumstantial evidence of the murder of a British police officer in Lahore and sentenced to death. Gandhi knew—even an American correspondent who had been in India only a year knew—that when a British policeman, official or soldier was murdered in India, an Indian life, or probably two or three or four Indian lives, would be taken in revenge and as a lesson, though not necessarily the lives of those who had done the murder.

But in Bhagat Singh's case, the evidence had seemed to the Indians so shadowy that the country had become aroused to a high pitch of indignation, and it had been understood in Gandhi's circle—and, I gathered, by the Mahatma himself—that if a peace settlement was concluded, the Viceroy would commute the death sentences of the three alleged terrorists in order to allay public opinion and preserve a relative calm for the coming Round Table Conference.

In the next few days Gandhi would beg the Viceroy to spare the lives of the three young men, but to no avail. On March 19 it was announced that Lord Irwin had rejected the appeals of the three men themselves, of Gandhi and other Indian leaders, and that the condemned trio would be hanged the following week. They were—in great secrecy—on March 24, their bodies hastily cremated within the prison grounds and the ashes tossed into the river Sutlej, sacred to the Sikhs and the Hindus. The British authorities justified the unusual action—usually the bodies were turned over to the families after execution for a proper religious burial—as necessary to avoid mobs getting out of control if a public funeral was held. All the next day India was in mourning over the execution of Bhagat Singh and his companions. A spontaneous *hartal* resulted in the closing of shops, offices and factories throughout the country. Nationalist tricolored flags flew at half-mast. In Lahore armed British police and a regiment of British troops patrolled the streets and kept the sullen crowds moving. In Karachi, to which I had gone to attend the forty-fifth annual convention of the Indian National Congress, the feeling of anger and resentment was so strong that it looked as if the Congress might repudiate the Gandhi-Irwin truce.*

That challenge and other consequences of the hangings lay ahead as Gandhi drew to a close in his dictation. No doubt he foresaw them, but I felt that despite his warning that he would raise no false hopes about saving the life of Bhagat Singh, he expected the Viceroy to be compassionate enough (and politically wise enough) to spare it. It was no secret that he had gotten along rather well with Lord Irwin personally. Their deep religious feelings had created a certain bond, and though otherwise they were as different as night and day (the austere, aristocratic English lord and the humble, ascetic Hindu), they had achieved a considerable respect for each other and even a little understanding. Now Gandhi was telling me, as he paused to collect his thoughts, that he wanted to close with a message to the young.

"One word to the youth of India," he began, "and I am finished.

"You ought to understand that we have entered into no peace treaty. It is a provisional, temporary settlement. I beseech you young men not to bid goodbye to common sense, to cool courage, to patience, to reason. I have claimed to be a young man of sixty-one. But even if I were to be labeled as a dilapidated old fogey, I have a right to appeal to your good senses. I do not want you to take for granted all that old men say to you, but I want you to consider it and weigh it, and if you find that we old men have bungled, that we have been guilty of weakness, get us to abdicate, and assume the reins yourselves."

He appealed to the young to observe a "disciplined obedience" after the suspension of civil disobedience. In fact he ended with a

*Though Nehru did not condone Bhagat Singh's alleged deed—he thought terrorism was out of date for the stage which the Indian revolution had reached by non-violence—he explained to me in Delhi why the young Punjabi had become a hero in India. If he had killed the British police officer in Lahore, the public thought he was only avenging the death of one of the Punjab's most beloved leaders, a former president of the Congress, Lala Lajpat Rai. While leading a peaceful demonstration in Lahore, he had been savagely beaten by a young British police officer and had died shortly after from his injuries. It was this officer whom the terrorists, whoever they were, believed they had killed.

typical homely lecture on the subject. It was one of his favorite topics.

"I beseech you to realize the supreme importance of discipline. Let it not be said that we are a people incapable of maintaining discipline. Indiscipline will mean disaster and make one like me who is pining to see India independent perish in sorrow and grief. We are as determined as ever to rule ourselves. It is for us to make the effort. The result will always be in God's hands."

I was so moved by some of his words and the simple, sincere way he spoke them that at moments I had difficulty in putting them down on my typewriter. If only the people of India—and of Britain, for that matter—could have *heard* them, I kept thinking. They sounded better than they read. I pulled the last page out of my machine, with the carbons, and handed them to Gandhi. With the help of Desai he sorted out the sheets and handed me one copy.

"Perhaps you can use something," he said and thanked me.

In retrospect there is something weird and unreal about those Delhi talks in the early spring of 1931. That they marked an important turning point in the Indian revolution seemed obvious at the time to Gandhi, and even to me. But not to the British. To them the Gandhi-Irwin pact had merely brought an end to a temporarily troublesome situation. They still had no inkling of the depth of the Indian revolution which Gandhi was unleashing nor of how it was being kindled by a resurgent Indian nationalism, a nationalism that across the Himalayas was also beginning to stir China to throw off foreign domination, and that one American historian, Hans Kohn, already believed was being turned into what he called "The Revolt of Asia."

At the beginning of 1931 the British government had no intention of giving up in any foreseeable future this gem and cornerstone of the Empire, which was India. It saw no need to. By playing the various Indian factions against one another, by a display of force when needed, it could continue to rule India indefinitely and milk what it could from it to help sustain the declining economy at home. In none of the talks I had in those days in Delhi with the Viceroy and his principal aides did I discern a feeling that time and the course of history might be running against them.*

*I would later see a little of Lord Irwin when, as Lord Halifax, he became British Foreign Secretary and, during part of the second World War, British ambassador in Washington. Though I still liked and admired him as a man, I could not help reflecting that the tumultuous events which were tearing up the world in the 1930's were largely beyond the comprehension of one with his narrow, aristocratic British breeding and resulting limited views. A steadfast character was not enough in these troubled times. A readiness to face the new and unexpected, a comprehension of the forces behind the strange twists history was taking, were needed.

Though Gandhi and the Viceroy got along personally quite well during their marathon talks that spring of 1931 in Delhi—their deep devotion to their respective religions seems to have forged a certain link between them—Lord Irwin, I felt, never quite grasped the revolutionary character of Gandhi nor of the revolutionary forces which the Mahatma was marshaling to bring an end to British rule.

Later, as Foreign Secretary, he showed an even more appalling ignorance of the revolutionary character of Adolf Hitler and of the forces of destruction which the Nazi dictator was unleashing in Europe toward the end of the 1930's. This would prove even more disastrous to British fortunes than the failure to understand Gandhi's India in time.

In the fall of 1937, when I was stationed in Germany, the new British Prime Minister, Neville Chamberlain, sent Halifax on a pilgrimage to Berchtesgaden to see Hitler, to try to size him up, ascertain what he was up to and wanted, and whether it would not be possible and even desirable for Britain to reach an understanding with Nazi Germany. Halifax, like Chamberlain after him, was charmed by Hitler and taken in by him. He reported to the Foreign Office in writing that "the German Chancellor and others gave the impression that they were not likely to embark on adventures involving force or at least war." And to Chamberlain himself Halifax reported orally that Hitler "was not bent on early adventures, partly because they might be unprofitable, and partly because he was busy building up Germany internally . . . Goering had assured him that not one drop of German blood would be shed in Europe unless Germany was absolutely forced to do it. The Germans gave him [Halifax] the impression . . . of intending to achieve their aims in orderly fashion."—Charles C. Tansill: *Back Door to War*, pp. 365–66.

By one of those ironies of which history is so full, Hitler had in fact on November 5, 1937, exactly fourteen days *before* he saw Halifax and prattled about peace, called in his generals and told them that he had decided "irrevocably" on war. (See the author's *The Rise and Fall of the Third Reich*, pp. 303–8.)

Hitler did not, of course, convey this historic decision to Lord Halifax; he contrived to give quite a contrary impression to his gullible British guest, and this impression, when conveyed to Chamberlain, greatly pleased the Prime Minister. "The German visit [of Halifax]," Chamberlain wrote in his diary, "was from my point of view a great success

Gandhi was sure of it. He hammered into me again and again that, though the British did not sense it, *time* was with him and his nationalist movement. *Time, and the course of history.* He understood what few Indians and fewer Englishmen realized, even in 1931, that the Great War, though Britain had emerged on the winning side, had fatally sapped the strength of the mother nation—the terrible loss in lives and treasure could never be made good. In its deteriorating condition Britain was bound to yield on India if he could show that a third of a billion people could not for long be held in subjection against their will by a weakened British power.

Though Gandhi was not a profound student of history—he had not had time to try to be one, he said once—he had within him something more important: a sense of history.

He had no illusions that the Viceroy and the handful of English officials who ruled India in the tea-party, polo-playing, hothouse atmosphere of Delhi and Simla (the summer capital), isolated from the ferment of the vast country, understood the depth of the awakening in India nor the historical force it was bringing to bear on the fortunes of the subcontinent. He was sure they did not. Nor did he expect the British government in London to have any more understanding. He had sometimes ruminated on the American Revolution and concluded that no British statesmanship, no more in the twentieth century than in the eighteenth, had the wisdom to give up what was impossible to keep, without a struggle.* The struggle in America had been bloody. His would be bloodless, but just as relentless.

That he would win it before he died, he had no doubt, though,

---

because it achieved its object, that of creating an atmosphere in which it is possible to discuss with Germany the practical questions involved in a European settlement."— Keith Feiling: *The Life of Neville Chamberlain* (Macmillan), p. 332.

*Gandhi would have been pleased, I think, had he lived, to hear Queen Elizabeth II's speech in Philadelphia on July 6, 1976, on the occasion of the U.S. Bicentennial. "We lost the American colonies," said the Queen, "because we lacked that statesmanship 'to know the right time, and the manner of yielding what is impossible to keep.'" The comment would have been apt for India in the 1930's.

as I reminded him once, he was approaching sixty-two and there was not much time.

"God willing, there are still a few years," he smiled.

That it would be only a few years—and while he still lived—before independence was won, he reiterated to me time and again in our talks and walks that spring and summer and fall of 1931. I would be sometimes taken back by his bubbling confidence, and accuse him of teasing me, as indeed he often liked to do.

"You will see, my dear Mr. Shirer!" he would say. "We shall gain our freedom—in my lifetime!"

"Well, the British still have the guns," I would retort.

"Yes, but we have something more important than guns. We have truth and justice—and time—on our side." And then more seriously: "You cannot hold down much longer three hundred and fifty million people who are determined to be free. You will see!"

And finally, at the end of a walk once in Delhi, he started to chuckle after he had repeated to me for the dozenth time his confident prediction.

"If I were a betting man," he said, laughing, "I would make you a bet."

"I would take you up on it, if you did," I said, "though it's a bet I would like to lose."

"Just remember this, my friend," he concluded. "Just remember what I've harped on so often, even though you don't believe me: *I shall see India free! Before I die!*"

"By the way," Gandhi had said that evening after his dictation as I was putting my typewriter in its case and preparing to leave. "When are you going to join me in one of my morning walks?"

"Whenever I'm invited," I said half jokingly.

"Five in the morning is a little early for you, isn't it?" he teased me, breaking into a grin.

"No. It's late for me," I said, explaining that because of the difference in time between Delhi and Chicago, I often worked until two or three in the morning filing my dispatches. "But it's easy to stay up until five."

Besides politics there was another matter I wanted to discuss with Gandhi. Two or three times he had touched briefly on what he called the value of comparative religion, suggesting that I give it some thought. Perhaps he had sensed my skepticism about my own Christian religion, which he himself said had so inspired him. Though a devout Hindu, he had explained that his religion was really a compound of the best in his own and other religions: in Buddhism, with its wisdom about man's lot on this earth; in Mohammedanism, which he liked for its appeal for brotherhood; and above all in Christianity, as revealed in the New Testament (he could not stomach the Old). He had promised to give me more of his thoughts on this as soon as he had time.*

The first walk with Gandhi took place in Delhi a couple of weeks later, on March 21. In the interval I accompanied him to a tumultuous homecoming in Ahmedabad and, at his request, on a jaunt through a countryside of tiny villages so far off the beaten track that he said few foreigners and indeed few Indians who lived in the great cities had ever seen them.

"You will never get to know the real India," he had remarked

---

* He had suggested that I read the Koran, and I bought a copy and dutifully perused it, but without finding much inspiration. I got much more, in poetry and in a philosophy of the meaning of existence, from the *Bhagavad Gita*.

To Carlyle the Koran was "as toilsome reading as I ever undertook, a wearisome, confused jumble, crude, incondite." Later, after further perusal, he found "merit in it quite other than literary." Apparently, though, in its original Arabic, it is a literary masterpiece. To Sir H. A. R. Gibb, the English Arabic scholar, ". . . no man in fifteen hundred years has ever played on that deep-toned instrument [the Arabic language] with such power, such boldness, and such range of emotional effect as Mohammed did."—H. A. R. Gibb: *Mohammedanism: An Historical Survey* (New York: Mentor Books, 1955), p. 37.

What bothered me most about the Koran was what distressed Gandhi about the Old Testament: the insistent harping on the fear of God's wrath and the consequences to man of incurring it.

one day, "until you get out of Delhi, Bombay and the other cities and see how the overwhelming mass of Indians, half starved and in rags, pass their lives in their wretched huts in half a million villages, toiling from dawn to dark in the nearby sun-parched fields to wrest a little food from a worn-out soil."

5

The days that followed the signing of the Delhi Pact that spring remain indelibly in my memory of the time in India.

They brought me closer to Gandhi, to further insights into his subtle mind and complex personality and his genius, and made me a witness for the first time to his tremendous—and yet, to me, mysterious—hold on the Indian masses. This last, this uncanny rapport that Gandhi had with huge gatherings of common people, most of them illiterate and ragged, which somehow made him, in their eyes, the manifestation of their collective conscience, was for me, when I first experienced it, an overwhelming experience.

Perhaps we will never understand the riddle of communication. The very great have it. Gandhi had it, more than any leader I have ever seen. He understood too that communication is a two-way phenomenon. He reached the masses, but they gave him back something that bolstered his confidence and his determination to continue the struggle to free them.

And their frenzied acclaim, their outpouring of affection for him, and their belief in him, their gathering by the tens or hundreds of thousands just to *see* him, were spontaneous. Later I would see Hitler wildly acclaimed by a mass of 200,000 Germans at a Nuremberg party rally. But that meeting was staged, the audience captive. The great crowds all over India that came on their own to hail Gandhi were unorganized and therefore sometimes disorderly, milling about in their excitement at merely being in the presence of the Mahatma. The Germans I saw in the Nazi time were deeply moved by the masterful oratory of Hitler. Gandhi was not an orator. He scarcely raised his voice and made no gestures. I doubt if the vast majority in the huge crowds I saw ever caught his words. They were fulfilled by the sight of him and especially by receiving his *darshan*. This puzzled me at first, and still does in memory. I witnessed the phenomenon; I cannot say that I fully understood it. The Indians, even the lowest, illiterate peasant, seemed to do so—instinctively. They felt in the presence of the great man that something immense was suddenly happening in their drab lives, that this saintly man in his loincloth cared about them, understood their wretched plight and somehow had the power, even in the face of the rule of the great white sahibs in Delhi and the provincial capitals, to do something about it.

From the moment Gandhi arrived in the early evening of March 8 at the Delhi railway station to catch the train to Ahmedabad, he was beset and acclaimed by great crowds of delirious men and women. Tens of thousands jammed into the station and the surrounding streets leading to it, and Gandhi only made it to the lone third-class passenger compartment in the decrepit baggage car usually reserved for railway workmen after a phalanx of police, with him in tow, worked its way through the shouting mob and delivered him at trainside. All that night and through the next day to the end of the twenty-four-hour journey as the train crept hundreds of miles along a narrow-gauge track over the Rajputana plateau thousands upon thousands rushed the rail stations en route and all but wrecked his dirty little compartment in their enthusiasm to get a glimpse of him. How the word of

Gandhi's coming penetrated the remotest villages no one knew. In India, I was beginning to think, there must be some underground means of communication. It baffled the authorities.

Gandhi got no sleep at all. All night long at every station stop hordes of villagers and peasants were waiting for him, swarming around the train until they found his compartment. Rail officials, police and soldiers exhorted the crowds in vain to step back so that the train might get under way. When it did manage to move, hundreds hung on to the steps of the cars in order to ride on to the next stop with the Mahatma. The train was falling behind schedule. A mile or two out of the station it would have to halt while the train crew and police brushed off the fanatical peasants like flies. At one station during the night a crowd of fierce-looking Rajputs with long beards descended upon the train. They kept flashing their lanterns into each compartment until they found their hero. Then in the melee, as the crowd pushed and shoved around Gandhi's compartment, several lanterns were smashed, fell under the coach and started a fire. It looked for a moment that the car would go up in smoke and that Gandhi would be lucky to escape with his life.

These poor peasants and villagers came not only to see Gandhi but to bring him offerings: coins, fruits, vegetables, clothes, spinning wheels and whatnot. Rail officials spent much of their time at each station stuffing the gifts into the baggage car until it was loaded to the top.

At midnight Gandhi began his twenty-four hours of silence. But the vast crowds, it was evident, had come not to hear him but to *see* him. At one station a college teacher joined us in our first-class compartment; he was trying to get to Ahmedabad for some conference and looked somewhat roughed up from pushing his way through the mob.

"How do you explain these crowds?" I asked him. "We've seen them station after station all night long."

"You see," he said in almost impeccable English, "well, you see, it's really quite simple. For these masses Gandhi holds out the only light, the only hope there is. They want to see the man who, they're told, goes around half naked like themselves and yet who dares to present their grievances to the mighty, bemedaled white Viceroy himself.

"And it's all the more remarkable because"—he paused—"I don't know whether you realize it, but you've been traveling most of the way through Rajputana, which is made up almost exclusively of princely states. There are nineteen of them, you know, all autocracies ruled by maharajas and nawabs. The people in these crowds see in Gandhi, first of all, a deliverer from the misrule of these damned princes. They may be ignorant, but they are not stupid. They know that these petty tyrants, once the British, who protect them, are gone, will be finished."

One of these princes, the Nawab of Palanpur, through whose state we passed before reaching Ahmedabad, got on the train when it stopped at Palanpur. He had wired Gandhi that he would be honored to accompany him through his dominion. So the bejeweled Nawab, who was a Moslem, climbed humbly into the filthy third-class compartment—he was accustomed, one of his aides told me, to traveling in a deluxe salon car of his own—and sat down with the greatest of the Hindus for an hour's chat, promising, Gandhi told me later, to throw his weight toward a settlement of the Hindu-Moslem problem so that the Indians could present a united front to the British in the coming negotiations in London. The Nawab must have been one of the more progressive princes, who saw the handwriting on the wall. There were a few, Gandhi had said, but they were distinctly in the minority.

It was nearly midnight before the little train, several hours late, steamed slowly into the station at Ahmedabad, the city from which just a year ago Gandhi had set out with a little band of disciples on the march to the sea to make illegal salt—a symbolic act which the British had at first pooh-poohed and which to most of us in the West who read about it had made no sense, but which had inflamed the imagination of the Indian people and launched the Mahatma on the first major step of his revolution through non-violent civil disobedience.

I doubt if he expected such a tumultuous, riotous welcome as he was about to receive, though he had been warned. At a suburban station a group of Congress leaders, accompanied by a police inspector, had waited on Gandhi and urged him to leave the train there. A howling mob of more than 100,000 men and women had taken possession of the main railroad station, they said. They feared he might get trampled to death. Already several persons had been injured, they said, as thousands fought to get as close to the station platform as possible.

Gandhi, who had no fear of anything so far as I could observe—not even of death—refused to budge. The good people, he said, had come to greet him. He would not disappoint them. He didn't. But he was lucky, I thought, to come out alive from the ensuing melee in the station. Not even the wildest scenes we had seen en route compared to those we now experienced as the train slowly came to a halt, and the crowd, half crazed with excitement, took over. Thousands fought to approach Gandhi's compartment.

They were jammed together like sardines, and as they pushed and shoved, they could not help tearing the clothes off one another and ripping the sandals from one another's feet. Gandhi appeared at the window of his compartment, beaming and clasping his hands together, and gave his *darshan,* but for once it did not seem enough to quiet the crowd. It milled about in front of him, everyone shouting and shoving. Had Gandhi stepped out onto the platform, as he several times started to do, I feared he would be torn to pieces. Already Congress Red Cross workers were beginning to carry out the injured, though they could make little progress through the vast sea of churning people. Finally, a group of Congress volunteers with red armbands on their sleeves—they had been trained in crowd control—surrounded Gandhi's compartment. Gradually they pushed back through the throng. And at last, long after midnight, they managed to make a narrow path to a side exit and spirit their leader away to safer parts.

The tumultuous welcome for Gandhi continued in Ahmedabad for the rest of the week. Before it was over hundreds more women and men had been injured as the crazed crowds got out of control, and Gandhi himself had been trampled upon and hurt and become ill from sheer exhaustion. Not too ill, though, to continue his politicking, rousing the masses with his promise of freedom soon.

His attitude toward the British was stiffening. On arriving in Ahmedabad, the textile capital of India, he had learned from the millowners (who were heavily financing his movement) as well as from the workers and from dozens of Congress party leaders who flocked from all parts of the country to confer with him, that they were far from pleased by his concessions in the Delhi agreement. Some of them told him frankly that unless he won the substance of independence in London, with Indian control of India's finances and a very limited transition period for control of the Army and foreign affairs by the British, he would have to launch another civil-disobedience campaign or risk losing his leadership of the nationalist movement.

Gandhi had reacted to this feeling among his supporters by assuring the crowds he addressed during the week that unless he got a definite promise of independence within a short time, he *would* relaunch the revolution. A good part of his week was also spent with Congress leaders discussing plans for it. Much of his time was also spent in an attempt at sheer survival among the unruly crowds, as tens of thousands of frenzied supporters fought to get near to him. He himself, he said, had never before seen anything like them.

The day after his arrival at Ahmedabad a vast assembly of 150,000 men and women gathered on the banks of the Sabarmati River to hear him speak. I doubt if many caught his words. The churning throng kept pushing toward the stand on which he was trying to address them. Gandhi finally cut his remarks short and, surrounded by a guard of Congress volunteers, tried to get out of the place alive. But he was instantly surrounded by thousands of shouting, excited fanatics, who brushed his escort aside. In the melee his right foot was trampled on and a toe was crushed. His doctors put him to bed and urged him to give up further meetings.

He had a fever and was suffering, they said, from complete exhaustion.

But he was up again the next day to keep an engagement that had a special significance to him. This was a meeting for women only, and Gandhi wanted to make of it an occasion to thank not only them but all the women in India for the part they had played in the civil-disobedience movement. Tens of thousands of them had been beaten in the streets by the lathis of the British-led police and then gone to jail. The awakening of women in a country where hitherto, protected as they were by ancient customs, which had confined them to the home and household cares, they had taken no part in the rough and tumble of public life had surprised the British and even the Indians, including Gandhi, who was now determined to keep them stirred up and to make them increasingly an integral part of his revolution.

These brave women in their attractive saris turned out to be as unruly as the men. Gandhi was to have addressed them in the city's principal vegetable market, a huge covered square. But with twenty thousand of them packed inside so tightly that they were gasping for breath—it was a scorching, hot day—and thirty thousand more outside clamoring to get in, there was utter confusion, and soon this mob of women got out of control, those outside fighting to get in, and those inside striving to press nearer to their idol so that they might catch his words. What followed, I suppose, was inevitable, but I had never seen anything like it before, nor have I since. Hundreds of slender little women were swept off their feet and were trampled on. In one spot they were piled up several deep. Dozens of Congress Red Cross workers, carrying stretchers, tried to get to them but were themselves swept off their feet. Gandhi, standing on a platform in the middle of the market, tried vainly to quiet the surging mass, but the cries of the women made such a hubbub that none could hear him. After attempting a few words he gave up and was escorted out by a squad of Congress volunteers. But outside the Mahatma tried to address the crowd there from an improvised platform. The ensuing affray was even worse than the one we had just seen inside. Hundreds more women were trampled down. Gandhi finally gave up and, sick at heart, allowed himself to be spirited away by his guards, but not until he too was badly pummeled once again. A few more meetings like this, I thought, and he would be torn to pieces.

All that week in Ahmedabad when I returned to my quarters to try in my dispatches to describe the tumultuous scenes of the day and then spend the rest of the evening trying to sort out my thoughts, I kept experiencing in my imagination an event that once had taken place in this very building where I had been put up. This was the Circuit House, which had been converted from a courthouse to a rest house for Europeans. Here in March 1922, exactly nine years before, Gandhi had been tried and convicted of sedition after one of the strangest and most eloquent pleas ever made in a courtroom—not in self-defense, for he pleaded guilty, but in defense of the right of India to be free—and sentenced to six years in prison. The trial and what Gandhi said at it launched him on the road he had followed to this day. His moving speech to the court constituted the most devastating indictment of British rule—and misrule—in India that had yet been heard in the land. It summed up with an inspired eloquence, which I believe will reverberate in India for centuries to come, the story of his life, why after first loyally accepting the Empire, he had turned against it and why he was devoting his life to freeing India from its grip. His trial, conviction and sentence was one of the crucial turning points on the road to revolution and Indian independence.

6

In this house, where I stayed the week in Ahmedabad, Mohandas K. Gandhi was being tried on a hot March day of 1922 before Mr. C. N. Broomsfield, I.C.S., District and Sessions Judge, and Sir J. T. Strangman, the Advocate-General, was stating the case for the prosecution, saying that the charge was that of bringing, or attempting to bring, into hatred or contempt, or exciting, or attempting to excite, disaffection toward His Majesty's government, established by law in British India, and that Gandhi was guilty of these things because of three articles he had written and published in his weekly magazine, Young India, though indeed it could be proved, if need be, that the accused had begun preaching disaffection long before the publication of the said three articles.

And Gandhi broke in: "I plead guilty to all the charges."

And the Advocate-General argued that the accused was guilty of launching a campaign to spread disaffection openly and systematically, to render the government impossible and overthrow it. The accused, he said, was a man of high educational qualifications and evidently from his writings a recognized leader. His writings were those of an educated man, *and not the writings of an obscure man, and the court must consider to what the results of a campaign of the nature disclosed in his writings must inevitably lead. They had examples before them in the last three months, the tragedies of Bombay* and Chauri Chaura,† leading to murder and destruction of private property. It was true that in the course of his articles the accused preached non-violence. But what was the use of preaching non-violence when he preached dissatisfaction toward the government or openly instigated others to overthrow it? These were the circumstances which he, the Advocate-General, asked the court to take into account in sentencing the accused, and it would be for the court to consider those circumstances, which certainly involved sentences of severity.*

And the judge said: "Mr. Gandhi, do you wish to make a statement on the question of sentence?"

Mr. Gandhi: "I would like to make a statement.

"Before I read my statement," Gandhi said, "I would like to state that I entirely endorse the learned Advocate-General's remarks in connection with my humble self. I think he was entirely fair to me in all the statements he has made, because it is very true, and I have no desire to conceal from this court the fact, that to preach disaffection toward the existing system of government has become almost a passion with me, and the learned Advocate-General is also entirely in the right when he says that my preaching of disaffection did not commence with my connection with Young India but that it commenced much earlier. And in the statement that I am about to read, it will be my painful duty to admit before this court that it commenced much earlier than the period stated by the Advocate-General. It is the most painful duty for me, but I have to discharge that duty knowing the responsibility that rests on my shoulders in connection with the Bombay

---

* At Bombay, on November 17, 1921, on the occasion of the arrival of the Prince of Wales (later King Edward VIII and thereafter the Duke of Windsor), riots broke out in which a large number of persons were killed and wounded. Gandhi had asked the masses to boycott the Prince's arrival, and when various Indians, mostly Parsis, insisted on taking part in the reception for the Prince, the mob attacked them.

† At Chauri Chaura, a village in the district of Gorakhpur, a mob, after having been fired on by the police, got out of control, charged the police, drove them back into the police station, set fire to the building, and clubbed to death all those who tried to escape. Twenty-two policemen lost their lives; most of them were burned to death.

occurrences and the Chauri Chaura occurrences. *Thinking over these deeply and sleeping over them night after night, it is impossible for me to dissociate myself from the diabolical crimes of Chauri Chaura or the mad outrages of Bombay. He is quite right when he says that as a man of responsibility, a man having received a fair share of education, having had a fair share of experience of this world, I should have known the consequences of every one of my acts. I knew that I was playing with fire, I ran the risk, and if I was set free I would still do the same. I have felt this morning that I would have failed in my duty, if I did not say this.*

"I wanted to avoid violence. . . . Non-violence is the first article of my creed. . . . But I had to make my choice. I had either to submit to a system which I considered has done an irreparable harm to my country, or incur the risk of the mad fury of my people bursting forth, when they understood the truth from my lips. I know that my people have sometimes gone mad. I am deeply sorry for it, and I am therefore here to submit not to a light penalty but to the heaviest penalty. I do not ask for mercy. I do not plead any extenuating act. I am here, therefore, to invite and cheerfully submit to the highest penalty that can be inflicted upon me for what in law is a deliberate crime and what appears to me to be the highest duty of a citizen.

"The only course open to you, the judge, is, as I am going to say in my statement, either to resign your post, or inflict on me the severest penalty, if you believe that the system and law you are assisting to administer are good for the people. I do not expect that kind of conversion, but by the time I have finished with my statement, you will perhaps have a glimpse of what is raging within my breast and which has made me run this maddest of risks which a sane man can run."

Gandhi paused, unfolded his statement, adjusted his steel-rimmed spectacles, looked about the room, filled with his followers, who sat still and motionless, and read:

"I owe it perhaps to the Indian public, and to the public in England, to placate which this prosecution is mainly taken up, that I should explain why from a staunch loyalist and co-operator I have become an uncompromising disaffectionist and non—co-operator. To the court too I should say why I plead guilty to the charge of promoting disaffection toward the government established by law in India.

"My public life began in 1893 in South Africa in troubled weather. My first contact with British authority in that country was not of a happy character. I discovered that as a man and an Indian I had no rights. More correctly, I discovered that I had no right as a man because I was an Indian.

"But I was baffled. I thought that this treatment of Indians was an excrescence upon a system that was intrinsically and mainly good. I gave the government my voluntary and hearty co-operation, criticizing it freely where I felt it was faulty but never wishing its destruction.

"Consequently when the existence of the Empire was threatened in 1899 by the Boer challenge, I offered my services to it, raised a voluntary ambulance corps and served at several actions that took place for the relief of Ladysmith. Similarly in 1906, at the time of the Zulu revolt, I raised a stretcher-bearer party and served till the end of the 'rebellion.' For my work in South Africa I was given by Lord Hardinge the Kaisar-i-Hind Gold Medal. When the war broke out in 1914 between England and Germany, I raised a volunteer ambulance corps in London consisting of the then resident Indians in London, chiefly students. Lastly in India when a special appeal was made at the War Conference in Delhi in 1918 by Lord Chelmsford for recruits, I struggled at the cost of my health to raise a corps in Kheda. In all these efforts at service I was actuated by the belief that it was possible by such services to gain a status of full equality in the Empire for my countrymen.

"The first shock came in the shape of the Rowlatt Act, a law designed to rob the people of all real freedom. I felt called upon to lead an intensive agitation against it. Then followed the Punjab horrors beginning with the massacre at Jallianwalla Bagh and culminating in the crawling orders, public flogging and other indescribable humiliations. . . . But in spite of the forebodings and grave warnings of friends, at the Amritsar Congress in 1919 I fought for co-operation and working the Montagu-Chelmsford reforms, hoping that the reforms, inadequate and unsatisfactory though they were, marked a new era of hope in the life of India.

"But all that hope was shattered. . . . The Punjab crime was whitewashed, and most culprits went not only unpunished but remained in the service, and in some cases continued to draw pensions from the Indian

revenue, and in some cases were even rewarded. {Gandhi was referring to General Dyer.} I saw too that not only did the reforms not mark a change of heart, but they were only a method of further draining India of her wealth and of prolonging her servitude.

"I came reluctantly to the conclusion that the British connection had made India more helpless than she was before, politically and economically. India has become so poor that she has little power of even resisting famines. Before the British advent, India spun and wove in her millions of cottages just the supplement she needed for adding to her meager agricultural resources. This cottage industry, so vital to India's existence, has been ruined by incredibly heartless and inhuman processes, as described by English witnesses. Little do town dwellers know how the semi-starved masses of India are slowly sinking to lifelessness. Little do they know that their miserable comfort represents the brokerage they get for the work they do for the foreign exploiter, that the profits and the brokerage are sucked from the masses. Little do they realize that the government established by law in British India is carried on for the exploitation of the masses. No sophistry, no jugglery in figures, can explain away the evidence that the skeletons in many villages present to the naked eye.

"The law itself in this country has been used to serve the foreign exploiter. My unbiased examination of the Punjab Martial Law cases has led me to believe that at least ninety-five percent of convictions were wholly bad. My experience of political cases in India leads me to the conclusion that in nine out of every ten the condemned men were totally innocent. Their crime consisted in the love of their country. In ninety-nine cases out of a hundred justice has been denied to Indians as against Europeans in the courts of India. This is not an exaggerated picture. It is the experience of almost every Indian who has had anything to do with such cases. In my own opinion, the administration of law is thus prostituted consciously or unconsciously for the benefit of the exploiter.

"The greatest misfortune is that Englishmen and their Indian associates in the administration of the country do not know that they are engaged in the crime I have attempted to describe. I am satisfied that many Englishmen and Indian officials honestly believe that they are administering one of the best systems devised in the world and that India is making steady though

slow progress. They do not know that a subtle but effective system of terrorism and an organized display of force on the one hand, and the deprivation of all powers of retaliation or self-defense on the other, have emasculated the people and induced in them the habit of simulation. This awful habit has added to the ignorance and the self-deception of the administrators.

"Section 124-A, under which I am happily charged, is perhaps the prince among the political sections of the Indian Penal Code designed to suppress the liberty of the citizen. Affection cannot be manufactured or regulated by law. If one has no affection for a person or a system, one should be free to give the fullest expression to his disaffection, so long as he does not contemplate, promote, or incite to violence. But the section under which I am charged is one under which mere promotion of disaffection is a crime. I have studied some of the cases under it, and I know that some of the most loved of India's patriots have been convicted under it. I consider it a privilege, therefore, to be charged under that section.

"I have endeavored to give in their briefest outline the reasons for my disaffection. I have no personal ill-will against any single administrator, much less can I have any disaffection toward the King's person. But I hold it to be a virtue to be disaffected toward a government which in its totality has done more harm to India than any previous system. India is less manly under the British rule than she ever was before. Holding such a belief, I consider it a sin to have affection for the system. And it has been a precious privilege for me to be able to write what I have in the various articles tendered in evidence against me.

"I am here therefore to invite and submit to the highest penalty that can be inflicted upon me for what in law is a deliberate crime and what appears to me to be the highest duty of a citizen. The only course open to you, the judge, is either to resign your post and thus disassociate yourself from evil, if you feel that the law you are called upon to administer is an evil and that in reality I am innocent; or to inflict on me the severest penalty, if you believe that the system and the law you are assisting to administer are good for the people of this country, and that my activity is therefore injurious to the public weal."

The judge seemed moved by Gandhi's words.

"Mr. Gandhi," he said, "you have made my task easy in one way by pleading guilty to the charge. Nevertheless, what remains, namely the determination of a just sentence, is perhaps as difficult a proposition as a judge in this country could have to face. The law is no respecter of persons. Nevertheless, it will be impossible to ignore the fact that you are in a different category from any person I have ever tried or am likely to try. It would be impossible to ignore the fact that in the eyes of millions of your countrymen you are a great patriot and a great leader. Even those who differ from you in politics look upon you as a man of high ideals and of a noble and even saintly life. I have to deal with you in one character only. It is not my duty and I do not presume to judge or criticize you in any other character. It is my duty to judge you as a man subject to the law, who by his own admission has broken the law and committed what to an ordinary man must appear to be a grave offense against the State.

"I do not forget that you have consistently preached against violence and that you have on many occasions, as I am willing to believe, done much to prevent violence. But having regard to the nature of your political teaching and the nature of many of those to whom it was addressed, how you could have continued to believe that violence would not be the inevitable consequence of it passes my capacity to understand.

"There are probably few people in India who do not sincerely regret that you should have made it impossible for any government to leave you at liberty. But it is so. I am trying to balance what is due to you against what appears to me to be necessary in the interest of the public, and I propose in passing sentence to follow the precedent of a case, in many respects similar to this case, that was decided some twelve years ago—I mean the case against Bal Gangadhar Tilak* under the same section. The sentence that was passed upon him, as it finally stood, was of simple imprisonment for six years. You will not consider it unreasonable, I think, that you should be classed with Mr. Tilak, that is, a sentence of two years' simple imprisonment on each count of the charge, or six years in all, which I feel it my duty to pass upon you. And I should like to say in doing so that if the course of

*Tilak, a Hindu of immense learning, was the outstanding Indian nationalist leader until Gandhi's rise to preeminence. He died in 1920 and Gandhi, in a sense, succeeded him, though their political ideas, especially in regard to methods, were not identical.

events in India makes it possible for the government to reduce the period and release you no one will be better pleased than I."

Gandhi, smiling at the sentence, wanted to add one word.

"I would like to say one word," he said to the judge. "Since you have done me the honor of recalling the trial of the late Lokamanya Bal Gangadhar Tilak, I just want to say that I consider it the proudest privilege and honor to be associated with his name. So far as the sentence itself is concerned, I certainly consider it as light as any judge would inflict on me, and so far as the whole proceedings are concerned, I must say that I could not have expected greater courtesy."

A local Indian reporter chronicled, in words which might have described the end of another great trial in Athens more than 2,000 years ago, the last scene in the courtroom:

"Then the friends of Mr. Gandhi crowded around him, as the judge left the court, and fell at his feet. There was much sobbing on the part of both men and women. But all the while Mr. Gandhi was smiling and cool and giving encouragement to everybody who came to him. After all his friends had taken leave of him, Mr. Gandhi was taken out of court to the Sabarmati jail."

7

There was a second anniversary those March days in 1931 in Ahmedabad that was very much on the mind of Gandhi in the snatches of conversation we had that week. The event it celebrated had brought him to the point he had now reached in his political struggle; its surprising consequences had brought me first to India the year before.

Exactly twelve months ago, as he recalled to me, on March 12, 1930, Gandhi, accompanied by seventy-eight men and women from his ashram here, had set out on foot on a two-hundred-mile trek to the sea. There they planned to defy the government by making salt from the seawater in disobedience of the Salt Act, which provided for a government monopoly of the manufacture of salt, levied a tax on its sale and prohibited Indians from making it themselves. The Salt March was a symbolic act which at first was lost on the British authorities and even on most Indians themselves. Gandhi was reported marching to the sea to make a handful of salt illegally—so what?

"We were bewildered," said Nehru. "We could not quite fit in a national struggle with common salt."

The British authorities treated it as a joke. They thought that Gandhi was losing contact with reality. They hoped this foolish prank might finish him. But as so often before, the genius of Gandhi had stumbled on a symbolic gesture, which, to the surprise of everyone but himself, would quickly catch the popular imagination and inflame India from one corner to the other.

At its party convention in December 1929, at Lahore, as we have seen, the Congress, convinced that the British government would not grant India even Dominion status within any measurable future, had come out for complete independence. It had instructed its members to withdraw from the national Legislative Assembly and all provincial legislatures and had sanctioned a campaign of civil disobedience, the date, the occasion and the reasons for it to be decided by Gandhi. But neither the Mahatma nor the members of the Congress had yet found a specific issue on which to begin a new struggle. That was why the Congress had left it up to Gandhi to find one. Gandhi mulled over the problem all through January and February of 1930, waiting, as he had often done before, he later told me, for his "inner voice" to give him the answer. By the end of February, apparently, it had.

On March 2, he addressed a long letter to the Viceroy, Lord Irwin.

DEAR FRIEND:

Before embarking on Civil Disobedience and taking the risk I have dreaded to take all these years, I would fain approach you and find a way out . . . I hold British rule to be a curse . . . Why? . . . It has impoverished the dumb millions by a system of progressive exploitation and by a ruinous, expensive military and civil administration which the country can never afford.

It has reduced us politically to serfdom. It has sapped the foundations of our culture. And by the policy of cruel disarmament, it has degraded us spiritually. I fear there never has been any intention of granting Dominion Status to India in the immediate future . . .

Gandhi went into the system in considerable detail of what he regarded as the milking of India, pointing out the inequities of the country's taxes in general and the salt taxes in particular. "The inequities [of these]," he wrote, "are maintained to carry on a foreign administration, demonstrably the most expensive in the world.

"Take your own salary," he continued, deliberately bringing up a subject which no Indian had ever dared to broach to a viceroy before.

It is over 21,000 rupees [$7,000] per month, besides many other indirect additions. You are getting over 700 rupees a day, against India's average income of less than two annas [4 cents] per day. Thus you are getting over 5,000 times India's average income . . .

On bended knee, I ask you to ponder over this phenomenon. I have taken a personal illustration to drive home a painful truth. I have too great a regard for you as a man to wish to hurt your feelings . . . But a system that provides for such an arrangement deserves to be summarily scrapped . . . Nothing but organized non-violence can check the organized violence of the British Government.

He then outlined his plans for non-violent resistance to British rule. "If the Indian people join me, as I expect they will, the sufferings they will undergo, unless the British nation soon retraces its steps, will be enough to melt the stoniest hearts." He invited the Viceroy to meet with him in a "real conference between equals."

But if you cannot see your way to deal with these evils and if my letter makes no appeal to your heart, on the eleventh day of this month, I shall proceed with such co-workers of the Ashram as I can take, to disregard the provisions of the Salt Laws.

Gandhi offered to postpone the launching of the civil-disobedience movement

if you care to discuss these matters with me . . . This letter is not in any way intended as a threat . . . I remain

Your sincere friend,
M. K. GANDHI

The letter was delivered to the viceregal palace in Delhi by an English friend of Gandhi's, a Quaker. The Viceroy flew back in a special plane to Delhi from the polo matches at Meerut to receive it. But after reading its contents, Lord Irwin chose not to reply. He had his secretary send a curt acknowledgment: "His Excellency . . . regrets to learn that you contemplate a course of action which is clearly bound to involve violation of the law and danger to the public peace."

Such British understanding!

Gandhi answered: "On bended knee I asked for bread, and I received stone instead."

The Viceroy refused to see him. But he refrained from arresting him. High British officials around the Viceroy in Delhi were sure that Gandhi was making a joke of himself to trudge two hundred miles to the sea with a ragged band of followers to make a handful of salt. They would let him hang himself. The bizarre act, they were confident, would ruin his hold on the Indian masses.

But it did not turn out that way; just the opposite.

It was one of the strangest treks ever witnessed in India or in any other country. And it soon became one of the most widely reported, as dozens of Indian reporters joined the two or three local newspapermen who were in at the outset, followed by correspondents from all over the world. The weird march began to hit the front pages of not only the Indian but the world press.

Following winding dirt roads from village to village Gandhi and his disciples marched two hundred miles from the Sabarmati ashram at Ahmedabad to Dandi, a small town near Jalalpur, on the entrance to the Gulf of Cambay, in twenty-four days. "Less than ten miles a day—without much luggage. Child's play!" Gandhi exclaimed. He was going on sixty-one, and the heat of the Indian spring, before the monsoons came, was stifling.

The procession soon became a triumphal march. The villages through which the marchers passed were festooned in their honor. Between the villages, peasants sprinkled water on the roads to keep the dust down and threw leaves and flower petals on them to make the going on foot easier. In nearly every settlement hundreds abandoned their work and joined the procession until the original band of less than one hundred swelled to several thousand by the time the sea was reached.

"We are marching in the name of God!" Gandhi told the villagers as his party rested for the night, prayers were said, and the Mahatma explained why he was setting out to break the iniquitous salt law. Some of Gandhi's followers began to compare the march to the journey of Jesus to Jerusalem, and there was much reading of the New Testament along the way. To add to the comparison someone in the party picked up a donkey to follow in the wake of Gandhi. Like Christ, Gandhi apparently had a presentiment of death at the end of the journey. On the evening of April 5, as they reached the sea, he told a large gathering: "Either I shall return with what I want, or else my dead body will float in the ocean." The evening was spent in prayers along the beach.

The next day, April 6, Gandhi waded into the sea, bathed and purified himself in the Hindu custom. He then picked up some salt which had been left by the waves on the beach (later auctioned for 1,600 rupees). He had broken the salt law. The word went out from scores of reporters to their newspapers all over India and the world.

Overnight the country was aroused. Thousands, then tens of thousands, swarmed to the beaches of India's lengthy coast to defy the government by making salt. In the streets of the big cities massive demonstrations were held, at which gobs of illegal salt were sold. Soon the mass protests branched out to other forms, especially to the boycott of British goods, which the Congress organized on a large scale. It became extremely difficult, if not impossible, for anyone to penetrate the thick picket lines of men and women the Congress threw around the shops selling British textiles and other goods. The British-led police would beat up the squatting picketers and cart them off to jail. Within an hour a new picket line would be formed.

But it was the Salt March itself that had caught the imagination of millions of Indians and aroused them to revolt. It was, as Vincent Sheean would put it, "a symbol of imperishable power over the imaginations of men." The British authorities at first were flabbergasted. They could not understand it. And none were more surprised than the leaders of the Congress. Nehru was a good example. He had not seen what making a bit of dirty salt had to do with the struggle for independence. The spectacle, as we have seen, "bewildered" him. He felt "a little abashed and ashamed," he admitted later, at having questioned the "efficacy" of Gandhi's march. He "marvelled at the knack of the man" for having seen how it would set the country ablaze with revolt.

In Delhi the British authorities waited a month, hoping that the excitement over breaking the salt law would subside. When it didn't, when it continued to spread up and down the country and to result in massive demonstrations that had to be put down by lathi beatings and mass arrests, rapidly filling the country's jails, the government decided at last to act.

Shortly after midnight on May 4, Gandhi was arrested as he slept under an old mango tree at his camp in Karadi, a village near Dandi. This time the Viceroy did not risk another trial. He did not want the Mahatma making another courtroom speech that would further inflame the people and add to the stature of the rebellious leader. There was therefore no trial and no sentence. Gandhi was simply put behind bars under Section XXXV of a law of 1827 that had been promulgated by the East India Company and which allowed for him to be held "at the pleasure of the government." Such an arbitrary act would have been impossible in England. But in India the English rulers had the power to get away with it. Actually, by again imprisoning Gandhi, they were playing into his hands. They were once more making a martyr of him, and by doing so raising him to new heights in the minds of his fellow countrymen. They were also making sure of the continued and increasing resentment of millions of Indians to such arbitrary foreign rule. Gandhi had counted on his arrest. It was part of his strategy.

And he felt fairly confident that this time, unlike ten years before, his followers would be disciplined enough to carry out his teaching of non-violence no matter how savage the oppression. With a few scattered, minor exceptions, the chief of which was at Peshawar, on the rugged North-West Frontier, where the trigger-happy Moslem Pathans used their rifles, this proved to be true.

One of the memorable examples of non-violent action in the face of extreme and bloody provocation was observed by a friend and colleague of mine, Webb Miller of the United Press, whose moving account of it was still being quoted in books on Gandhi forty years later.* Miller, one of the great American foreign correspondents, was a sensitive man, but in his dispatches he somehow managed to keep his emotions more in check than most of the rest of us did. This time, however, he could not hold them back.

On May 21, less than three weeks after Gandhi's arrest, he had followed a group of 2,500 Congress volunteers, led by Mrs. Sarojini Naidu, on an attempted raid on the government's Dharasana Salt Works, 150 miles north of Bombay, defended by four hundred Indian police under the command of six British officers.

In complete silence the Gandhi men drew up and halted a hundred yards from the stockade. A picked column advanced from

* As for instance in Erik H. Erikson's *Gandhi's Truth*, published in 1969.

the crowd, waded the ditches, and approached the barbed-wire stockade. . . . Suddenly, at a word of command, scores of native policemen rushed upon the advancing marchers and rained blows on their heads with their steel-shod lathis. Not one of the marchers even raised an arm to fend off the blows. They went down like ten-pins. From where I stood I heard the sickening whack of the clubs on unprotected skulls. The waiting crowd of marchers groaned and sucked in their breath in sympathetic pain at every blow. Those struck down fell sprawling, unconscious or writhing with fractured skulls or broken shoulders. . . . The survivors, without breaking ranks, silently and doggedly marched on until struck down. . . .

They marched steadily, with heads up, without the encouragement of music or cheering or any possibility that they might escape serious injury or death. The police rushed out and methodically and mechanically beat down the second column. There was no fight, no struggle; the marchers simply walked forward till struck down.

Even when they were down, they were put upon by the police, carrying out the barked orders of the British officers. "The police," wrote Miller, "commenced to savagely kick the seated men in the abdomen and testicles and then dragged them by their arms and feet and threw them into the ditches."

One was dragged to a ditch where I stood. The splash of his body doused me with muddy water. . . . Hour after hour stretcher-bearers carried back a stream of inert, bleeding bodies. . . . By 11 A.M. the heat had reached 116 degrees, and the assault subsided.

Miller went to a temporary hospital set up by a Congress medical team. There he counted 320 wounded, many still unconscious, others writhing in agony from body and head blows. Two were dead. Mrs. Naidu, whom Gandhi on his arrest had appointed acting president of the Congress, was arrested and sentenced to prison.

The Dharasana Salt Works was saved. British authority prevailed. But the story was flashed around the world—Miller's graphic United Press dispatch was published in more than a thousand newspapers at home and abroad. The violence of the British-led police aroused widespread revulsion, even in England. It kindled resentment up and down India—but also pride. The instrument of militant non-violence which Gandhi had forged had proved its power in action. All that late summer, after I arrived in India, and through the fall and winter, I would see it work in the streets and squares of a dozen cities. It was slowly undermining British rule. It was making the Indians, so lethargic for so long, stand up. It was filling them with hope that some day, and soon, they would again be masters in their own country.

A symbolic act—the making of salt illegally, of all things—the significance of which only Gandhi at first had understood and which had been derided by so many, had fired the imagination of the Indian masses and set them on a course the Mahatma was confident would lead to independence before he died. Even on the scene in India in those days of mass beatings and arrests I was slow to recognize what Gandhi felt intuitively: that on rare occasions in history—and this was one—when the circumstances are propitious, the power of an idea can sweep all before it.

It happened once, Gandhi pointed out to me that week in Ahmedabad, in our own American colonial days under the British. The Boston Tea Party, he argued, had been a symbolic act, somewhat similar to his Salt March. He had even recalled that to the Viceroy recently in Delhi. While having tea with him one day at the viceregal palace, he had dropped a pinch of illegal salt that he carried in an old brown bag into his cup "to remind us," he said he told Lord Irwin, "of the famous Boston Tea Party."

I did not remember that "famous" tea party too well, and when I returned to Bombay I scurried to books on American history at the university library there. Some parallels with what had taken place in India before my eyes rather astonished me. The Indians, Gandhi had said, were trying to break the government's salt monopoly just as the American colonists had tried to break the British government's monopoly of tea, and both attempts had led to rebellion.

In 1773, I found, to bail out the East India Company, which had a surplus of 17 million pounds of Indian tea in its warehouses in England, the Commons in London had voted to give the Company a virtual monopoly of the tea trade with the American colonies, which had previously bought their tea on the markets of London and Amsterdam. So the American colonists, I learned, had had their own experience with the East India Company and were fully aware of its "relentless barbarity, its black, sordid and cruel avarice," as one of them put it, in India! And they had responded to the tea monopoly by dumping 342 chests of tea into Boston harbor. In Annapolis they had gone further. They had not only burned the tea, but the ship that brought it.

The day after the Boston Tea Party John Adams had predicted that it would arouse the country and have "important consequences." He considered it "an Epocha in history." Gandhi's making illegal salt at Dandi the spring before was also turning out to be "an Epocha in history."

And it was a shining moment in Gandhi's tumultuous life. Years later Jawaharlal Nehru, mulling over the many pictures in his mind "of this man, whose eyes were often full of laughter and yet there were pools of infinite sadness," remembered above all the sight of Gandhi trudging down the dusty road to the sea.

> The picture that is dominant and most significant is as I saw him marching, staff in hand, to Dandi on the Salt March in 1930.
>
> Here was the pilgrim on his quest of Truth, quiet, peaceful, determined, and fearless, who would continue that quest and that pilgrimage, regardless of the consequences.

The week I accompanied the Mahatma on a trip through the countryside, visiting some of those 700,000 villages which he told me were the real India, he did not seem so much the pilgrim as a father figure, almost a god, to whom the peasants poured out their tales of woe and waited patiently for his blessing and for his advice about what, if anything, could be done. For seven days and nights in a decrepit car we bumped along the rutty bullock trails of the Kaira and Bardoli districts, far from a main road or a railway line, the paths packed from village to village with peasants gaping up at the shaven head of the little man and bowing as he gave them his *darshan*. Often we traveled late at night, because it was cooler then, and thousands stood in the darkness along the lonely trails, holding up their lanterns to light the way. The women seemed to outnumber the men, and often in the dim lantern light they would hold their babies high above them, as Gandhi passed, to receive the blessing which the very sight of him would give. Sometimes men and women would spring on the running board of his car and kiss it, and often they would simply squat on the road and refuse to budge until the Mahatma had stuck his head out the window and greeted them. There were afternoons when the tropical sun made the earth a furnace, and Gandhi would squat on a sweltering platform under a rude canvas shelter, hearing the people out as he spun, listening carefully and sympathetically to their complaints, which were varied and long, for one had had his cattle seized by the police for not paying his taxes, as Gandhi, they said, had urged them, others had lost their homes or their tracts of land for the same reason, this woman's husband had not been released from jail despite amnesty, that woman's sons and daughters were still behind bars.

Gandhi would listen patiently, and patiently explain that under his pact with the Viceroy, they should have their property restored and their men- and womenfolk out of jail and that he would see to it that they were. He told them how proud he was that these very districts had led the countryside in the non-payment of taxes. Since he realized that these peasants were obviously more politically awake than most in the country,* he gave them a political message

*And better off economically too. I did not see any of the starving skeletons Gandhi had mentioned when he told me of the terrible plight of the downtrodden peasantry. At least these people seemed to have enough to eat, though by American or English

that he was already sending up and down India through the thousands of Congress volunteers recently released from prison. My notes jotted down that week remind me of what it was:

> Complete independence is not yet won. We must use this armistice to prepare for resumption of our struggle. The fight for *Swaraj* will continue—and on a greater scale than ever before, unless our demands are granted.

Gandhi did not go so far as to tell these peasants what he repeated to me privately that week: that the more he thought about the situation since leaving Delhi, the more he was forced to conclude that there was not much hope for gaining his goal by negotiation. The decision of the Conservative Party in England the previous week not to participate in any further talks on India obviously had stiffened his attitude. For the first time he confided to me that unless the Tories changed their position, he might not go to London for a second Round Table Conference after all, despite his formal promise to the Viceroy.

Gandhi enlarged on his misgivings about the British during our early-morning four-mile walk in Delhi on March 21, a few days later. As we trudged along a dusty road that led past the old fort of Delhi, where Akbar, the great Mogul emperor, had ruled India before the British came, I found it difficult at first to keep up with Gandhi's rather nimble steps, but gradually I caught my second breath, managed to keep pace, and could concentrate on what he

---

standards they farmed and lived primitively in their parched fields and thatched huts around stagnant ponds in which their water buffaloes dozed up to their necks to escape the day's heat, and which provided not only drinking water, but a place to bathe and to wash clothes. The soil seemed fairly fertile for India, and though it was dry and the crops seemed somewhat burned out, the coming monsoon would shortly take care of that. When I remarked to Gandhi that these peasants seemed to be far from starving, he said that this particular rural district had been "rather prosperous," that it was not very typical of the Indian countryside, in most of which, as he would show me sometime, people really lived wretched lives.

was saying. He seemed in a more somber mood than usual. He thought the British government was tricking him over "safeguards," which obviously were meant to preserve British rule in India indefinitely. Two or three days before in speeches in Parliament, Wedgwood Benn, Secretary of State for India, and Lord Chancellor Sankey, who would preside over the coming Round Table Conference, had reiterated that the Labor government would insist on safeguards in the new constitution for a "self-governing" India that gave the Viceroy control of the Army, foreign affairs, finance and minorities.

"If the British government's word on these safeguards is final," Gandhi said, "and we are not free to open the whole question as to what reservations are really needed to protect India during the transition period, then I think it is futile to attend a further conference."

In fact, Gandhi said, he had told the Viceroy as much in a private communication he had sent him the day before.

"The truce agreement," Gandhi continued, "stipulated that we would discuss only safeguards in India's interests. Now the British appear to me to be on the point of breaking these terms of the truce."

The British, Gandhi said, did not seem to realize how late the hour was.

"It is only a question of months," he went on, "when either the power must pass into the hands of this nation, or it must, God forbid, re-embark, if another course is not open, on the well-trodden course of suffering. I realize, of course, that we must solve our internal problems first, notably the Hindu-Moslem question. But I am hopeful of reaching some measure of accord before tomorrow night when I depart for Karachi and the annual convention of the Congress."

As it turned out, Gandhi was overly optimistic about reaching an understanding with the Moslems, but it did not seem so that day. All through that spring and summer of 1931, my dispatches show, both sides continually claimed that they were on the verge of an agreement and would be able to present a united front to the British in demanding self-government for India at the coming conference in London.

After our week in the countryside, Gandhi had driven down to Bombay and after a tumultuous welcome by a quarter of a million people had spent the next two days conferring with Maulana Shaukat Ali, the Mohammedan leader, in a desperate effort to achieve, finally, a Hindu-Moslem accord. Shaukat Ali was a big, bearded, hale fellow, who, ten years before, along with his brother, Mohammed, had been close to Gandhi in the Congress movement and then, breaking away from the Congress, had become, under the prodding of the British, I gathered, a fanatical champion of Moslem demands against the Hindus.

After two days of talks, Shaukat Ali told me that Gandhi had met all his demands. The chief issue had been whether Hindus and Moslems would vote in separate or joint electorates for elections to the provincial and national legislatures. The Moslems, fearing that they would be swamped by the Hindu majority in joint electorates, had insisted on separate ones. This way, with one-fourth of the population (80 million out of 320 million), they would at least be assured of one-quarter of the legislative seats. But Gandhi offered them a guarantee of at least one-third of the seats if they accepted joint electorates. He was against anything that kept the two communities separated politically.

"Gandhi gave us more than we asked," Shaukat Ali told me at the end of the parleys. "So now we will receive one-third representation, instead of one-fourth, and on that basis we have agreed provisionally to joint electorates. Then, if they work, we will accept them finally." He was very happy, and Gandhi beamed. It seemed to both of them that at last they had obtained a solution to the country's most tragic problem, the strife between Hindus and Moslems, which had cost thousands of lives in the last few years and wrecked all chances of Indian national unity. They were drawing up a "peace pact," they said. It would be signed in Delhi that very weekend.

In Chicago, the headline over my dispatch in the *Tribune* reflected the optimism of that day in Bombay.

HINDU-MOSLEM
CHIEFS IN INDIA
AGREE TO PEACE

Old Religious War Ends;
Will Sign Pact.

The "peace pact" was never signed. Moslem fanatics saw to that. Not all Gandhi's genius, not all his strivings over the years, could bring the two communities together. He would win independence for India, but he could not win over the majority of Moslems, or at least their leaders, to join him in a united India, free at last of the British. They would break away to form their own Moslem nation.

This failure, as Gandhi often said, was the greatest cross he ever bore.

8

The Moslem leader who, above all others, eventually frustrated Gandhi in this was Mohammed Ali Jinnah, who befriended me during my two years in India, often inviting me to his mansion on Malabar Hill in Bombay for long talks and plentiful drinks and to meet his friends and followers.

Like Gandhi and Nehru, Jinnah as a young man also had studied law at the Inner Temple in London and had been admitted to the bar. Unlike Gandhi, Jinnah in those days, at the beginning of the 1930's, was a debonair barrister, completely Westernized in dress, tastes and habits, sporting a monocle like a true British gentleman, purchasing his clothes in London's Bond Street and wearing them impeccably, and indulging his love of good food, fine wines, choice whiskeys and expensive cigarettes.

He was contemptuous of the poor and the unwashed, with whom Gandhi lived and worked—no filthy third-class railway compartments for him or miserable hovels when he was traveling. He went first-class and stayed with the richest maharajas or put up at the best Europeanized hotels.

He seemed to me at that time indifferent to his religion. He rarely worshiped at the mosque on Fridays. He had no compunction about breaking the laws of the Prophet, including those that forbade the eating of pork, the drinking of alcohol and marrying outside the faith. His fanaticism for Islam would come later, and it would be entirely politically motivated. This man, who one day would become the father of the Islamic nation of Pakistan, found himself a Moslem almost by accident. As with Gandhi, his family came from the Kathiawar region, and for long had belonged to the same Hindu caste as the Gandhis. For reasons Jinnah did not know, or remember, his grandfather had been converted from Hinduism to Islam. So Jinnah had been born and raised a Moslem. But up to and including the time I knew him in India, he did not seem to take his religion seriously. He had the same tolerance for other religions as Gandhi had. He had married a Parsi, a follower of Zoroastrianism, the ancient religion of Persia before it was replaced by Islam.

It was politics, not religious zeal, that had made Jinnah one of the leaders of the Moslem community and a power in the Moslem League. In his early years he had joined the Congress. And even after he left it at the end of the first World War and threw in his lot with the Moslem League, when it too came out for Indian self-government, he worked with Gandhi and the Congress for two principal goals: a Hindu-Moslem accord and independence for India. But he broke with Gandhi during the first civil-disobedience campaign in 1921. His zeal for the law had left him little sympathy for deliberate lawbreakers, and his fastidious tastes were revolted by the spectacle of sweating Gandhi-ites squatting in the filthy streets and being carted off to foul jails. He complained to Gandhi that he was appealing to the "ignorant and illiterate" and not to the educated elite, which would have to take over India when the British left. A strict constitutionalist, he believed that self-government could be won by lawyers framing a new constitution.

When I argued with him one day that, in the light of history, including that of my own country, you could win independence only by struggle, he stuck to his guns. "Believe me, my friend," he said with some heat, "we have the same goal as Gandhi and his followers. We too insist on an India in which Indians are masters in their own household. Only, we think we can get it by constitutional means. And we intend to get it at the Round Table Conference in London."

This was a chimera. But Jinnah, an immensely stubborn man, would not admit it.

I heard no talk at Jinnah's house in those years of creating a separate Indian Islamic state as the only solution to the Hindu-Moslem problem. I do not believe the idea had ever occurred to him. Even two years later, in 1933, when the idea was broached to him at a meeting of Indian Moslems in London, Jinnah told them it was "an impossible dream." He would have nothing to do with it. This attitude would gradually change over the years as Jinnah increasingly convinced himself that the 80 million Moslems would be submerged and crushed in a Hindu-dominated independent India. In the end he became so convinced of it, so fanatical, that he alone, against all the pleadings of the British, of Gandhi and Nehru, and of many of his own Moslem followers, held out to the bitter end for the partition of free India, and, by a remarkable display of stubbornness and will power, won.

Clever lawyer that he was, Jinnah took the independence that Gandhi had wrested for India from the British by rousing the masses to non-violent struggle and used it to set up his own independent but shaky Moslem nation of Pakistan, destined, I believed then, to break up, as shortly happened when the eastern Bengali part, separated from the western part by a thousand miles of India's territory, broke away to form Bangladesh; destined too eventually, I believed, to simply disappear.

For surely, sooner or later, it would reattach itself to a richer and more powerful India, the second most populous nation in the world, and, like all great powers in the world, strictly secular.

"No large nation, founded on a religious basis, as Pakistan is," Nehru insisted to me once, after India became independent and he, as Prime Minister, ran it, "can survive in the twentieth century. The Turks found that out after the first World War."

Nehru was proud that nearly as many Moslems lived in India as in Pakistan. At the time of this writing, there are some 61 million of them, giving India the third-largest Mohammedan population in the world, and they enjoy the same freedom of worship as the predominant Hindus and all other religious communities, including the Christians, and live in peace with them.

They had not always lived in peace with the Hindus during the three centuries of British rule. The strife between the two communities, the appalling bloodshed that often occurred when they flew at each other's throats, was a curse on India, worse, it seemed to me, even than the hunger of the masses, the wretched plight of the 70 million "untouchables," * and the invidious, rigid caste system, which kept a Hindu in his economic and social place from birth to death—he could not break out of it.

In my own brief time in India, in the midst of the great civil-disobedience movement against British authority, there were outbreaks of Hindu-Moslem riots in some of the cities that made my blood curdle by their savagery. Hundreds upon hundreds on both sides were simply butchered to death—men, women and children.

It was difficult to find out how many of these quarrels were incited by the British in their effort to keep both communities at each others' throats so that they could not unite in the drive for self-rule. The British chief of police in Bombay once told me— almost as a joke—that it was very easy to provoke a Hindu-Moslem riot. For a hundred dollars, he said, you could start something really savage. Pay some Moslems to throw the carcass of a cow into a Hindu temple, or some Hindus to toss a dead pig into a mosque,

*Literally outcastes from Hindu society. For a caste Hindu to be touched by one of them, even to have the shadow of one of them fall upon him, was to be polluted. In the cities and towns the untouchables were restricted in their work mostly to street sweeping and cleaning of latrines. In the countryside they were little better than serfs, brutally mistreated by their Hindu masters as if they were cattle. "Untouchability," Gandhi told me once, "is a device of Satan and the greatest of all the blots on Hinduism."

and you could have, he said, a bloody mess, in which a lot of people would be knifed, beaten and killed.

Whatever the British role may have been in inciting many of these massacres, it did not excuse the leaders of the two communities. There seemed to be plenty of unscrupulous and irresponsible fanatics among them who would turn their followers to butchering those of the other faith.

Actually, the majority of the Moslems were racially the same as the Hindus; they shared a common background. Their ancestors had been converted to Islam either by force during the reigns of the Mogul emperors or, as in most cases, by the appeal of a religion proclaiming universal brotherhood, and one which promised equality to those from the lower Hindu castes and especially to the untouchables, who were excluded from any caste. Islam promised them an escape from their miserable lot, freedom from the inequities of the Hindu caste system. Thus most of the converts came originally from the lower classes. In places like Bengal I found it difficult to distinguish a Moslem from a Hindu. They looked racially the same, spoke the same language, Bengali, had the identical fiery Bengali temperament and love of poetry, and observed in common the many Bengali customs and manners. The 50 million of them there were divided almost equally in numbers, with the Moslems, who lived mostly in East Bengal, having a slight majority. They were separated only by their religion.

Religion did constitute a great divide in India. No two religions in the world were more unlike, more in conflict. Hinduism, I learned, somewhat to my astonishment, had no established church, no liturgy, no special form of worship, no revealed truth beyond that in the Vedas, no one founder, no one God. A Hindu could worship any number or combination of a million divinities. He saw God in many forms, human as well as animal—the worship of cows was but one example, but there were also sacred elephants, monkeys, snakes, phallic forms (such as one saw along the roads every mile or two)—and there was a myriad of gods and goddesses who were believed to preside over the weather, the changing seasons, the crops, the fertility of men, women, and cattle, and the various ailments of mankind. There was of course in Hinduism the great trinity—Brahma, the Creator; Shiva, the Destroyer; and Vishnu, the Preserver—and the object of life for a devout Hindu was to achieve an understanding of the relationship of these three fundamental forces which, if truly comprehended, would lead to the achievement of the Absolute, a perfect balance. (Gandhi was more devoted to attaining the truth. "Truth," he used to tell me, "is the supreme God for me. Truth is God.")

The Islamic faith was much more simple than the Hindu. There was one God, Allah, the One and Merciful, and one founder, Mohammed the Prophet, and one revealed truth, to be found in the Koran. Islam forbade idols and idolatry; Hinduism glorified them. The Moslems worshiped as a body in a mosque, praying in unison and chanting the verses from the Koran. A Hindu worshiped alone at home or in a small temple, in which there was no public saying of prayers or verses from the sacred works.* Mohammedanism was a spare, severe, dogmatic monotheistic religion. Hinduism was not only a polytheistic, undogmatic, tolerant religion but a way of life, suggesting not only a means by which one with the gods and the cosmos could be reached, but laying down the earthly social structures of life, of caste, of the family. The caste system was an integral part of Hinduism and the Moslems disliked it intensely.

It provided a further barrier between the two communities. Some of the taboos that made a caste Hindu feel he was polluted by the slightest contact with an untouchable were applied also by Hindus to Moslems, and the latter resented it. An orthodox Hindu would not partake of a meal with a Mohammedan or even share drinking water from the same well. In the villages, where the two communities lived together fairly peacefully, in their shared

---

* At Gandhi's evening prayer meetings, which I usually attended when I was with him, and which were open to all faiths, there was a public chanting of sacred verses, not only Hindu (usually from the *Bhagavad Gita*), but Christian (from the New Testament) and Islamic (from the Koran). Gandhi also liked to lead the gathering in singing Christian hymns, his favorite being "Lead, Kindly Light."

poverty, there was a well for Hindus and a well for Moslems. Difference in diet was also a cause of irritation between the two communities. Hindus were predominately vegetarians. They would not eat beef; the cow to them was sacred. It was a mortal sin to kill one, and it nauseated them to think of anyone eating its flesh, as the Moslems, like the British, did.

One of the mysteries to me of my days in India was the Hindu worship of the cow, and I have never gotten over the sight in every city, town and village I visited or lived in of these hapless skeletons of animals wandering through the streets—even the streets of the great cities, Delhi, Calcutta and Bombay—and lanes and fields, foraging for food that might have kept millions of Indians from hungering had they got it first. Woe to him, even a white sahib, who harmed these useless beasts—he would be set upon by angry Hindus, who regarded them as sacred.

It made no sense to me, though I knew that, like cults everywhere, the worship and preservation of cows had, far back in the mists of ancient history, served an important purpose. The Aryan invaders, sweeping down to the plains of India from Central Asia, had depended at first for their sheer livelihood on their herds of cattle, as beasts of burden, suppliers of milk, butter, and cheese, and probably in the beginning of meat as food. When famine struck, herds were slaughtered. To prevent this, to preserve the cattle necessary for continued life, the early Hindu seers had simply made them sacred. From then on killing a cow was forbidden.

So the animals had multiplied and gotten out of hand, and they wandered off to fend for themselves. No one knew how many there were, but Professor Shah told me the estimate was more than 100 million, perhaps 150 million. India, with its majority of people living on the edge of starvation, did not have the resources to support this immense herd of beasts. A quarter, perhaps, Shah thought, of this vast array of cows produced a trickle of milk, providing some much-needed food, especially for babies and the young; another quarter served as beasts of burden for the peasants, pulling their primitive plows and bullock carts. The rest, at least one-half, 50 to 75 million, were not only useless but consumed food dearly needed by millions of human beings. Shah, a Hindu himself, thought they ought to be destroyed. But he knew that the vast majority of his fellow Hindus would be up in arms at such an act.

Gandhi, with his odd contradictions, would have been among them. He sometimes startled me by his staunch stand for the protection of the cow. He was sure God wanted it.* If there were a God, I argued, He should take pity on these poor skeleton cows and allow man to put them out of their misery. And take pity too on the millions of poor, starving human beings, who were of such concern to Gandhi, and who sorely needed the food these wandering, worthless beasts deprived them of.

Gandhi, to my surprise, also defended—though somewhat inconsistently, I thought—the Hindu caste system, which seemed to me an anachronism in the twentieth century and indeed an evil system to perpetuate the terrible inequalities of Hindu society. I understood well enough the historical reasons, good and bad, for it in early times.

When the Hindu Aryans, two millenniums before Christ, poured down into the plains of India, they found them occupied by a darker-skinned, primitive people, the Dravidians, whom they

---

*Early in life he had taken a vow to his mother to refrain from drinking milk. But during the Great War, in the midst of a recruiting campaign in Kheda, he had fallen gravely ill and was, as he put it, "at death's door." Doctors, as well as Hindu medicine men (Vaidyas), told him that unless he resumed drinking milk he might not survive his illness. But he could not, he told them, break his vow. A compromise, of which later he was always a little ashamed, suggested itself to him. His mother, he told himself, had surely meant only cow's milk. She had never mentioned milk from a goat. ". . . as I wanted to live," he recounts in his autobiography, "I somehow beguiled myself into emphasizing the letter of the vow and decided to take goat's milk. I was fully conscious, when I started taking mother goat's milk, that the spirit of my vow was destroyed."— Gandhi, op. cit. p. 273.

Nevertheless, even when he was in the best of health, as he usually was, he continued to stick to the new milk. During the time I knew him in India and for a couple of months in London at the Round Table Conference, he drank at least two pints of goat's milk a day with his meals.

quickly subjugated. To keep them subjugated and apart, these ancient Hindu invaders erected a caste system, which excluded the dark Dravidians from their society and made them their serfs. The Sanskrit word for caste is *"varna,"* which means *color.* Thus caste originally was a color bar, and in India, as later in America, served at first to separate free men from slaves and remained when servitude was abolished, a strong barrier between people of different-colored skins.

But caste became much more than that. Gradually over the centuries it became the foundation of a religiously ordained social fabric for the Hindu people. It assigned to each caste, and to each of the myriad subcastes, the place of its members in society from birth to death, prescribing in what field of work they could earn their living, how their families were to be organized and related to others, and laying down the customs they must follow. Caste kept each group a separate, exclusive entity and all but prohibited social intercourse between them. No one could marry outside his caste or even dine and share a drink of water with those of other castes.

The Vedas, the most ancient of the Hindu scriptures, sanctified the caste system as having sprung from Brahma, the Creator, and so made what was essentially a social structure a part of the Hindu religion. The scriptures defined the four main castes: *Brahmans,* at the top, who provided the priests and other religious leaders; next, the *Kshatriyas,* the warriors and princes; third, the *Vaisyas,* to which Gandhi originally belonged, who were landowners, cattle breeders and tradesmen; and last, the *Sudras,* by far the most numerous, who were the craftsmen and artisans. Beyond the pale, and next to the *Sudras* in numbers, were the untouchables, who were excluded from Hindu caste society and confined to being scavengers, street sweepers and cleaners of latrines.

There were literally thousands of subcastes—Gandhi belonged to a *Vaisyas* subcaste called *Modh Bania.* Many of these were strictly occupational castes for those engaged in every conceivable line of work—ironmongers, wood-carvers, bakers, barbers, builders, weavers, painters and so on. And each of these was hereditary. One was born into a trade or occupation and had to remain in it the rest of his life. There were also hundreds of odd subcastes, one of them a caste of robbers *(Kullars)* whose members regarded their calling as a hereditary right, were proud of it, and zealously guarded its prerogatives.

With all its rigidities, inequalities, superstitions, absurdities and even abominations, the caste system knit Hindu society together. It gave it coherence and order. If every man and woman knew his place, which was predetermined by caste from birth to the end, they also knew that under such a system every person was deemed to be useful to society. Each had a function to fulfill, a job to do. No curse of unemployment, of forced idleness, hung over them.

Much of the strength of the caste system lay in it being considered by Hindus as part of their religion, and therefore sacred, its strict rules inviolable because they were laid down by the gods. The Vedas had promulgated a myth Hindus still believed: that each of the four main castes had sprung from a different part of the body of Brahma, the Creator—the *Brahmans* from his mouth, the *Kshatriyas* from his biceps, the *Vaisyas* from his thigh, the *Sudras* from his feet. Without the sanction of religion among a people for whom politics, religion and social custom were inseparable (as they were for Gandhi), the system of caste might have withered and died, as so many social systems down the ages did, succumbing like the old tribal order in Europe to the inexorable forces for change in history. Religion helped keep the caste system from disintegrating or from being destroyed by an outside hostile force.

Caste held Hindu society together through countless wars, revolutions and upheavals—through, above all, foreign conquest and occupation. Not even the Mohammedan conquerors, who imposed Islam on so much of the world with the sword, could impose it on the Hindus when they invaded India and ruled it for several centuries. The British, who perhaps did not understand Hinduism fully, could not undermine it either; their Christian missionaries made few converts. In the end this failure would be their undoing. As the twentieth century came, it was not only the ferment of Asian nationalism but the resurgence of Hinduism, for both of which Gandhi became the principal instrument, that brought their three centuries of rule abruptly to an end.

Still, valuable as the caste system had been in preserving the Hindu nation for a couple of thousand years, it seemed to me it had now, in the twentieth century, as India struggled again to be free, outlived its usefulness. It had become, in many ways, a curse, a hindrance to the development of a modern society. Young leaders of the Congress, like Jawaharlal Nehru, Hindus themselves (Nehru was a Brahman), were sure of it. Nehru envisaged a free India becoming a socialist republic, without caste, and eventually without classes. But Gandhi, who often remarked that he didn't particularly like socialism (Nehru said he didn't understand it), disagreed. He wanted to reform the system of caste, as he wanted to reform everything else, including man, but he did not believe it was wise to do away with it. Fundamentally, he argued, it was sound, and still necessary. His views, which he would impart to me on occasions, were all the more interesting because early in life, he told me, he had suffered what most Hindus regarded as the supreme humiliation. He had been kicked out of his subcaste, *Modh Bania,* for refusing to obey a command of its leaders. He had been made, he said, an outcaste—a fate the majority of Hindus regarded as worse than death.

On the eve of his departure in 1888 for London to study law, the elders of his caste had called him in and forbade the journey on the grounds that its rules prohibited voyages abroad. They could not, among other things, permit him, as Gandhi once rather laughingly recalled, to eat and drink with Europeans. Gandhi refused to obey and was promptly excommunicated. On his return from England three years later, Gandhi found that his closest relatives were forbidden to receive him in their homes, even for a drink of water.

He never sought readmission to his caste. This experience, he said, led him to a broader view of the system than most Hindus held. He was never "troubled by castes." This made his task easier later when he insisted on having a family of untouchables live in his ashram at Ahmedabad, an act that horrified orthodox Hindus. Still, as he often insisted to me, he believed in the caste system. Sometimes I would be a little taken back at the sweep of his support.

One day, a week or so after we had had a lengthy discussion on the subject, Gandhi gave me a collection of pieces he had written in *Young India* over the years about caste.

"I would not change a word today," he said. "This is what I believe, however unpopular it may be to some of our restless young men." I'm sure he meant chiefly Nehru, but he mentioned no names. I have preserved a few quotations which best sum up Gandhi's thoughts on caste. As will be seen, they are not without some Gandhian contradictions.

> Some argue that the retention of the caste system spells ruin for India and that it is caste which has reduced India to slavery. In my opinion, it is not caste that has made us what we are. It was our greed and disregard of essential virtues which enslaved us. I believe that caste has saved Hindustan from disintegration.

But then, in a typical contradiction, he declares: "I have frequently said, I do not believe in caste, in the modern sense. It is an excrescence and a handicap to progress. Nor do I believe in inequalities between human beings. We are all absolutely equal." However:

> I do however believe in *Varna* [caste], which is based on hereditary occupations: imparting knowledge, defending the defenseless, carrying on agriculture and commerce, and performing service through physical labor. These occupations are common to all mankind.
>
> I consider the four caste divisions alone to be fundamental, natural and essential . . . I am certainly against any attempt at destroying these fundamental divisions. The caste system is not

based on inequality, there is no question of inferiority, and so far as there is any such question arising, as in Madras, Maharashtra, or elsewhere, the tendency should undoubtedly be checked. But there appears to be no valid reason for ending the system because of its abuse . . .

As to his surprising support of hereditary caste, he returns to elaborate on it.

I am inclined to think that the law of heredity is an eternal law, and any attempt to alter that law must lead, as it has led before, to utter confusion. I can see very great use in considering a Brahmin to be always a Brahmin throughout his life. If he does not conduct himself like a Brahmin, he naturally will cease to command the respect that is due to the real Brahmin.

That so liberating a force as Gandhi would support so outmoded and confining a custom as "eternal law," since to me it condemned Hindus to a straitjacket in their life and work, simply because of their birth, somewhat surprised me. But even more surprising to me was his objection to the agitation among some of the Hindu young, like Nehru and his youthful followers, in favor of interdrinking, interdining and intermarrying between the castes, which was taboo among most Hindus.

"Doing such things between castes," Gandhi contended in one of his sermonlike articles, "is not, I hold, essential for the promotion of democracy. I do not contemplate under a most democratic constitution a universality of manners and customs about eating, drinking and marrying . . . I decline to consider it a sin for a man not to drink or eat with any and everybody."

Sin or not, Gandhi himself did not follow the Hindu custom. In his ashrams, or on the road, he shared a meal with "any and everybody"—Hindus of all castes, untouchables, Moslems, English, Americans, Europeans.

Old fogey as he appeared to me in his belief in these old and outmoded Hindu customs, such as the protection of cows and the preservation of caste, he was quite different in his adamant opposition to Hindus perpetuating the diabolical custom of regarding one-fifth of their fellowmen as untouchables. He fought against it to his dying day, and gave no quarter, incurring the wrath and contempt of orthodox Hindus, who considered his agitation for the outcastes, his breaking bread with them, a mortal sin. Again and again, he told the Hindus that India did not deserve to be free until it had freed itself from untouchability, pounding into them that it was a "device of Satan and the greatest of all the blots on Hinduism."

How often in the days in India I heard him return to the same theme, as he addressed the crowds from one part of the country to the other!

"Self-government," he would say, "is inconceivable and unattainable without the removal of untouchability, as it also is without Hindu-Moslem unity . . . Untouchability cannot be given a secondary place on our program. Without the removal of this taint, self-government is a meaningless term. In my opinion we have become 'pariahs of the Empire' because we have created 'pariahs' in our midst. We shall be unfit to gain independence so long as we keep in bondage a fifth of the population of Hindustan."

To Gandhi, the untouchables were *harijans,* "the Children of God."

On sex, on the other hand, Gandhi's ideas and preachments seemed to me outlandish and almost inhuman, and Nehru, for one, not only refused to accept them but denounced them. Gandhi's personal struggles with the problem of sex, of which he wrote, and sometimes spoke, with great frankness, and, further, what many in India regarded as an inexplicable lapse from his vows of *Brahmacharya* in the last years of his old age, will be touched on briefly later, when I attempt to sum up the man, his mind, his personality, his character, his genius, and his singular impact on the world, on India and on me.

By the time I left India in 1931 I had the impression that Mohammed Ali Jinnah and Gandhi, despite their common determination to rid India of the British and to solve the Hindu-Moslem problem, were drifting apart. This was mainly because of the Moslem leader's growing conviction that the kind of independent India Gandhi was struggling for would be so dominated by the Hindus that the great Moslem minority would be overwhelmed. But it was partly due, I began to feel, to Jinnah's increasingly personal dislike of the Mahatma. He could not stand what he called "Gandhi's Hindu fads."

"Why does Gandhi," Jinnah would say, "have to squat on my good Persian rugs when he comes to see me, and break our talk by sipping goat's milk out of a filthy cup he has preserved from prison? Why does he have to preach the evils of eating meat, drinking alcohol, smoking tobacco? I like a good cut of beef, the best Scotch I can find, a vintage wine, my cigarettes. I hate all this Hindu nonsense about cows being sacred and the Hindus telling us that we Moslems have no right to kill them for beef. I despise this antiquated Hindu caste business that Gandhi still defends. I resent a Hindu feeling it's unclean to eat with me, a Moslem, or even to shake my hand. Of course, Gandhi doesn't go that far, I admit, but he has his Hindu peculiarities."

As the years went by, Jinnah's dislike of the Hindus, I heard later from friends in India, grew. But in the time I knew him, he had not yet become embittered at them. He was more amiable then, less stern, rigid, fanatical than he later became. His face had not yet taken on that gaunt, ascetic look that so struck friend and foe in the last tumultuous years before independence. He still had a sense of humor. His parties at his palatial residence overlooking Bombay were attended by the most beautiful Indian women I had ever seen, many of them chic Parsis, as his late wife had been, and there was much imbibing of the strong drinks prohibited by the Koran.

Yet Jinnah did, occasionally, lapse into a sadness, and his face seemed to tell you of some kind of personal sorrow that he was bearing. He never spoke of his personal life, at least to me, but I sometimes wondered whether these moments of sadness did not spring from the breakup of his marriage two or three years before and of his wife's untimely death a year later.

At forty-one, he had fallen in love with a strikingly handsome and vivacious young Parsi, and over the strenuous objections of her father, who was an old friend of his, not to mention those of the Moslem community, he had married her as soon as she became eighteen. Gay and party-loving, she was also a political activist, who spoke her mind, throwing herself, like Jinnah, into the movement for Indian independence. I never learned the reason for the breakup of what struck the fashionable and political circles in Bombay as the most attractive of marriages. Women at his parties would hint to me that perhaps it was in part the age difference and also Jinnah's inability to adjust to such an impetuous and irrepressible young woman. At any rate, they said, there began a falling out. And finally, in 1928, after ten years of marriage, she left him, and a year later died of an overdose of morphine. Jinnah apparently never recovered from the blow. He never married again. He began to devote his whole life to the Moslem cause in India.

History, of course, is full of paradoxes. Jinnah, the most irreligious of men, would become a terrible, unbending fanatic for a religiously ordered Islamic state. Gandhi, the most religious of Indians, would hold out to the bitter end for a secular India, which would tolerate all religions, but whose constitution and government would be beholden to none.

9

The kind of constitution and government Gandhi envisaged for an independent India was spelled out at the forty-fifth convention of the All-India Congress, which began at Karachi on March 27, 1931. It was a party political convention the like of which I had never seen before—nor seen since—with its ringing revolutionary proclamations acclaimed by some 350 leaders, men and women, just out of jail, squatting in the heat under a tent in a semicircle at Gandhi's feet, all of them, like Gandhi, spinning away like children playing with toys as they talked. They made up the so-called Subjects Committee, selected from the five thousand delegates to do the real work of the convention, though in reality, it was Gandhi alone who dominated the proceedings, writing most of the resolutions and moving their adoption with his customary eloquence and surprising firmness.

His manner and words were generally humble, as almost always, but listening to him day after day, I noticed too that he could be tough and even a bit authoritarian with those who did not always agree with him. When opposition to some of his proposals sprouted, he did not shrink from using his acknowledged authority to get what he thought he needed. At the Karachi convention of the Congress that year, one saw in Gandhi the consummate politician rather than the saint.

He had no trouble at all in getting the unanimous support of the convention for the main demands of the Congress which he, as its representative, would present to the British at the coming Round Table Conference in London. These were: complete independence; Indian control over the Army, foreign affairs, and financial, fiscal and economic policies during the interim of the transfer of power; an impartial tribunal to determine how much of the national debt would be assumed by India and by Great Britain; and the right of India to secede from the British Empire.*

But on two major issues Gandhi ran into some determined opposition among the delegates, and it was fascinating to watch how skillfully and tactfully—and forcefully—he overcame it. A good many of the delegates opposed the resolution approving the Delhi Pact, and even more of them objected to giving Gandhi full powers to negotiate with the British on behalf of the Congress.

_____

*This revolutionary program was a far cry from the innocuous one first propounded by the founder of the Congress, a retired English member of the Indian Civil Service by the name of Allan Octavian Hume. With the approval of the Viceroy and the British government, Hume had called in a few educated Indians in 1885 to help him organize the Congress, whose chief aim was to be the "consolidation of the union between England and India." For some years its slowly growing membership did nothing but accede to the views of the English masters, whose dictatorial powers over the country they saw little hope of eroding. By 1907, however, egged on by a group of Young Turks, the Congress called for a self-governing India within the British Empire, to be achieved "by constitutional means."

Nothing came from this bold bid. And it was not until after the Great War, when a growing number of Indians, both Hindu and Moslem, saw that the British government had no intention of honoring its wartime pledge to grant India self-rule, that the Congress raised its sights. At a special convention in Calcutta in 1920, Mahatma Gandhi, back from his long struggle for Indian rights in South Africa, captured control of the Congress and quickly turned it toward a more radical path to Indian freedom. Whether holding office or not, whether in prison or outside, he had dominated the Congress ever since.

They offered an amendment requiring that any agreement entered into by Gandhi in London be subject to final approval by the Congress itself.

The Mahatma bridled at this restriction of his powers.

"I venture to suggest to you," he said, "with all the force at my command, that this amendment is not only unnecessary but unbecoming of the Congress . . . Those who go to the Conference are expected to have full credentials and full authority to bind their principals. But if they go there and have to say: 'We have come here, we will discuss; but we cannot bind our principals' . . . the procedure becomes . . . wholly ineffective. Hence it is absolutely necessary not to put in any such proviso."

So long as the Congress delegates negotiated within the general instructions given them at the convention, Gandhi argued, "it would be improper for you to repudiate them.

"Hence I suggest to you," he concluded, "that it is not only superfluous, not only unnecessary, for you to attach the condition of ratification to this resolution, it is unbecoming of you . . . Therefore I hope you will, without further discussion, withdraw this particular amendment."

This was a not-so-humble Mahatma sternly admonishing his fellow politicians—a side of him not many outsiders saw. I looked around the assembly to see what his opponents would do. "Without further discussion," they did as he asked. They withdrew the amendment. Gandhi was given full powers to negotiate, and any agreements he made would be binding on the Congress.

Gandhi, as I have noted of our talks in Delhi, often resorted to soaring generalities, but at Karachi he begged the delegates to be realistic about what he could obtain in London and not be disappointed or embittered if he returned empty-handed.

"If our delegation goes to the conference, it does not mean," he warned, "that it will bring back in its pocket complete independence. If it does not bring it back, it does not mean that it returns humiliated. Nothing of the kind. All that we expect to do is to tell the British what we want, and if we do not get it, we are bound to return empty-handed and receive your compliments, not your curses.

"You have threatened to oust us in case we return empty-handed," he went on. "You may not do so because I make no promise to return with complete independence. I can only promise that we won't return with slavery, that we will not sell out the interests of the country."

And then, as if to soften his authoritarian tone, Gandhi's mood turned to humbleness and he assured the delegates that he did not regard himself as indispensable.

"Do not endorse the settlement," he said, "because you feel that you cannot do without the 'Mahatma.' If you cannot win independence without the 'Mahatma,' neither can you retain it. It is idle to think that the 'Mahatma' is indispensable."

But of course that was exactly what the delegates thought, and Gandhi knew it. He might be self-effacing and humble, but, like all great men, he knew his worth. He realized, I had no doubt, that at this juncture in India's struggle for indepencence he *was* indispensable. Still, like the good politician he was, he concluded his long speech with an appeal for support.

"If you feel that I was right in making the truce and deserve your support, I ask you to give it to me not halfheartedly but wholeheartedly."

The delegates did. As Gandhi left the rostrum, they leaped to their feet and acclaimed him wildly. They then voted unanimously to make him the *sole* delegate to represent the Congress at the London parleys.

"It's the best arrangement," Gandhi remarked to me later, "the most efficacious and most economical." There was not the slightest trace of egotism in his words. There *was*, I thought to myself, a sense of destiny. Why not?

Despite the heat and the occasional wrangling, the long-windedness of some of the speakers and even a little violence on the part of a tiny Communist fringe, Gandhi kept his remarkable sense of humor throughout the proceedings. On his arrival at the railway station in Karachi from Delhi he was greeted by a band of Marxist youths called the Red Shirts, who accused him of selling out to the British in the Delhi Pact, and set upon him as if they were out to clobber him to death. Yelling, "Down with Gandhi! Down with the traitor Gandhi!" and flourishing their black flags, they rushed at him. One fanatical youth seemed to me about to bang the Mahatma over the head with his flagpole. The indomitable Sarojini Naidu, flaunting her bright orange-colored sari, stepped in front of Gandhi and asked the mob to calm itself. Then Gandhi, looking rather frail in his loincloth, faced the youths and smiled.

"You have a perfect right," he told them, "to demonstrate for anything you wish. But why try to break my head?"

There was one figure in Karachi, little known in the West but a power in India, who deserves mention. Next to Gandhi, it was Vallabhbhai Patel, India's nearest thing to an old Tammany Hall boss, who ran the convention. Under Gandhi's guidance it had been Patel, a bald-headed, walrus-mustached, tough-minded, pragmatic peasant lawyer, who built up the Congress to a formidable national political party, the only one there was in India. He was the boss of the machine.

I had first met him a few weeks before during the Gandhi-Irwin talks in Delhi. It was obvious at once that he carried a good deal of weight in the Congress Working Committee, with which Gandhi conferred daily during the negotiations. Several other things about Patel also became fairly clear to me: that the Mahatma leaned on him as much as he did on Jawaharlal Nehru, that Patel and Nehru were rivals for power in the Congress (and as different as two men could be), and that Patel was cut from quite another cloth not only from Nehru but from Gandhi and indeed from Jinnah. Eventually it would be these four men, three Hindus and a Moslem, who would decide the fate of India.

Of the four, only Patel had come up from the mass of the Indian peasantry. Like Gandhi and Jinnah, he was a Gujarati—the three shared a common mother tongue. And like the other three, Patel had gone off to London to study law and become a lawyer. But he had had a harder time making it.

The son of a poor farmer in a Gujarat district north of Bombay who had fought in an Indian unit against the British during the great Mutiny of 1857, Patel had left the soil to work in the textile mills of Ahmedabad, where Gandhi would later organize the first strike in Indian history. Frugal, hardworking and ambitious, he had continued his studies at night, after working hours, saved most of his wages and at thirty-three had accumulated enough to pay his way to London and the expenses of studying law at the Inns of Court. Returning to Ahmedabad as soon as he had been admitted to the bar, he set up a law practice and quickly acquired among his clients the millowners for whom he had once worked as a common laborer. He flourished—for the first and last time in his life— joining the Ahmedabad Club, the center of social life for wealthy millowners, merchants and professional men, playing cards and enjoying the good life of a successful and much sought-after barrister.

But not for long. As happened to so many affluent Indians, especially lawyers, to Jawaharlal Nehru and to his father, Motilal Nehru, for instance, Patel's path crossed Gandhi's, and his life abruptly took quite a new and drastic turn. In 1918 Gandhi had been called in to listen to the grievances of the workers at the textile mills in Ahmedabad. When the employers refused his proposal for impartial arbitration, Gandhi advised the workers to strike and they did. Among those who offered to help him was Patel, notwithstanding that several of the millowners were his legal clients. Something in Gandhi's personality, in the Mahatma's selfless dedication to the downtrodden and to the awakening of the masses, struck a responsive chord in Patel, and he threw himself into organizing the strike with the same ardor that he had previously shown in representing the millowners in the courts. Gandhi quickly recognized Patel's flair for organizing. But good as it was, it was not enough. In the end, when the strikers faltered and began to drift back to work, Gandhi resorted for the first, but not the last, time to a new tactic which would prove very effective in the later independence struggle. He began a fast. The Hindu millowners were horrified. Within three days they capitulated.

Patel had not liked winning a strike in such a manner. He was skeptical of resorting to such a medieval Hindu practice in a twentieth-century labor dispute. He preferred slugging it out with the owners. But being an exceedingly practical man, he conceded that without the fast in the end the strike might have failed. Gandhi, for his part, took note of Patel's surprising ability to bring order into what had been a chaotic movement of workers to band together to improve their lot.

He at once called on Patel to organize a civil-disobedience campaign in the Kheda district north of Bombay, where a crop failure had made it impossible, he thought, for the peasants to pay their taxes. When the government nevertheless insisted on their payment, Patel went from village to village to advise non-payment and to organize the peasants in a massive no-tax campaign. So thorough and painstaking was his work that the government in the end agreed to a compromise by which the rich landowners paid the taxes of the poor peasants. From that time on Gandhi assigned Patel to a more important task: organizing the Congress party into a truly national body, with roots in every province in India. By the time of the Congress convention in Karachi that spring of 1931, Patel, who presided over it as president, had succeeded brilliantly in this task.

It was Gandhi's genius, to be sure, that had inspired the Indian masses, given them the technique of *Satyagraha* with which to stage a non-violent revolution, and hit upon the Salt March as a symbol to arouse them to action. But it was Patel's ability as an organizer that had molded the Indian Congress into a nationwide political machine capable of carrying on the civil-disobedience campaign, even after thousands of its leaders had been incarcerated, until the Viceroy agreed to negotiate.

Pride in this achievement, it was evident, more than compensated for the sacrifices Patel had made in throwing in his lot with

Mahatma Gandhi

Kasturbai Gandhi was illiterate and lost in the world her husband was shaking, but she was a woman of indomitable character.

Kasturbai married Gandhi when both were 13. Here they are seen some 30 years later, in 1915, on their return to India from South Africa.

Jawaharlal Nehru was Gandhi's closest aide and the first Prime Minister of independent India. He held the post from 1947 to his death in 1964.

Vallabhbhai Patel was India's nearest thing to an old Tammany Hall boss—without the corruption. Under Gandhi's leadership, Patel built the Indian National Congress into the most powerful political party in India.

Gandhi and Mrs. Sarojini Naidu were close friends and political associates. Mrs. Naidu, a celebrated poet, was the leading woman in Gandhi's civil-disobedience movement, an eloquent speaker and a shrewd negotiator.

Mohammed Ali Jinnah, an eminent Bombay lawyer and Moslem nationalist. In his last years he became the fanatical leader of the Moslem League. I knew him in his more tolerant, less ascetic days when he was a genial host at some of Bombay's finest parties.

WLS

Dr. B. R. Ambedkar, the embittered leader of India's 70 million untouchables. Educated at Columbia University in New York, Dr. Ambedkar became an able, tough lawyer and often quarreled with Gandhi, despite the Mahatma's lifelong struggle to liberate the untouchables.

Miss Madeline Slade (Mirabai) was the daughter of an English admiral. She became a devoted disciple and close friend and aide of Gandhi, throwing herself into the civil-disobedience movement and sometimes getting herself jailed.

Lord Irwin (later Lord Halifax), Viceroy of India, leaving the country at the termination of his mission on April 18, 1931. He jailed Gandhi without trial, and later negotiated the Delhi Pact with him, a truce that suspended the civil-disobedience movement and brought Gandhi to the Round Table Conference in London in the fall of 1931.

WIDE WORLD PHOTOS

Lord Willingdon, successor to Lord Irwin as Viceroy, inspecting the Guard of Honor on May 17, 1931, shortly after his arrival in Bombay. An old hand in India and a mediocre one, he too jailed Gandhi without trial.

Gateway of India, Bombay. It was one's first sight of India, arriving by ship. The Viceroys and other British notables landed there and took ship from there. On the arrival of the Prince of Wales (later King Edward VIII and subsequently the Duke of Windsor) at the Gateway in 1921, there was a riot in which several persons were injured or killed. The British authorities blamed Gandhi for it.

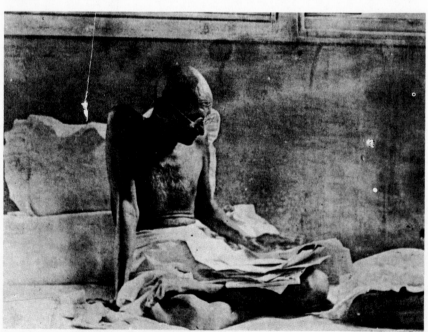

Gandhi spinning on the verandah of the home of his host, Dr. M. H. Ansari, Delhi, 1931. It did seem to me that Gandhi was always spinning. He did so during many of our talks and he often spun as he addressed public meetings. It was a symbolic act of great importance to him, and he and all good nationalists wore exclusively *khadi*, or homespun cloth. Gandhi set himself a daily quota of 200 yards of yarn to spin—no matter how busy he was or how late at night he might have to begin.

Reading his papers at Dr. Ansari's home. This photo shows how emaciated Gandhi was as the result of his fasting.

Gandhi walking the countryside outside of Delhi in the spring of 1931. To keep fit, Gandhi began his day with a four-mile walk, usually accompanied by his secretaries and close associates, who would discuss with him the day's schedule and business.

Gandhi holding a prayer meeting on the lawn of Dr. Ansari's home in Delhi, March 1931. Each day toward dusk, no matter where he was, Gandhi held a prayer meeting, at which hymns from the Hindu *Bhagavad Gita* and from the works of other religions were chanted and prayers said. It was at such a prayer meeting that Gandhi was later assassinated. Dr. Ansari, Gandhi's host and close friend, was a noted physician, a Moslem and a former president of the Congress Party.

Gandhi addressing a Congress Party convention. I took a photograph at the party's convention in Karachi in the spring of 1931. The delegates voted overwhelmingly to reiterate the Congress demand for complete independence for India and instructed Gandhi to take nothing less.

Many orthodox Hindus would not think of drinking from a well used by Moslems or other non-Hindus. They thought it polluted them, just as they believed that even the shadow of an untouchable falling on them defiled them. So the local authorities often provided two wells, though the source of the water was the same. At the right in upper photograph, James Mills of the Associated Press.

WATER FOR HINDUS अमृत

WATER FOR MOHAMMADENS पानी मुसलमानों

WLS

WLS

Gandhi addressing a crowd of a hundred thousand people on the banks of the Sabarmati River at Ahmedabad, March 1931. After the signing of the Delhi Pact with Lord Irwin on March 4, Gandhi returned to his home base at Ahmedabad to receive a hero's welcome.

I did have my quiet moments alone in India in 1931.

Exclusively IN TOMORROW'S GREAT CHICAGO SUNDAY TRIBUNE

WILLIAM SHIRER'S

IMPORTANT LONDON DISPATCH ABOUT

GANDHI

WILLIAM SHIRER
Chicago Tribune Correspondent

Tomorrow's Tribune will bring to you another colorful news story by William Shirer, Chicago Tribune correspondent, now in London writing of the activities and utterances of that world-important figure—Mahatma Gandhi. Don't miss this important dispatch by the same Chicago Tribune man whose exclusive interview with Gandhi at Marseilles first gave the world the news that Gandhi's demand from Great Britain would be complete independence for India.

WILLIAM SHIRER, when America knew only the rumblings of the Indian revolt, told in unbiased, vivid reports to the Chicago Tribune the story of Gandhi's fight for freedom and of the operation of the British policy. Shirer has a personal acquaintance with India's leader which enables him to obtain first the news of Gandhi's actions and policies. Tomorrow's dispatch throws new light on the London conference. Be sure to read it.

THE GREAT CHICAGO SUNDAY TRIBUNE

THE WORLD'S GREATEST NEWSPAPER

A full-page advertisement in the *Chicago Tribune*. Gandhi was big news in Chicago.

The Mall in Simla was a piece of Old England transplanted to the summer capital in the cool foothills of the Himalayas. Here the British officials and their wives gathered to shop, pick up their mail and the newspapers, discuss the day's social and sporting activities, and then adjourn for tea at one of the numerous teashops.

The Viceregal Palace in New Delhi, now the Presidential Palace.

Lord and Lady Louis Mountbatten. He was the last British Viceroy in India.

Nathuram Godse, the Hindu assassin of Gandhi.

Mahatma Gandhi lying in state in New Delhi after his assassination on January 30, 1948.

Gandhi. In Delhi one day the Mahatma had mentioned to me that when Patel plunged himself into the no-tax campaign in Kheda, he had "suspended a splendid and growing practice at the bar. He was never able," Gandhi said, "to resume it." He had given over his life entirely to the struggle for independence.

Though a brilliant lawyer and an even more brilliant politician, Patel proudly retained something of his peasant origins. I find a dispatch of mine from the Karachi Congress describing him as "a Lincoln-like character"—"a simple, rawboned peasant lawyer." He had a peasant's distrust of the intellectual and this I think was one basis for his differences with Nehru. They remained political rivals and sometimes enemies to the last.

"I'm really not interested in the things that interest the intelligentsia," he told the Congress in his speech of welcome as president. "The peasantry do not understand them. While I would respect the rights of landlords, rajas, maharajas and others to the extent that they do not hurt the sweating millions, my interest lies in helping the downtrodden to rise from their state and be on a level with the tallest in the land."

Nehru thought only a socialist India could help the downtrodden, but Patel disagreed. He thought socialism was utopian, with little practicality for a poor, peasant nation with no large industrial proletariat such as India, and besides it was a foreign idea, and therefore doubly suspect. Patel, the most Indian of Indians who dominated the Congress, had little interest in foreign ideas or indeed in the outside world. Foreign affairs, which so fascinated Nehru, did not arouse even his curiosity. World opinion did not matter to him, as it did to Gandhi. We foreign correspondents seemed irrelevant to him. He was helpful enough to me. But he seemed to wonder why I had come out to India in the first place— wasn't there enough to interest me at home? So Patel puzzled me but also fascinated me. Among a group of disparate Indian nationalists whose heads often seemed to be in the clouds—and Gandhi, like Nehru, was no exception—he remained down to earth, close to the Indian soil, practical, pragmatic, skeptical of high-flown talk in which the Hindus so often indulged, knowing that it took one power structure to overthrow another and that if the Congress did not develop that power the country would never get free. It was a good thing for Gandhi and for the country that such a single-minded, hardheaded organizing genius was at hand. He forged the political machine Gandhi and Nehru needed to win independence.

Finally, under Gandhi's guidance, the convention proclaimed an Indian Bill of Rights, which the Congress declared would have to be a part of the future constitution of India and eventually was. It laid down for the first time ever the fundamental rights of the Indian people in what seemed destined to me to become—and did become—the world's most populous democracy, the only one on the mainland of Asia.

For a people who for millenniums had lived under autocratic tyranny, these "fundamental rights," as Gandhi called them when, with considerable eloquence, he moved their adoption, were sweeping. It struck me that the British had taught Indians like Gandhi a good deal about democracy and civil rights though they had denied them to India. I scribbled down the essential points. Freedom of association, of speech and of press. Freedom of conscience and of religion. Religious neutrality on the part of the State. Adult suffrage and equal rights for both sexes.

Two of the provisions were directed against the Hindu caste system, providing that neither caste, nor religion or sex, could bar any citizen from public office or employment or in the exercise of any trade or calling, or in the use of public roads, wells, schools and other places of public resort. In theory at least, this freed the untouchables for the first time in Indian history.

Other clauses provided for free primary education, "a living wage for industrial workers, limited hours of labor and protection against the economic consequences of old age, sickness and unemployment." Any vestige of serfdom which prevailed among the untouchables or among others in the princely autocracies was to be abolished. Women workers were to be protected and given maternity leave; child labor was prohibited, and the right of workers to organize in unions was affirmed.

Finally, the Congress called for a "total prohibition of intoxicating drinks and drugs," which was not surprising since both Hindu and Moslem religions prohibited the drinking of intoxicating liquor.

All told, I thought, this Bill of Rights went further in its guarantee of individual freedom than that of our own American Constitution. Notable to me, and, as Gandhi told the convention, especially pleasing to him, were the provisions for equal rights for women, not only in politics but in public and private employment and in the social structure of the nation. This was all the more remarkable, I thought, in a country where millions of women (mostly Moslems) were still confined by their men to *purdah,* and millions more, among the Hindus, were regarded as inferior by their men and confined to the kitchen, the keeping of the household and raising children. Gandhi pointed with pride to the fact that the Congress had never permitted sex discrimination in its organization and that two women, Mrs. Besant (who was English) and Mrs. Naidu, had been its presidents. "In the future free state," he said, in a remarkable prophecy, "it will be open to us to have women presidents." And in fact India would have a woman Prime Minister, with more power than the president, long before Great Britain, which did not have one until May of 1979.

The proclamation of fundamental rights for the citizen impressed me more than anything else at the Congress convention, but as I left Karachi I wondered, given the cussedness of human beings all over the world, if such a splendid and enlightened program would ever become a reality. I could not help remembering that the Weimar Constitution had given the Germans after the Great War similar freedoms, which they were foolishly throwing away, and that in Soviet Russia another constitution had guaranteed the people fundamental rights that the government would never honor. Perhaps in India, once it was free, the government would honor its constitutional commitments. If Gandhi, Nehru and Patel were still around, I felt fairly sure it would.*

The forty-fifth annual convention of the Congress at Karachi that spring of 1931 added a little more to my knowledge of India and the Indians, their mounting drive for independence, and my grasp of Gandhi's genius. To see the Mahatma in action as a revolutionary politician in the midst of a political convention added to my insights. Nehru thought that at Karachi I had seen the politician in Gandhi at his best.

I marveled during that week in the deadening Indian heat at Gandhi's unflagging energy, his capacity for work, his grasp of detail, his skill in drafting the wording of the resolutions and in explaining to the delegates what was important, his hold over them and over his inner circle of advisers and indeed over the masses which attended the general sessions in the stadium, where sixty thousand men and women gathered to hear him speak.†

His aides said that he was getting no more than four hours' sleep a night, for after the long sessions of the day were over, he sat up for hours each evening with the members of the Working Committee and other key delegates, settling their differences, listening to and reading reports, drawing up agendas for the next day's meetings, dictating the wording of resolutions, making mental notes for his frequent speeches (I never saw Gandhi read a

*It did for a time under independence, but then Prime Minister Indira Gandhi, daughter of Jawaharlal Nehru, of all people, made a mockery of it when in June 1975 she resorted to rule by arbitrary decree, scrapping or changing most of the constitution to suit her needs, and jailing without trial thousands of her political opponents, many of them close associates of Mahatma Gandhi (to whom, despite her name, she was not related). But her surprising attempt to destroy Indian democracy and set up a dictatorship for herself was short-lived. In the spring of 1977, the Indian people voted her out of power.

†Thanks to an innovation of Patel's, the crowds could now actually hear him. Patel had installed twelve loudspeakers in the stadium. It was the first time I myself had experienced the amplifying of voice by means of a microphone and loudspeakers, this technological development everyone now takes for granted. It changed the nature of political (and other) meetings throughout the world. For the first time a large gathering could hear what a speaker said. For Gandhi, with his rather thin, small voice, this was a godsend.

speech or even speak from notes), and managing to find time for his spinning, his prayers, his matinal four-mile walk, and even a few minutes each day to chat with us correspondents. Fatigued as he must have been, he never showed it. Day after day in the stifling heat, he seemed fresh and relaxed, bubbling with confidence and often humor—how often those days, as I recall them and as my notes show, he broke into a peal of laughter.

What supported him so magnificently? It could only have been, I concluded, an overwhelming inner feeling that at last, after so protracted and wearying a struggle, he was now, at sixty-one, well on his way to making his beloved land free before he died.

During the Karachi convention some things happened, there and elsewhere, which reminded me that Gandhi's ideals and goals were not yet completely shared by all Indians, even in the Congress.

In his presidential address at the packed stadium Patel had paused to issue a stinging denunciation of untouchability, calling it "this stain which blackens Hinduism" and declaring that "no independence would be worth having unless untouchability is removed."

His words, strong as they were, evidently fell on some deaf ears. Suddenly I was astounded to see some fifty untouchable women, in their mud-colored saris, being driven from the stadium like hogs. It was outrageous.

Much more depresssing to Gandhi had been the news that reached Karachi the day before, on the eve of the opening of the convention, from Cawnpore. In that dusty manufacturing city of a quarter of a million, eight hundred miles away on the holy Ganges in north-central India, thousands of Hindus and Moslems were slashing each other's throats, pillaging, raping, burning.

By the time I got to Cawnpore, as soon as the Congress meeting was over, the rioting had stopped. Both sides had exhausted themselves, leaving only as evidence of the slaughter block upon block of smoldering ruins, demolished Moslem mosques and wrecked Hindu temples. Many bodies of the slain, men, women and children, still lay putrefying in the heat in blood-soaked gutters. Tales of atrocities on both sides were so sickening I could scarcely stomach reporting them in my dispatch. Town officials were busy toting up the casualties. The hospitals were jammed with the wounded. The number of known dead was 295, of whom 19 were children, 38 women and 238 men. The Moslems had killed 155 Hindus, the Hindus killed 119 Moslems, and the religious identity of 21 bodies was declared "doubtful." Their remains were so charred or mutilated that even the stamp of religion, so strong and inerasable in India, had been obliterated and neither side would risk claiming them for fear of making a ghastly mistake.

The slaughter at Cawnpore cast a gloomy spell over the Congress. In Karachi, Gandhi called a special prayer meeting for all faiths to mourn the dead. He was obviously shaken. He hastily dispatched three Moslem and three Hindu leaders to Cawnpore to try to bring an end to the bloodshed. But either they arrived too late or were unable to quiet the mobs. Some of the Congress delegates blamed the British authorities for not stepping in sooner to halt the slaughter. It was very convenient for them, they said, to have this happen while the Congress was assembling to reiterate its demand for the end of British rule. A few delegates even hinted that it must have been British officials at Cawnpore who instigated the trouble in the first place. Possibly, but after I had been to Cawnpore I doubted it. This Hindu-Moslem quarrel, with its senseless butchery, was a curse upon India and the Indians, and it seemed to me it was up to them, and not the British, to settle it.

Gandhi, at least, recognized that. After the prayer meeting, someone asked Gandhi if in view of the growing Hindu-Moslem strife he would be willing to let the British government settle the age-old problem when the Round Table Conference began in London.

"Certainly not!" he replied with some heat. "I can imagine nothing more humiliating or degrading than to refer our domestic troubles to the British."

In April that year there was a change of viceroys.

Lord Irwin, looking tired and haggard after his hectic five years in office, departed for home, and Lord Willingdon, a former governor of Bombay province, and more recently Governor-General of Canada, arrived to take his place. I went back to Bombay to witness the pomp and ceremony of the changing of the guard and also to see Gandhi, who had mentioned to me that the retiring Viceroy had invited him to come to the great port city, from which he would sail, for a farewell talk. Irwin had fought him and jailed him, but Gandhi still liked the stern, pious Englishman and respected him as a human being. Irwin had also told him he wanted to arrange a meeting between him and Willingdon as soon as the new Viceroy arrived. Irwin hoped that the rapport he had established with the Mahatma would be continued with his successor. Gandhi hoped so too, but, that, of course, remained to be seen. I gathered Gandhi was a little skeptical. Willingdon was an old hand in India. In his time a high British official talked only to friendly Indians who accepted British rule.

All the lords, ladies, knights, dames, maharajas, rajas, nawabs, and other potentates and notables who managed to wax so fat off this sweltering land of starving millions had assembled in Bombay to say farewell to Lord Irwin and to welcome his successor. There were glittering parties at some of the great houses in Bombay and in the new ornate ballroom of the Taj Mahal Hotel one could watch an array of British officers and officials in formal dress and decorations offering up toasts with champagne and, despite the heat—there was no air conditioning then—dancing the night through to the tunes of two jazz orchestras. Outside the hotel, on the street that ran into the great square in front of the Prince of Wales Museum, you could see, if you looked, the gutters filling up with brown hulks turning in for the night, making pillows of the curbstone, pulling their rags over their skeleton bodies to keep off the evening's chill and the malaria mosquitoes.

That was one of the contrasts between the rulers and the ruled, of which India, I was learning, was so full. I noted others. Lord Irwin had arrived from Delhi in the Viceroy's deluxe special white-and-gold train, reviewed the honor guard of British and Indian troops, and then had driven in a coach-and-four to Government House where the notables, British and Indian, were gathered to welcome him. Gandhi had arrived at about the same time, climbing out of his shabby third-class compartment at a suburban stop and trudging a couple of miles through the broiling sun to the home of a friend. He had wanted to avoid any mass demonstrations that might have marred the arrival of the Viceroy.

When I called on him that evening I found him spinning away and in high spirits. One of his doctors had told me as I entered the house that he had tried vainly to send his patient to bed—he was running a fever and was on the verge of sheer exhaustion. But Gandhi would have none of it. He had spent an hour with Lord Irwin in the afternoon, and the meeting obviously had pleased him greatly.

"Not that we agree on very much," he remarked to me, his eyes lighting up impishly. "But we understand each other."

Actually Irwin had made a speech to the millowners that afternoon, criticizing Gandhi and the Congress for taking advantage of the truce.

"They are reorganizing their forces for a further struggle," Irwin warned. "This contains the germs of trouble and is a menace to peace. It imposes on the government a duty to prepare a counteraction."

Gandhi did not seem to mind, when I reported the speech to him. He could not see anything wrong, he said, with "reorganizing" his forces. That was indeed what he was doing. There was no secret about it. That very afternoon, he said, he had conferred with a group of Indian textile dealers about a plan to re-export $25 million worth of foreign cloth, mostly British, and replace it with Indian goods. That would be a further blow to Manchester's business with India, already hard hit by his boycott. Once again I was struck by Gandhi's grasp of such mundane matters. There was no talk this time of God and love. Indian businessmen, politicians, lawyers, students, academics, kept tripping in all evening to consult with him about this and that. To each he listened carefully; to each he had some suggestion to make.

Next day British warships and shore batteries boomed a thirty-one-gun salute as Willingdon's ship, looking dismal, as all the P. & O. boats did in their faded brown paint, came up the bay, and the new Viceroy alighted at the arched Gateway to India at the water's edge. Dressed in formal attire, he reviewed the battalions of British and Indian troops drawn up in the square and then drove off in a coach-and-four to Government House. Few Indians lined the carefully guarded streets to greet their new ruler.

There were more pomp and ceremony and more thunderous gun salutes the next day as Lord Irwin took ship home and Willingdon was sworn in as the new Viceroy, but this time Gandhi stole the show. While a couple of hundred loyal Indians stood behind solid police lines in front of the university convocation hall to watch Lord Willingdon take his oath of office to "serve well and truly King George V, Emperor of India," a hundred thousand cheering Hindus and Mohammedans jammed outside the City Hall to acclaim Gandhi as he received a municipal address on behalf of the city of Bombay. The city fathers, showing their political acumen, had presented addresses to the incoming and outgoing viceroys the day before, and it was now Gandhi's turn. The gesture of putting the frail Indian leader on a plane of equality with the great British viceroys was not lost on the crowd. Moreover, city officials, for the first time, had set up loudspeakers in the great square to carry the Mahatma's words to the vast assemblage. The clamor became even louder when he began to address them in his native Gujarati, the common language in Bombay. No English for them. It was a foreign language. They did not understand it.

"I take it," Gandhi began, turning to the city officials, some of whom had just come from the viceregal ceremonies still clad in their long coats and British decorations, "that in honoring me you are honoring the starving millions I try to represent."

Eschewing politics out of regard for the feelings of the new Viceroy, Gandhi turned to a subject he knew no Viceroy would ever touch. He made a fervent appeal for the improvement of the welfare of the working classes and of their education and that of their children. Bombay had the largest industrial proletariat in the country, and much of the crowd was made up of workers. They hung on to every word. It was fascinating to feel the rapport between Gandhi and this massive audience. He resorted to no soaring oratory; of that he was incapable. He never raised his voice. But somehow, by the mystery of communication, his simple words got through to his listeners. They heard him out silently, and when he had finished, they broke into a roar of applause that seemed to reverberate far through the city.

Some of Gandhi's aides were resentful that the new Viceroy had declined to see Gandhi, as Lord Irwin had just before his departure, but if the Mahatma was sensitive to the snub, he did not show it. He may have felt that something he had told me on his arrival in Bombay—my dispatch on it had been cabled back to the local press—might have put Willingdon off. He had informed Lord Irwin, he said, when he saw him that day for the last time that he had no intention of wasting his time in London in any of the technical committees that would meet first to draft a new constitution.

"I intend to seek a general agreement first," he said he had told Irwin. "We can discuss details later. I have to know first what the British government is prepared to give us. If it's independence, as I shall demand, it will be easy to work out the details. If it's not independence, why waste time on technicalities? Why bother to draft a constitution until you know what it's for? It's the old story of putting the cart before the horse."

Gandhi's position made sense to me, but I was told at Government House that it had not pleased the new Viceroy, nor, in fact, the departing one. It was another example, one British official complained to me, of the wily Mahatma trying to upset the applecart.

That evening Lord and Lady Willingdon left in the Viceroy's special train for Delhi. Gandhi also departed, in a third-class compartment for Ahmedabad. Though Willingdon had persisted in not seeing the Congress leader, it was secretly arranged through aides, I heard, that in a month or so they would meet in Simla. The new Viceroy, a veteran professional colonialist of the old school, obviously was in no hurry to come to grips with the man who had caused so much trouble to his predecessor. I wondered if he knew there was a revolution going on in India—and that perhaps time was ticking away.

10

Gandhi in Simla! It was bizarre. Simla was bizarre. You had to see it to believe it—this odd summer capital of India, this make-believe piece of Old England transplanted to Asia, perched eight thousand feet above the burning Indian plains on a narrow ridge in the foothills of the towering Himalayas, the highest mountain range in the world.

This was the ultimate contrast in British India. Here on the cool heights of Simla the remoteness of the white rulers from their perspiring brown subjects below became complete. And for the greater part of the year. For seven months out of the twelve, British officials and their ladies could well imagine themselves living back home amidst the splendid greenery of England. Every year since 1864, during the viceroyalty of Sir John Lawrence, when the hot weather set in at the end of March, the Governor-General and his officials had departed Delhi with their families, servants and baggage, followed by mountainous piles of government records, for Simla, remaining there until the end of October, when the plains below began to cool, and they could return there to work in comfort.

For thirty-nine years the annual trek had been an arduous one, but apparently worth the trouble. The terrain from Kalka sixty miles up to Simla was so rugged that British engineers had made little progress in building a road for wheeled vehicles. The trip had to be made on mountain ponies and bullock carts and, later, two-horse tongas, with much of the baggage, including thousands of cases of canned dainties, French wine and Scotch whiskey, and all the official files, lugged up the mountains on the backs of thousands of coolies.

Then in 1903, after years of labor and the expenditure of millions of dollars, a narrow-gauge railway up the mountains to Simla from the railhead at Kalka was completed, and British officialdom could move to the summer capital with greater ease. It gave you a breathtaking ride, the train darting through a hundred tunnels, over trestles so high above the ravines that it made you dizzy to look down, as it did when you cavorted around dozens of hairpin bends that clung to the steep sides of the rocky cliffs. Finally, after the last tunnel, you suddenly saw Simla, perched like a jewel on a pine-covered ridge, with the snows of the Himalayas rising high in the skies to the north.

It was breathlessly beautiful. But it was a weird capital for the most populous country, next to China, in Asia. All that summer I counted the days when I could get away from it for good. There was so much about it that was depressing, and even revolting.

God knows, life was pleasant and comfortable enough, if you had nothing on your mind. The clear, cool air of the mountains was delightful, a tonic to the mind and body of a Westerner after months of remorseless heat on the plains below. The Cecil Hotel, where I put up, was one of the best in India. After dinner the English gentlemen and ladies danced the evening through to the music of two jazz orchestras in its spacious ballroom, the men in tails, white tie and white gloves, the English misses in their dainty evening gowns. If they were high enough up on the social scale, they would be invited to the balls at the Viceregal Lodge, the most important social events of the summer, though scarcely less so than those at the residence of the Commander-in-Chief and that of the Governor of the Punjab, who also summered in Simla. Uniforms or full dress and decorations were required.

The Viceroy, the Commander-in-Chief and the Governor of the Punjab were the only persons permitted by law to have and to use motorcars and carriages. Everyone else in Simla got about in rickshaws, pushed and pulled by four panting coolies, or walked. You could ride horseback along the mountain lanes if you were followed by an Indian groom on foot, but not in the town itself, which had one sole street running along its ridge, the Mall.

The Mall! Pure English. It ran for a mile or so from the Tudor Christ Church Cathedral past picturesque storefronts, banks and tea shops with their Tudor façades of wooden beams and stucco, just like at home, to the Cecil Hotel. The English gathered on the Mall during the day to shop, to pick up the morning *Statesman* of Calcutta or *The Times of India* of Bombay and their mail, pausing in the shade to exchange a word or two and usually adjourning to one of the tea shops. On Sunday mornings, when the shops were closed, they would arrive by the hundreds in their rickshaws to attend services at Christ Church, joining the Viceroy and the commanding general in belting out the familiar Christian hymns and listening complacently to the sermons, in which often they were reminded of British Christian virtues in this vast pagan land. Sundays, and weekdays too, the English had the Mall pretty much to themselves. Until the Great War, I was told by old-timers, no Indian was permitted to show himself on the street. Times had changed, of course, and now the Mall was open to the "natives," provided they were properly dressed. That summer I saw many a poor Indian in his rags chased by police from the Mall.

Sport was not lacking in this summer citadel of British rule. Without it how could an Englishman go on living? At Anandale, in a pleasant valley a thousand feet below the town, the only flat space for miles around, British officers and officials had built a splendid playground. There all day long they played polo, cricket and tennis, staged gymkhanas and bet on the races. There was not enough space for a golf course, but one was found on the Naldera spur, twelve miles away. And there was the shooting. Apparently it was not too good so high up in the hills, but what there was gladdened the heart of many an old Indian Army colonel. They would tell you that there was no shooting in the world that compared with bagging a kaleege pheasant, apparently a difficult bird to corner. Occasionally, they said, they got a Himalayan black bear or a leopard and more frequently a chamois or a barking deer. "Great sport!" they assured me.

There was nothing sporting about the human beasts of burden who pulled and pushed the rickshaws up and down the steep hills until their lungs gave out. Nor about those stocky Kashmiri Pathans who, because vehicles—even wagons or carts—were forbidden except for the use of the three highest British officials, transported on their backs the heavy goods carried in more civilized places by carts, wagons and trucks. They provided a sorry sight I had never seen before, nor seen since, and that I never forgot.

Almost any day while strolling up the Mall you could see these husky Pathans struggling by under loads that would have broken the back of a mule. One day I saw one of them bent under a large haystack and moving it gingerly up the street. Hay for the horses of the white sahibs. Nearly every day during the first few weeks when the British officials were settling in you could see four sweating coolies staggering up the Mall with a grand piano on their backs. It seemed that every bungalow had to have its piano. Every day you saw these Pathans bearing on their backs whatever the commerce demanded: sacks of grain, cement, sand, coal; cases of canned goods, wines, spirits; stacks of chairs, tables, beds; finished lumber or unfinished logs.

There was no limit to their loads. A hundred pounds a man was considered light. Often it was twice that. Sometimes a group of English men and women, shopping along the Mall, would pause to chuckle at the sight, perhaps at a haystack moving past or a piano, and the standard joke among them was of a slender young coolie sauntering smartly along the Mall with a grand piano on one shoulder and a bungalow on the other.

That summer the Indians on the municipal council tried to pass a law limiting a coolie's load to one maund (eighty-six pounds), but they were overruled by their British superiors. This disturbed one English woman, the society editor of *The Pioneer* of Allahabad.

"Long residence in India," she wrote, "dulls one's finer feelings and is apt to deaden one's English outlook on things like this . . . Familiarity with the seamy side of life has bred indifference."

She told of a woman friend, visiting Simla for the first time, being shocked "at one of the most horrible sights she had ever seen, a crated piano on the stooped backs of four coolies. She thought the plight of these human carriers was a blot on enlightened civilization."

The good society editor thought so too, and before moving on to chronicle the levees at Viceregal Lodge, the balls there and elsewhere, the bridge parties and the activities of the Simla Amateur Dramatic Club, she gave her support to the Indians on the municipal council and urged that the "coolies' loads be limited to one maund, and not the three or four maunds I have seen."

Three maunds, I calculated, would be 258 pounds and four maunds would be 344 pounds.

I got to Simla in time to see the new Viceroy arrive. Unable to shake off some malaria and dysentery, I had been urged by an Indian doctor friend of mine in Bombay to try the summer capital for a change. Besides, I wanted to see what sort of a fellow Lord Willingdon was and whether he had been given any leeway in London to seriously negotiate with Gandhi, who would be arriving in a few weeks to try to ascertain that for himself. The Mahatma, after the snub Willingdon had given him in Bombay, did not seem too hopeful. Writing in *Young India* that week, he had found "ominous signs on the horizon."

Even in the rarefied air of the Himalayas, in this make-believe summer capital, the usual pomp and ceremony were accorded the man who was virtually the ruler of one-fifth of the human race. The artillery fired another salute, the troops presented arms, Lord and Lady Willingdon drove up the Mall in a golden coach and were greeted on the lawn of the Viceregal Lodge by a thousand British officers and officials, resplendent in their uniforms or in formal civil attire, their breasts heavy with decorations, their wives in their finest frocks and floppy hats. The invitation had stipulated that "levee dress is required," but since I had none, I went along with what I had, a white linen suit that could have stood some pressing. In such garb I was not encouraged to get near the Viceroy and his lady, but later in the week he invited me for lunch and a talk, with no stipulation about dress.

Considering what I had written about India and the displeasure it had caused in government circles, Lord Willingdon received me cordially enough. I found him a little pompous and somewhat shallow, a typical representative of those who gloried in helping govern His Majesty's far-flung empire. He had not particularly distinguished himself as Governor-General of the Bombay Presidency during the Great War nor as Governor-General of Canada thereafter.* But he had had whatever it takes to move up the ladder of imperial governors. As Viceroy he had now reached the top, and the prospect of ruling India for the next five years was obviously extremely pleasant for him. He seemed to me not to have any idea of the extent or the depth of the nationalist revolution in India. He kept stressing that Gandhi was just one Indian politician and the Congress merely one political party among many that he would be

---

*Years later John Kenneth Galbraith remembered Willingdon in Canada. "He had a thin, gray, deeply depressing face and a narrow, trembling frame. The inadequacy of his presence was emphasized by the uniforms, top hats, medals and carriages by which he was clothed, decorated or moved. One wondered even then, if, behind it all, there lurked some intelligence." Later Galbraith concluded that his wonder was unfounded, that "nothing so lurked. He went on to be Viceroy. His most pregnant thought was how easy India was to govern."—Galbraith, *The New York Times Book Review*, July 14, 1974, p. 2.

dealing with. Still, behind his words I felt that he took Gandhi more seriously than he wanted me to believe. He kept coming back to the point whether I thought Gandhi would attend the Round Table Conference. Apparently the government in London was pressing him on that.

"You know the old man rather well, don't you," he said, not making it a question. Obviously he had been briefed on what I was reporting.

"I don't suppose any Westerner can say he knows him very well," I said, and then, just for the hell of it, I added, "including some of your highest officials here."

"You think so?" he said breezily, tweaking his mustache.

I left the Viceregal Lodge that day, as I did two or three subsequent times, with the impression that Willingdon did not have the mind or the imagination, as Lord Irwin to a certain extent had had, to deal boldly with the drive of the Indians for self-rule. He would be rather good at putting them off. He would move no faster than London desired. Progress toward self-government would be kept at a snail's pace.*

Anxious to take his own measure of the new Viceroy, Gandhi arrived at the rarefied heights of Simla on May 13. The strange Himalayan capital of British officialdom, so fixed in its English ways, had never seen anything quite like what followed. Suddenly the India of the Indians, so remote to these polo-playing, tea-

---

* How ludicrously slow to Indians, if not to him, that pace would be came out one day when Willingdon proudly revealed to me a plan drawn up by Sir Philip Chetwode, Commander-in-Chief of the Indian Army, to "Indianize" the country's armed forces. After months of study Sir Philip concluded that one complete all-Indian division of 25,000 men could be built over the next twenty-five years, and ready for active service at the end of that period, or in 1956. The rest of the 200,000 men, or seven-eighths of it, even after 1956, would be British-officered and consist of 5,000 British and 125,000 Indian troops. That was the plan. Willingdon thought it was "splendid" and showed "how far" the British were prepared to go in turning over affairs in India to the Indians. I could scarcely believe him. At any rate, history would shortly make a mockery of this farce.

partying English rulers, imposed itself, if only for a few days, upon this Asian English town.

It was the first time Gandhi had visited Simla since 1921, just ten years before, when he had come up the mountains to tell the then Viceroy, Lord Reading, that unless the government terror in the Punjab was halted he would go on with the civil-disobedience movement, which he had recently launched, and for which the noble lord would shortly clap him behind bars, with a sentence of six years.

I went down the mountains to Kalka to see what sort of a reception the hill folk, a little remote themselves from the searing plains below, where most Indians lived, would give the Mahatma. It turned out to be no different, no less tumultuous, than all the others I had seen from one end of the country to the other. From the moment Gandhi abandoned his third-class compartment on the Simla Express at Kalka to enter a small, rather beaten American motorcar, which took him up the precipitous serpentine road leading to Simla—it had been much improved in recent years—he received one ovation after the other. Word had spread among the simple hill folk by that mysterious grapevine which I have mentioned and they flocked down the mountains to hail him. At almost every turn of the road they showered him with flowers and shouted a greeting slightly different from what I had heard elsewhere: *"Be taj badsha ki jai!*—Victory to our uncrowned king!"* Mrs. Gandhi and Miss Slade flanked him in the little car. Some in the crowd seemed surprised to see the tall, gaunt, white-skinned English lady at the Mahatma's side, but this did not lessen their wild enthusiasm at the sight of him. A couple of hours later, when the small party reached Simla, a number of English ladies and gentlemen, who had gathered on the Mall out of curiosity to see what the little man who had caused so much fuss looked like, took a dimmer view of their wellborn compatriot sitting at the side of the seditious rebel in a loincloth. I heard and overheard their contemptuous comments at dinner that evening at the Cecil.

They had not liked either an official ruling—could it possibly have been by the Viceroy himself?—which permitted Gandhi's ragged group to motor down the Mall on its way to an Indian home where it would stay. That had never happened before in Simla. It was somehow ominous, they thought. Would Gandhi, they asked that night around the Cecil bar, be allowed, in the face of the law, to motor to the Viceregal Lodge when he saw Lord Willingdon? They hoped not. That had certainly never happened before either— even for the most prominent officials, even for a general, and certainly never for an Indian.

The authorities made a further concession to Gandhi that did not sit well with the sahibs. For the first time, ever, they threw open to him for a mass meeting the Ridge, a square previously reserved only for dress parades. Horrors! The troubled talk around the Cecil that evening was that if this kept up they would wake up soon and learn that the Viceroy had named Gandhi Prime Minister and was turning India over to the Indians. It was unbelievable!

Later that evening I went over to Gandhi's house. Despite the fatigue of the journey, he was in fine spirits. He was going to keep the British guessing, it developed, as to whether, after all, he would attend the Round Table Conference in London. I thought that had been settled by the Delhi Pact, but the old man said No.

"I have not yet made up my mind about going to London," he told me when I asked him. There were several obstacles, he said. For one thing, the government was not observing the terms of the Delhi Pact. It was still holding several hundred men and women in jail. He had just spent three hours, he said, with the Home Minister, and had presented him with a long list of government violations of the truce. But the most important obstacle, he said, was purely Indian: the Indians themselves had not yet reached an agreement on the Hindu-Moslem problem.

"I don't want to go to London," he explained, "unless I have the united voice of India behind me. That means Moslems and Hindus must settle their differences and back me unitedly."

"But is there time for that?" I asked.

"I am hopeful," he smiled, as if remembering how often he had said that to me. "I'm hopeful that within a fortnight the communal problem may be in a fair way toward settlement." I thought he was being hopeful indeed.

For some weeks my editors in Chicago had been pestering me with cables asking if Gandhi planned to visit America after the London conference. The news agencies had got headlines at home by saying that he had. So I put it to him that evening.

"I long to visit your great country," he said. "I have had the most tempting invitations to do so. But I must deny myself that luxury until my task of achieving independence is finished. I would like to carry my message of non-violence and love to America. But I cannot do so until I have been able to show the American people that such a doctrine has triumphed in India, and that it offers the whole world a new instrument for winning the rights of man peacefully and insuring the brotherhood of all nations."

I took down his words and incorporated them in my dispatch that evening. I wondered how his "message of non-violence and love" would go down with my fellow countrymen at home, if he ever carried it there.

The cat-and-mouse game that Gandhi played with the British during the next days in Simla, and then for weeks after he had left, about whether or not he would attend the London conference, did not amuse the fat cats on the Himalayan heights nor, I gathered, in London. The meeting there would be a fiasco without Gandhi. Yet even the Viceroy could not quite pin him down, at least not for long.

The day after his arrival, Gandhi addressed a rally of Indians on the Ridge. It was the first mass meeting of Indians ever held in this Indian summer capital, and despite a pouring rain, ten thousand hill folk showed up to hear the frail leader. He began to shiver in the chill mountain air and Miss Slade, ever at his side, threw a homespun shawl over his bony shoulders and raised a big black umbrella over his head. He told the crowd it would be "useless" for him to go to London unless Indians of all creeds united solidly behind him. But even if he went?

"If we cannot get complete self-government then we must be ready to renew the war against the British, which I beseech God may not become necessary."

Apparently Gandhi was much less intransigent the next day when he saw Lord Willingdon. At any rate, the Viceroy gave it out that the Indian leader had definitely committed himself to attending the Round Table Conference. He was reported highly pleased by the way his first meeting with Gandhi had gone.

The Indian community in Simla was far from pleased, indeed it was indignant, at Lord Willingdon's failure to offer Gandhi one of the many viceregal automobiles or to allow him to use his own little car in which to make the six-mile trip from his lodgings to the Viceregal Lodge. There had been, I was told, a lively debate in the Governor-General's council on the matter and the decision was made that the frail little man must walk, if he did not wish to ride in a rickshaw.

Gandhi's friends had urged him to take one, but he had refused. "I will never allow my brother men to become beasts of burden for me," he had replied rather sternly. "I shall walk."

And he did, up and down the hilly roads in a chilling, drenching rain for the six miles to the lodge and the six miles back, wading through deep puddles, plodding along with the help of a staff, soaked to the skin long before he reached the Viceroy's office. It was nothing, he quipped to us newspapermen trudging alongside, after the two hundred miles or so he had walked to the sea to make salt. Still, his doctor that evening was fearful he might catch pneumonia from the thorough soaking in the chill mountain air.

The pettiness of British officials, the sheer callousness—the final decision was said to have been made by the Viceroy—depressed me, if not Gandhi. He was sixty-one, he had been seriously ill from fever and exhaustion a week or two before, he had been invited by Lord Willingdon to come here for a talk, not a grueling walk.

Common courtesy, common decency, called for the British to make a simple gesture of allowing the old man, the acknowledged leader of the vast majority of Indians, to ride. But these particular British had not had it. Ruling India brought out the worst in them.

If receiving Gandhi in his drenched rags aroused any feelings in Lord Willingdon, he kept them to himself. His press officer, who briefed us on the meeting, was highly indignant that the correspondents would ask about it. Typically, the Mahatma showed no resentment at all at having been made to walk twelve miles through the rain. That evening he brushed aside with a laugh every attempt of the correspondents to get him to comment on it.

Apparently his condition had not dampened his sharpness during the talk with the Viceroy. He told Willingdon bluntly that the government was not carrying out all the terms of the Delhi truce—hundreds of prisoners had not yet been released, for example—and got from him a promise that he would personally see to it that they were. He received also an assurance that despite what the Tory diehards were saying in London, the Indian leader would be free to bring up any issues he liked, including safeguards and the Congress' demand for independence.

Gandhi, I gathered, found Lord Willingdon more amiable than he had expected. And more liberal. When the Governor-General told him he looked forward to becoming India's "first constitutional Viceroy," Gandhi retorted: "You can start your regime now along constitutional lines by shaping the government to the will and to the aspirations of the Indian people."

He had no illusions, I'm sure, that this ruler of India would heed his advice. It would not be long before his confidence in him began to sag, and with reason.

Mrs. Gandhi, who was illiterate and no politician, though some of her husband's political aspirations had rubbed off on her, was equally tart when Lady Willingdon received her the next day. It was the first time a vicereine had ever invited in the wife of the Indian leader, causing eyebrows to be raised among the British officials and their wives. Kasturbai Gandhi had ridden to the lodge in a rickshaw, which her husband had disdained the day before. But that was the extent of her concession.

When Lady Willingdon told her she would like to obtain some khaddar cloth, the coarse homespun material which Gandhi had popularized as one means of hurting the British textile trade with India, Mrs. Gandhi replied she would be happy to send her some.

"I want to get in closer touch with the Indian people that way," said Lady Willingdon. "Could you send me something in mauve?"

"Certainly, I'll send you lots of mauve," said Mrs. Gandhi. "And by the way, I like your idea of getting in closer touch with the Indian people by sampling our homespun materials. You would also know them better if you lived down in the plains, where they dwell, instead of up here on these mountain heights."

Gandhi and his party left Simla to spend a few days at a mountain resort at Naini Tal, leaving up in the air whether he would go to London or not. The Viceroy thought the Indian leader had definitely committed himself to go during their talk. But now he began to wonder. On May 22, a week after that parley, I found great confusion at the government offices. London provisionally had set June 29 for the opening of the meeting and had reserved cabins for the Indian delegation on the P. & O. boat sailing from Bombay on the thirteenth. But Gandhi had wired the Viceroy on this May 22 that the sailing date was too soon. It gave him only three weeks to settle the Hindu-Moslem question and the still existing differences over compliance with the Delhi truce. Other telegrams came in that day. Sir Tej Behadur Sapru, the Liberal leader, who had been acting for months as a mediator between the Congress and the government, wired the Viceroy that it would be futile to hold the London conference without Gandhi. I phoned the Mahatma at Naini Tal. He was out, but Desai, his secretary, told me Gandhi would give his definitive answer on June 3. They were leaving their retreat, he said, for Borsad, in Gujarat, where the government was still refusing to return confiscated property to the peasants.

Two days later, on May 24, Desai telephoned to tell me that

Gandhi refused to be stampeded into going to London. He declined also to become involved in any more talk for the moment about weighty constitutional matters.

"Read this week's issue of *Young India*," said Desai, "and you'll see the chief has other things on his mind."

What Gandhi had on his mind that torrid week was rather astonishing, I thought, when I read through the magazine. The Mahatma had written almost the entire issue himself, as he often did. There was a long piece again condemning *suttee*, the horrible old Hindu custom of having young widows burn themselves to death on the funeral pyres of their departed husbands. I had not realized that such abominations still went on in this country. Gandhi had penned another long piece about happy marriages. And another about the right count in spinning and how to make your yarn weaveable. And still another commenting on a cable he had received from a certain American named Dr. Harry Ward, advising Gandhi not to come to the United States because "American newspapers have become increasingly sensational and would misrepresent and exploit you." Not a word about politics. Not a hint about whether he would go to London. The old fox, I thought, as I thumbed through the issue. The government in London was burning up the cable lines to Simla demanding to know if the Viceroy could produce the Mahatma. And the Mahatma was composing lengthy pieces about *suttee*, the spinning of yarn, and happy marriages!

Finally on May 30 I sent a rather frantic telegram to Gandhi at Bardoli.

MAHATMA GANDHI

BARDOLI

VIEW OF FACT FEDERAL STRUCTURES COMMITTEE DEFINITELY RECONVENED LONDON SEPTEMBER FIFTH AND BECAUSE MANY CONFLICTING REPORTS EMANATING FROM BARDOLI STATE YOU WILL OR WILL NOT JOIN THAT COMMITTEE OR THAT YOU INTEND GOING LONDON ONLY AS OBSERVER AND NOT AS NEGOTIATOR COULD YOU KINDLY MAKE YOUR POSITION

CLEAR ABOUT YOUR PARTICIPATION ROUND TABLE CONFERENCE STOP IF
YOU CONSENT DO SO YOU WOULD GREATLY CLEAR UP MUDDLED WORLD
OPINION WHICH IS WONDERING WHETHER YOU INTEND NEGOTIATE
PERMANENT SETTLEMENT AT LONDON OR NOT AND WHY.

WILLIAM SHIRER HOTEL CECIL SIMLA

Gandhi's reply reached me by wire on the evening of June 1.

RECENT REPORTS MY POSITION UNAUTHORIZED BEING UNINTELLIGENT
ANTICIPATION STOP SO FAR AS I CAN SEE ABSENCE [HINDU-MOSLEM]
COMMUNAL SOLUTION BLOCKS MY PARTICIPATION ROUND TABLE CON-
FERENCE STOP DELICATE SITUATION GANDHI-IRWIN SETTLEMENT MAKES
MY IMMEDIATE LEAVING INDIA DIFFICULT STOP APART FROM THESE DIFFI-
CULTIES I'M ANXIOUS ATTEND ROUND TABLE CONFERENCE AND TAKE FULL
SHARE DELIBERATIONS AND PRESS CONGRESS DEMANDS STOP AM THERE-
FORE SEEKING WAY OUT OF DIFFICULTY STOP BUT IF COMMUNAL QUESTION
ISN'T SOLVED HERE AND SETTLEMENT DIFFICULTY IS OVER AND IF I AM
REQUESTED PROCEED TO LONDON TO EXPLAIN CONGRESS POSITION TO
RESPONSIBLE STATESMEN AND PUBLIC IN GREAT BRITAIN I HAVE TOLD
FRIENDS I SHOULD HOLD MYSELF READINESS PROCEED LONDON STOP IN
SHORT I AM ANXIOUS SECURE PERMANENT PEACE BY NEGOTIATION CONSIS-
TENT WITH FUNDAMENTAL POSITION CONGRESS.

M. K. GANDHI

I read it that evening and reread it before I sat down to write my
dispatch to Chicago. What was one to make of it? After chewing it
over and over I decided to make as optimistic an interpretation as
possible.

"Gandhi is ready and anxious," I began my dispatch, "to secure
permanent peace in India by negotiation. He is ready to go to
London and participate in the Round Table Conference—on
conditions. Tonight he broke his long silence on his intentions in a
telegram to your correspondent from his headquarters in Bardoli."

That evening at the Cecil I ran into a British official who said the
government was still in the dark about Gandhi's intentions, despite

a wire to the Viceroy similar to the one the Mahatma had sent me—I had forgotten that the British authorities had access to all messages I received as well as to those I sent. The official did not think Gandhi had made himself very clear.

"But when has he ever?" he added, with a weary smile.

The Hindu-Moslem question was not solved that summer despite Gandhi's determination to settle it so that the Indians could present a united front at London. The issue separating the two sides seemed simple enough to an outsider, but not to the Indians. It was whether there should be joint or separate electorates for election to the federal and provincial legislatures in an eventual self-governing India. The Congress, which had a good many Moslems in it, but still a minority of them, feared separate electorates would prolong the differences between the two communities indefinitely. Besides, it opposed the principle of dividing the electorate by religion. The Moslems insisted on separate electorates for themselves as the only means of preventing them from being swamped by the Hindu majority.

In his meeting with the Moslem leaders in Bombay in March Gandhi thought he had solved the problem by offering to guarantee the Mohammedans one-third of the seats in the legislatures, which was considerably more than the one-fourth proportion of Moslems to Hindus in the country, in return for their acceptance of joint electorates. Shaukat Ali, the fiery Islamic leader, had told me himself in Bombay that he had accepted Gandhi's offer, at least provisionally. It would give him and his co-religionists a greater representation in the legislatures than their numbers called for.

But apparently Ali, who once had been Gandhi's principal aide in the Congress and a fierce champion of Indian independence, had changed his mind. Congress circles believed he had secretly sold out to the British. At any rate when the so-called loyalist Moslems met the nationalist Moslems at Simla at the end of June to iron out *their* differences, Shaukat Ali was in a belligerent anti-Hindu mood. I had never seen him so wild-eyed.

"If the Hindus don't meet our demands this time we're going to make war on them," he fairly shouted at me. "We ruled the Hindus once," he stormed, referring to the great days of Mogul dominion in Delhi. "We at least don't intend to be ruled by them now."

He told me his Moslems had already drawn up plans to fight the Congress boycott of British goods unless the Hindus gave in to him. They would counterpicket, he said, the Congress' picketing of shops selling foreign wares.

It was for me a sad encounter, for I had taken a liking to this wild and woolly man, a direct descendant of the warring Arabians who in the time of Mohammed had taken up fire and sword to spread Islam over half of Asia. No one in India had been more adamant in demanding the British turn over India to the Indians. Now, if he hadn't sold out to them, he was acting as if he had.

Dr. Sayyed Mahmmud, the general secretary of the Congress and a leading Moslem himself, was outraged.

"The belief spread by the British and now, I regret, by some of my Islamic brothers," he told me, "that the Moslems never supported Gandhi and the Congress is simply untrue. Many did hold back because their leaders feared Hindu domination. But the world ought to know that twelve thousand Moslems were jailed during the civil-disobedience campaign, and five hundred Moslems have been killed since Gandhi started his march to the sea a year ago."

At Simla that end of June the two warring Moslem factions could not get together, and their meetings broke up without an accord. If they could not agree among themselves on the only major issue at stake, how could they reach an accord with the Congress and the Hindus? Gandhi, who had said in advance he would accept whatever demands the Mohammedans could unite on, was sick at heart. The British, whose continued rule, as Gandhi kept trying to tell his fellow countrymen, depended on keeping the Indians at one another's throats, were pleased.

In the end Gandhi with great reluctance gave in to the mounting pressure from the British, from some of the more progressive Indian princes and from several Indian moderates and agreed to go to London to present the Congress case for Indian independence now. From my numerous talks with him that summer I knew he had no illusions that the Round Table Conference would give him anything like what he wanted. But he thought he should make the gesture of good faith and good will, and go. The conference, he felt sure, would fail. The British in 1931 were not about to give back India to the Indians. Then, Gandhi had made it plain, he would have to renew the struggle.

But it would be a long one. He had no illusions about that either. And fascinated as I was by this revolution and the experience it had given me with Gandhi, the most interesting and inspiring man I had ever met, or was likely again to meet, I could not stay on for long in a country whose scorching climate had already laid me low. In truth, I wanted to get back to Europe, which was really where I was most at home, and which now seemed to me to be beginning to slide downhill toward fascism, chaos and war. Hitler and Nazism were on the rise in Germany. In Rome Mussolini was making belligerent noises. What happened in Europe, it seemed to me, would decide the fate of the world, including that of my own country, and indeed that of Britain and India. I wanted to get back to reporting that.

By the end of June that year the dysentery and malaria picked up during my first tour of duty in India and which I had been unable to shake the past few months had become worse. I lay in bed in Simla with fever for several days, unable to work. There was not much to write about anyway. The story had petered out. It would come to life again in September, when Gandhi arrived in London. I got permission from Chicago to return to my post in Vienna and take a cure for my tropical maladies. The cold and imperious Colonel McCormick, lord of the *Chicago Tribune,* melted enough to send his good wishes for my recovery.

"But I want you to pick up Gandhi in London in September," he instructed me. That I was happy and anxious to do.

I picked Gandhi up in Marseilles on September 11, 1931, when he disembarked from the liner *Rajputana,* out from Bombay, to take the boat train to London. As the ship swung backward into the dock at dawn Gandhi could be seen standing alone on the aft upper deck gazing at the great port and obviously surprised at the cheering of two or three thousand French below on the pier and at the din of factory whistles blowing a note of welcome. In the early-morning chill he had thrown a rough homespun shawl over his skinny shoulders. He looked much fitter than when I last saw him in India a couple of months before. Later, he said the sea voyage had greatly improved his health.

Pleasantly surprised as he was at the impromptu reception accorded by the French as the boat was being docked, he was obviously startled by that given him by several hundred European and American reporters and photographers who closed in on him in the ship's lounge, pushing and shoving and shouting. He had never experienced that before. In India we were too few and too attuned to Gandhi to turn his press conferences into a bedlam.

Finding it impossible to hear the questions or to make himself heard above the din of the clamoring photographers and reporters, Gandhi finally retreated to his second-class cabin. There I eventually found him, sprawling on his bunk, his thin little legs dangling over the side, and—this did not surprise me as it might have the other reporters—spinning away. He greeted me warmly. He seemed excited about touching down in Europe for the first time in seventeen years and he was as radiant as ever. But he became more sober when I pressed him to tell me what he intended to do in London. Sober, but not hesitant.

"Since you have been good enough to report my words truthfully from India," he said, and then for a second flashing his infectious smile, "even though they have often confused you, my dear Mr. Shirer, I will tell you."

What he now said almost startled me, for his stand had hardened since our talks in India. It left little chance, I thought, as I scribbled the words down, for his reaching any understanding, much less any agreement, with the British government in London. He would ask the British for three things, he said.

FIRST—complete independence for India. Dominion status is not sufficient.

SECOND—The status of India within the British Empire to be only on a coequal basis.

THIRD—Safeguards during the transitional stage, if the first two conditions are accepted.

This was the first time Gandhi had come out flatly against Dominion status, which after all would mean virtual independence for India, as it had for Canada, Australia, and South Africa. So I asked him to explain his position a little further.

"My idea of independence," Gandhi replied, "does not exclude an alliance or partnership with the British. It does exclude, absolutely, Dominion status. Two years ago I personally would have accepted Dominion status. Now I believe it is impossible for India."

"Why?" I asked.

"Because Dominion status, as I understand it, implies a family of nations made up of the same people," Gandhi explained. "Now, we are not of the same family as the English. Our race, culture and religion preclude that. We will take on a partnership with the British, but not Dominion status."

I was, I guess, a little incredulous.

"But do you think you have a ghost of a chance of putting such demands across with the British in London?" I asked.

"Frankly not," Gandhi said. "Looking at the external side of things, there is not much chance for them to be ready to grant what I ask.

"But my position is clear," he added soberly. "I am against Dominion status, mind you. I am not going to London to ask for that. I hope to be able to explain my position to the British statesmen, if they are accessible. That is all. Then, if there is any basis of accord—I mean, on independence—the details can be filled in."

Gandhi was wrecking, even before he got to London, I thought, any possibility that something serious might come out of the

Round Table Conference. The British government, hard pressed though it was by mounting unemployment, the slipping of the pound sterling, growing social unrest and the prospect of a new election, certainly had no intention of letting go of India, the bulwark of its Empire. Gandhi, one of the shrewdest men in the world, knew that perfectly well. But I was not seeing him to give my own views, which were of no importance. Gandhi knew them well, from our long talks in India, and had borne listening to them with infinite patience.

"You cannot be very optimistic," I said, "in view of what you have just said." In fact, I wondered why he had made the long trip to England.

"You know me well enough," he smiled, "to know that I am always optimistic." He grinned through his two teeth and his eyes lit up mischievously. "I admit," he went on, "I do not see land in sight yet. But neither did Columbus, so it is said, until the last moment."

We turned to other topics. I asked Gandhi about press reports saying he hoped to make a barnstorming tour of England, making speeches everywhere in an effort to gain backing from the people.

"I don't intend even to make a speech at the Round Table Conference," he said. I took that piece of information with a large grain of salt.

"I will try," he said, "to present my position to the cotton-mill workers of Lancashire, hundreds of thousands of whom are out of work due largely to our Indian boycott." He would tell them, he hinted, that if their government gave India its independence the boycott would end and their factories might start humming again. There was something of the *banian* trader in Gandhi, reflecting the caste from which he came.

All the while we talked Gandhi's aides were carrying out the makeshift baggage of his party, a couple of spinning wheels, changes of loincloths, mattresses, bedding and the prison utensils with which the Mahatma ate his meals. One group was dispatched to the ship's refrigerators to fetch cans of goat's milk which they had brought along to provide Gandhi with one of the staples of his meager diet.

Also sitting on the floor as we talked were the inimitable Sarojini Naidu, as ebullient as ever, and Madeleine Slade, or Mirabai, as she now preferred to be called. Mrs. Naidu, of whom I had become very fond, kept butting in occasionally to crack a joke. Attired in an orange silk sari, she looked elegant.

"I hear you came first-class deluxe," I teased her.

"Certainly!" she flashed back. "Not for me these cramped steerage quarters. I find them unbearable!"

Gandhi, who had a great love for her, beamed.

"You will never learn to live like the rest of us," he said.

"Why should I?" she shot back.

Gandhi had remarked, in answer to a question of mine, that, contrary to reports, he was not going to America. "I would like to," he said, "but I don't feel it's proper at this time. I am not ready for it, and perhaps your country is not ready for me."

"I'm going to America!" Mrs. Naidu broke in. "Unless the British jail me first. And I'm not going to lecture on poetry."

I talked for a moment with Mirabai. In her coarse homespun sari, her head still shaved, her eyes staring out of a cadaverous face, she resembled a ghost. I asked her how it felt to be back in Europe. She looked so sad.

"I'm not thrilled to be back," she said. "I have been away six years now, six happy years. My past life in England is dead and buried, and let it be. I had no desire to return. I came back only because Gandhiji asked me to. It is the last time." She did say she would see her mother, Lady Slade, in London. I wondered what kind of a meeting that would be.

I hurried back to my hotel to write up the interview and get it off by cable. That done, I took a taxi to the local office of the P. & O. shipping line to get a ticket for the all-Pullman boat train in which Gandhi would be leaving for London at the day's end.

"Sorry!" the local P. & O. manager apologized to me. He was under strict orders, he said, to issue tickets only to passengers on the ship.

"But what about us journalists assigned to cover Gandhi?" I asked.

"Sorry. But I've been forbidden to sell you a place on the train."

He was a decent enough chap. Lord Inchcape himself, who controlled the Peninsula and Oriental Line, had laid it down, he said: No journalists, not even English, were to be sold tickets on the boat train. Inchcape, I remembered, had made a fortune in the India shipping trade. He was known in India as violently opposed to Gandhi.

I registered my protest with the manager and, a little dejected by the rebuff, took a taxi back to the hotel. So this was the first move on the part of British interests to prevent Gandhi from stealing the show. It was starting right here in Marseilles.

Gandhi and his party had taken rooms in the hotel. I went up to see him, apologizing for taking more of his time when he had been so generous to me during the morning.

"But I think you ought to know," I said, "that the British obviously are determined to prevent, insofar as they can, the world press from covering your mission to London. Lord Inchcape, for example, has barred us newspapermen from your boat train."

Gandhi perked up his ears.

"They wouldn't sell you a ticket on the train?" he asked.

"They refused," I said. "They said no journalists would be allowed on your train."

Without another word, Gandhi turned to a canvas bag that lay on the floor next to him. It was crammed with papers of one sort or another. He finally extracted a large manila envelope and took out a bunch of tickets.

"There you are," he smiled, checking a pair of tickets. "One for the railroad, I think, the other for the sleeper."

I took out my billfold to pay him.

"Don't ask me how much it is," he laughed, and turned me over to Mahadev Desai, his chief secretary, and by this time a good friend of mine. It took us some time to figure out how much to pay.

As I stood at a window of the plush *wagon-lit* as Gandhi's boat train slowly pulled out of the Marseilles station a few hours later I could not say that my journalistic colleagues, even some of my close friends among them, who had been excluded from the train, gave me anything like a friendly glance as they stood on the platform and watched my smiling face in the car window pass by.

This was one more kindness that Mahatma Gandhi, no matter how busy he was, had done me since we first met. He had been strenuously occupied the whole day, going over hundreds of telegrams that had awaited him in Marseilles, dictating replies to his secretaries, who were also constantly on the phone to London, arranging his schedule there. He had had to go off to the City Hall for an official reception and make a speech. He had a steady stream of visitors, and talks with other Indian delegates to the conference. Somehow he had found time for me, time to make an announcement of his demands that for his own reasons he wanted made public before his arrival in the British capital, time to scratch into his bag for a boat-train ticket for me in defiance of Lord Inchcape and as a gesture of his regard for me.

I went up to his compartment toward dusk as the train sped north through France. He was spinning, and gazing out the car window at the green fields. I went back to my own compartment and typed out a new lead for my dispatch. I had a new dateline: "Aboard Gandhi's Train from Marseilles to London, Sept. 11— Puttering away at his spinning wheel as he watched the sun set over the green fields of France, so unlike the parched and sun-baked plains of India, Mahatma Gandhi sped north toward London tonight. . . ."

For three or four hundred francs, the kindly porter of my Pullman car agreed to drop off my new dispatch with the stationmaster at the first stop and arrange for him to put it on the wires, collect, to my Paris office. I added a hundred francs for the stationmaster.

It had been quite a day.

Next day my editors would cable congratulations on my scoop. The *Chicago Tribune* would boast of it in a full-page ad.

11

Gandhi in London! The imperial capital had never witnessed anything quite like it. Despite the efforts of some of the Conservative press lords to cut the Indian leader down to size in their newspapers, the Mahatma kept breaking into the headlines as crowds turned out by the thousands to greet him wherever he went and hordes of photographers and reporters kept at his heels. The crowds were invariably friendly—no matter to them that this little man had come to London to defy the British Empire. The tumultuous welcome was a new experience for Gandhi in London and he obviously enjoyed it. He had been a shy, unknown, unnoticed student when he had first come to the city in 1887. Even in 1914, twenty-six years later, when he had returned briefly to London on the eve of the war, he was little known to the public, and then only vaguely as a Hindu agitator who had stirred up a fuss in South Africa by clamoring for civil rights for his Indian fellow countrymen there.

Now he was a world figure, and the strangest one Londoners had ever seen, walking the streets in his loincloth with an old homespun shawl over his bony shoulders to protect him from the autumn chill, smiling broadly at all who greeted him and preaching love and non-violence.

Some of the newspapers had appealed to their readers not to poke fun at his scanty dress. On the day after his arrival the *Sunday Times* wrote solemnly: "There is in Gandhi's dress and mode of life an invitation to empty minds to regard him as something of a figure for fun. In the interests of common courtesy, let those who are so tempted hold their hands."

There were some taunts at his loincloth, especially when he appeared in it at Buckingham Palace to have tea with the King-Emperor. A few Britons regarded this as showing a lack of respect for the sovereign. But Gandhi took it all lightheartedly. Asked by an English reporter if he thought his loincloth was "appropriate" for Buckingham Palace, where formal dress was required, Gandhi quipped: "The King was wearing enough for us both." He had had a good laugh, one of his aides told me, when a retired British Indian Army colonel had had delivered to him as his ship stopped at Suez a silk petticoat with a note: "Cover Your Nudity!"

The British authorities did their best to spirit Gandhi into London as inconspicuously as possible. Thousands of Indian and British sympathizers had crammed into Victoria Station to greet him when the boat train arrived. But at Folkestone, after the Channel crossing, officials of the India Office persuaded him to make the journey up to London by car to avoid demonstrations, some of which, they warned, would be hostile. Thousands of Lancashire cotton-mill workers, it was said, put out of work by the Indian Congress boycott, had come down to London to demonstrate against the Indian leader. So, chauffeured by a high official of the India Office, no less, with two Scotland Yard detectives in the back seat to protect him, Gandhi, sitting in front aside his distinguished driver, was driven through back streets into the capital, unnoticed in the gray drizzle, and deposited at the doorway of Kingsley Hall in the drab East End, where he had been invited to stay. A few hundred persons were gathered outside in the rain to greet him there. Inside there were 1,500 invited guests representing the three political parties in Parliament, the government, the King, the churches and the trade unions. An army of reporters and photographers, invited or not, had forced its way in.

Gandhi, though obviously tired from the journey, lost no time in telling the assembly what he had come to London for. Apologizing for his fatigue, he asked to be allowed to speak seated. But there was plenty of power in his voice, which carried through amplifiers to every corner of the large hall.

"I have come here," he began, "to win freedom—freedom for the dumb, semistarved millions whom I represent."

The British, he went on, were saying that he did not represent India. He begged to differ.

"I claim to represent the nation of India. I claim to represent the dumb, semistarved paupers who make up India. I have not come to London to bargain. I have a specific mandate from the Congress, which gives me little freedom of action. In all the fundamentals I am hidebound." And he proceeded to outline what that mandate was: complete independence, etc.

"I know you have your budget troubles," he concluded, "but the budget never will be honestly balanced until the balance between India and Great Britain is set right."

Just as he had told me the day before in Marseilles, he was not going to beat around the bush in London. His audience, which included many admirers and well-wishers, was stunned by his bluntness. It greeted his words in silence. The good people assembled there, I felt, had expected him to be more diplomatic and conciliatory. They were disappointed.

In a brief question-and-answer period that followed his short speech, less controversial subjects were brought up. London, where forty-eight years before he had studied law, dancing, French and the violin, and gone out to parties in formal dress, looked just about the same to him, he said, in answer to one question.

"Perhaps I have changed," he smiled. When someone asked him

if he would wear a loincloth in London, he replied that he would. He would continue, he said, to do his two hours of daily spinning, regardless of other claims on his time. (I had watched him get his two hours in for the day while crossing the Channel.) He would continue to observe Monday as a day of silence.

"But the Round Table Conference opens on Monday. Won't you speak out?" someone asked.

"No," Gandhi replied, with an impish smile. "I'll keep my silence. It will make me an even better listener than I am on other days."

He was as good as his word. All through the ceremonial opening of the conference in St. James's Palace, with speeches of welcome from the Prime Minister and Lord Sankey, the Lord Chancellor and chairman of the meeting, and courteous statements by half a dozen Indian degates, Gandhi sat in his homespun rags as silent as the Sphinx. The next day he made up for it.

Speaking extemporaneously, without a single note, he delivered what I, who had listened to so many of his speeches, have always considered to be the greatest one of his long political life.* From the moment he started speaking, sitting simply at his place, humble in manner, his voice even and low key, choosing his words carefully and blending them into an eloquence the like of which I had never heard, I had a feeling in my stomach that he was going to

---

*The conference secretariat, set up by the India Office, refused to give the correspondents a complete text of Gandhi's address. The day before we had asked its press chief if he would be good enough to supply us with this. He had politely refused. Gandhi, he said, must be treated like all the other delegates. Summaries of their speeches and extracts from them would be provided, but not complete texts.

"But Gandhi's speech may have worldwide importance," I protested. "There is much interest in it on both sides of the Atlantic. Many of us would like the complete text."

"Sorry," said the press chief, "but we must stick to the rules. They apply to all the delegates, Indian and British."

Since there was little interest in what the others said, this was a patent attempt by the British authorities to water down what Gandhi might say and dampen its impact. I engaged a shorthand stenographer, but could not get him a press pass. During the speech I took as full notes as I could and checked them with Gandhi's secretaries, one of whom had taken shorthand notes as best he could, though he was not very expert.

rise to the occasion and soar to heights he had never before achieved.

"Today," I scribbled in my notebook, "Gandhi is not the 'holy man,' not the Mahatma, but the masterful politician, culminating, as it were, a life of political struggle." Many great men, it occurred to me, muff the great opportunities for one reason or another, perhaps out of nervousness, or from overstriving. Gandhi, it became evident at once, was going to make the most of his.

England's great legal minds, Lord Reading, Lord Sankey, lord chief justices past and present, sat fascinated and intrigued as the frail little Indian leader, who had received his early training in the law in the same Inns of Court as they, crouched in his seat and built up his case for independence for India.

He would take nothing less, he said simply. If he could not get it he would bother them no longer with his presence. But before the British decided, he hoped they would hear him out. Several members of the cabinet and scores of leaders of Parliament, who had crowded into the great hall of St. James's Palace to see what the little rebel was really like, leaned forward to catch his words. Like everyone else present they seemed gripped by the spell Gandhi began to weave.

But they were scarcely prepared, it was obvious, for his blunt, if softly spoken, defiance of the British government and the British Empire, his castigation of British rule in India and his uncompromising demand that it be ended forthwith. No one from the colonies, unless it be Ben Franklin a century and a half before, had ever come to the imperial capital and publicly spoken like that to the British authorities. For it became clear at once that Gandhi was addressing himself principally to the British government and Parliament, which would make the decision either to hold on to India or to free her.

"India has been held by the sword," Gandhi reminded them. "I do not for one moment minimize the ability of Great Britain to hold India in subjection under the sword.

"But which would be better—an enslaved but rebellious India or an India as an esteemed partner with Great Britain to share her sorrows and take part side by side with her in her misfortunes? An India that, if need be, of her own free will, can fight side by side with Britain, not for the exploitation of a single race or a single human being, but, it might be, for the good of the whole world.

"So I said to myself while nearing the shores of this beautiful island of England: 'Perchance it may be possible for you to convince the British ministers that India can be a valuable partner, not held by force but by the silken cord of love. Then again I thought that India might be of real assistance in balancing your budget.'"

Gandhi paused, and smiled toward the British delegates and the members of the cabinet and Parliament. You could almost see some of them wincing. Was this playing cricket to try to take advantage of them now that the country was in the grip of the worst financial crisis since the war, with the budget badly unbalanced, the pound sterling slipping on the money exchanges, unemployment soaring, labor and social unrest threatening to get out of hand—there had just been what no true Englishmen believed possible, a mutiny in the Navy, the very pillar of the British Establishment, and another walkout of the coal miners was imminent. It must have seemed to some of them that the Mahatma would never wipe the smile off his face.

He went on, picturing a glorious future for the two nations, with Great Britain and India working together in equal partnership. I had never heard Gandhi indulge in such flattery, given his dim view of the British.

"What could we not do together—yours a nation with bravery perhaps unequaled by any nation, and noted for having fought slavery and protected the weak, and ours a nation with its glorious and ancient past.

"Take these two nations together, and I ask you whether India free, completely independent, as Great Britain is now independent—whether an honorable partnership would not be beneficial, even in terms of your domestic affairs."

He would not let go of that theme. I had never heard him so tenacious. And all the while he was delivering his jabs so humbly! But in his humbleness he did not shave off a fraction of his demand for complete independence.

"I have come here in a spirit of cooperation," he continued. "I have no wish to embarrass the government's authority. I am but a poor humble agent acting in behalf of the All-India National Congress."

And as if to counteract the powerful propaganda of the London press, which had carried numerous articles stating that Gandhi was but one of several Indian delegates and should be treated as such at the Round Table Conference, Gandhi launched into a long account of the history of the Congress party, how it was founded by an Englishman, Allan Octavian Hume, and how Hindus, Moslems, Parsis, Christians, and even women had been at its helm as presidents, and finally how it had won its present powerful hold on the country.

"I hope I won't jar you by my party's mandate, which I have come to plead," he said, again stopping to smile at the English delegates.

He then read the text of the mandate drawn up at Karachi by the Indian Congress in April, emphasizing that he was "instructed" to take nothing less than complete independence, meaning immediate control over the Army, foreign affairs, and finance, and a "scrutiny" of how much of the Indian national debt each of the countries should shoulder.

"If you can convince me that these claims are inimical to the interests of the dumb and half-starved millions I represent, then I will revise them. I am open to conviction."

Gandhi next proceeded, with a few biting words, to reject completely the conclusions of the first Round Table Conference the previous year.

"I have carefully studied its conclusions," he said, "as well as Prime Minister MacDonald's statement giving the considered policy of His Majesty's Government. It falls far short of our claims.

"In the Delhi Pact with Lord Irwin we accepted the principle of federation, responsibility at the center, with safeguards in the interests of India."

Gandhi paused, and then said slowly:

"But I will never be satisfied with a mere political constitution which, when read, would seem to give India all she desires, but in reality gives her nothing."

Nor could he accept any agreement that did not provide for India seceding from the Empire or the Commonwealth if she desired.

"If we are intent on complete independence, it is not from any sense of arrogance, and not because we want to parade before the world how we broke away from the British. We contemplate only a partnership.

"There was a time," Gandhi went on, "when I prided myself upon being a British subject. I have ceased for many years to call myself a British subject. But I aspire to be a citizen not of the Empire, but of the Commonwealth—in true partnership, but not one superimposed upon one nation by another. Hence the Indian National Congress insists that either party have the right to sever the connection."

I glanced at the faces of the British statesmen gathered in the great hall. They reflected sheer incredulousness at the astounding idea of an India, which they had held by the sword so long, withdrawing from the mighty Empire or Commonwealth. Why, their faces seemed to say, it was nothing but gall for this curious little Indian to even assume that there would be Dominion status for India and membership in the Commonwealth in the foreseeable future. Gandhi may have noticed the expression on their faces, for he harped back to the theme he had been trying to exploit for an hour: Britain's precarious financial plight and how India might help to alleviate it if she were set free.

"I understand," he said, beaming at the delegates, "that British statesmen today are wholly engrossed in their domestic affairs and are trying to make both ends meet. We could not expect them to do anything less. I thought that by coming here at such a time we might be looked upon as interlopers. And yet possibly not. It is possible that British ministers might consider the Round Table Conference of primary importance even in terms of domestic affairs."

Gandhi then went on to another unpleasant subject for the British: how much of India's national debt Britain should assume. Uncharacteristically, he fairly jumped on the timid Parsi delegate who on the opening day had assured the British that India would never bring up the debt question. On the contrary, he said, he insisted on bringing it up now. And he summarized from his remarkable memory the report drawn up for the Congress by Professor K. T. Shah and his associates which concluded that Britain should assume three billion of India's national debt of four billion dollars. Most of the three billions, Gandhi asserted, was expended by the Indian government in fighting Britain's wars, including the East India Company's war against the Indians at the time of the Mutiny of 1857. A half billion dollars, Gandhi noted slyly, was simply assessed India by the British government as a further "contribution" to Britain's war effort during the Great War, though the government of India had provided an overseas army of one million men and paid for their upkeep and supplies in a conflict about which the Indian people, having no responsible representatives in the government, had had no say. The British government in India had simply declared war in 1914 without consulting them.

"If there is stocktaking," Gandhi argued, "between incoming and outgoing partners, their transactions are subject to audit and adjustment. The Indian National Congress is not guilty of a crime in asking that the nation should understand what it is taking over."

And then, rather slyly again, I thought, he added:

"I know that the British people do not want to saddle India with a single burden it should not legitimately bear. And I say that the Congress never dreamed of repudiating a single claim or burden it should justly discharge. If we are to live as an honorable nation, worthy of commanding credit from the world, we will pay every farthing of our legitimate debt."

Judging by the expression on their faces it seemed evident that the last thing the British authorities in the hall expected to hear from the lips of the saintly Mahatma was this excursion into the intricacies of government debt, finance and credit. What could this amazing Hindu bring up next!

But he was almost through. In one concluding sentence he attempted to demolish the whole British approach to the conference: that it discuss all the details of a constitution before getting down to the fundamentals of what sort of a nation the constitution would govern.

"This is my position, then," Gandhi said, sitting back in his chair. "You cannot expect me to fill in all the details and tell you what I mean by control over the Army, finance, fiscal and economic policies. We have to know first what the British government is prepared to offer India. Then if it is acceptable we can easily fill in the details."

There was little applause as he finished. The spell Gandhi had cast still hung over the hall. Applause would have seemed almost inappropriate. Everyone seemed to feel that. But Gandhi's words, so simply spoken, the enormity of his demands, the sharpness but also the confidence with which he put them, seemed to me, at least, to have shaken the British Empire, or at least its rulers in this assembly.

But British diplomacy was almost equal to the occasion. After the veteran Brahman, Pandit Malaviya, a gentle but subtle white-haired old man, had risen to second Gandhi's remarks and pledge his support to the Mahatma's demands, Sir Samuel Hoare, Secretary of State for India, rose gingerly to his feet.

He was glad, he said, "to hear the very frank expressions from the new members. Obviously they contain very controversial issues. But this is no time to enter into general controversies. We must get down to work on the details."

So in the afternoon the so-called Federal Structures Committee, which was the main body of the conference, began its work on the details. Gandhi attended, but he did not open his mouth.

Not content to listen to the boring, meaningless debates at the conference, which he thought were a waste of time, Gandhi took his message directly to the members of Parliament and the trade unions, to churchmen, to the dons at Oxford, and finally to the cotton-mill owners and workers of Lancashire, whose plants were largely idled by the Indian Congress boycott of British textiles.

Aware that the Commons would have the last word about Indian independence, Gandhi sought to make the most of the invitations to meet with its members. To them he again stressed that an independent India would be more beneficial to Britain and the Commonwealth than an enslaved, rebellious India. He fielded the sharpest of questions with patience but also frankly. He was appalled, he told me later, at the ignorance of the M.P.'s of the history of the British in India and of the current situation there. He had expected to find more knowledge in members of Parliament. He said he had had to tell them that they had been raised on false history.

"I had to tell them," he said, "that British rule in India, contrary to what they seemed to think, had not been beneficial, that we Indians called it 'misrule.'" Gandhi said he was also surprised that so many members, even among the Laborites, judging by their questions, had swallowed the "Churchill line" that the Indians were simply unfit for self-rule.

This had vexed him most. Though the members of Parliament had listened to him courteously and probed him with questions, he had been unable to make any headway with them on his demand for complete independence. Somehow they considered that ludicrous, not the least the Labor Party members.

The M.P.'s, I concluded from my talks with them, found Gandhi a fascinating but strange man. He certainly was not like an Englishman. At the first meeting in a large committee room of the

House he had shown this, as one member put it, by abruptly breaking off a question-and-answer discussion to hold a prayer meeting. Promptly at 7 P.M., the hour of his evening prayers, he had waved his hand and asked permission to be excused for a few minutes. Accompanied by Madeleine Slade and Sarojini Naidu, he squatted on the bare floor, took off his sandals, and proceeded with his devotions. The M.P.'s stood in rather surprised silence as the chanted cadences of the *Gita* echoed through the corridors of the staid House of Commons. Nothing like that, I imagine, had ever been heard before in Westminster. The prayers over, Gandhi resumed his seat and asked if there were any more questions.

My dispatches from London during the next few days recall, on rereading them nearly a half century later, the weird contradictions of this meeting of East and West. Gandhi kept clamoring for the British government to show its hand on how far it would go in meeting his demand for Indian independence. The government blithely ignored his appeals. At the conference itself British and Indian delegates passed the days in meaningless debates. Gandhi was not fooled. The British delegates and some of the Indian, and most of the London press, chided the Mahatma for being "unrealistic." I thought he was utterly realistic. He kept insisting that the conference get down to substance.

On September 17, two days after his historic speech to the conference (which was largely ignored by the Rothermere press, while *The Times* buried its account on an obscure page), I began my dispatch: "Gandhi simply will not be put off." All day long the knights of the Round Table had confined their discussion to the wording of an oath of allegiance to the King-Emperor in a "constitutional" India. Gandhi, a man of infinite patience, had finally exhausted his large store of it and had broken in to say that the endless talk on such a subject was "depressing" him.

"You have been talking for hours today about a proposed oath of allegiance. How can I give an opinion on that now? It depends on what we are getting. If it is complete independence, the oath will be of one character. If the oath is to be taken by us as subjects of India, then I have no place here."

Turning directly to Lord Sankey, the chairman, he challenged the British government to "lay its cards on the table."

"Might I lodge a gentle, humble complaint against His Majesty's advisers?" Gandhi asked, a broad smile breaking over his face. He was aware, I'm sure, that no other Indian delegate addressed the British chairman like that.

"Having brought the committee together, knowing that we are all busy men, is it not possible for the government to give us a lead? Why can't the government let the committee know its mind? I would be delighted if it would bring forward concrete proposals. Let the government put its cards on the table. If this is done, we can reach some conclusions, good or bad . . . But here we are dealing with subheads when we don't know what franchise we are going to get. I offer my suggestions in terms of a mandate by the Indian Congress party. But if the committee does not know where it is sailing, my observations are naturally of little worth . . . If the members of this committee simply dissolve themselves into a debating society, we will never get anywhere. Perhaps the Chairman can bring this to the attention of his advisers."

Lord Sankey, without batting an eye, said he would. But Gandhi must have known by this time that it would not do the slightest good. He was insisting on serious negotiations. The British government was putting him off. The other Indian delegates were of no help; they seemed satisfied with sounding off about the dreariest of trivia and seeing their names in the newspapers the next day. This obviously vexed the Mahatma and he suddenly turned on them.

"As I studied the list of Indian delegates here," he said, "I suddenly realized that they were not the chosen ones of the nation but the chosen ones of the government." Gandhi was referring to the fact, hushed up by the London press, that the Indian delegates had been chosen not by parties but by the Viceroy. With the exception of those from the Moslem League, the untouchables, the Chamber of Princes and of course himself from the Congress, they represented no one but themselves. They were grateful to the British to have been invited.

After the meeting I had a few words with the Mahatma. He divulged that since the conference was getting nowhere he was setting up private meetings for himself with the principal British political leaders. It was the only way, he thought, to get some sort of response to his proposals. He had already arranged, he said, to see Prime Minister MacDonald, Stanley Baldwin, the Conservative Party leader in the Commons, and Sir Herbert Samuel, the Liberal leader and Home Secretary. I was sure he had no illusions that these private meetings with those who held the political power would bring any results. But if he was to get a No to his claims, he wanted to get it from those who had the authority to give it. In the meantime, he said, he would continue to attend the meetings of the conference, at least for a few more days, and speak out.

Actually, shortly before adjournment that afternoon, he had tangled with Lord Peel, the Lord Privy Seal, who had dwelt on the "dangers" of direct elections in a country whose inhabitants were largely illiterate.

"I am wedded to adult suffrage," Gandhi had retorted. "Why, I have found some of the noblest specimens of humanity among the poorest illiterates. I do not like a test of literacy for voters. I would prefer them to know the three R's, but if we wait for that we will wait until the Greek kalends. Personally, I am not prepared to wait that long."

He was not prepared, either, to wait very much longer in London.

On the evening of September 20, six days after the opening of the Round Table Conference and just before he began his Monday's twenty-four hours of silence, I found Gandhi in a more perturbed state of mind than I had ever seen before.

"I spoke gently last week," he told me. "But I don't see how I can bear much longer this hopeless uncertainty, for which there is no reason. Truly, the government is like the Sphinx. It is so cautious that it is impossible to learn where it stands."

I asked him what he intended to do about it.

"I want to be patient. I realize the obvious difficulties of the government just now," he said.

It had not escaped his notice that most of the headlines in the London press the past few days were devoted to the government's fight to save the pound, balance the budget, restore the balance of trade and allay unrest in the Navy.

"I want to be patient," he repeated. "But we cannot make progress until we know the government's view and how far it is prepared to go. The government cannot sit on the fence forever."

But of course it could, and would—at least for a good long time, and Gandhi knew it. He had become a very frustrated man—most unusual for him. I had never before seen him show the slightest sign of frustration, despite all his setbacks. He had always seemed to me to be supremely confident of where he was going and how he intended to get there. Now, he felt stymied.

His malaise was not assuaged the next day when the British government, without consulting the Indians, announced it was linking the Indian rupee to the falling pound, and thus forcibly devaluating it. The following day, his twenty-four hours of silence over, he expressed at the conference his indignation at Britain's action.

"While we all sympathize with the British nation in this crisis," he said, "I must express my surprise and sorrow at the manner in which this action was taken in India.

"What pains me is that the decision was taken over the head of the Indian Legislature in striking proof of the unbending attitude of the government toward India. Evidently in the matters of the greatest importance to us, we are not yet considered fit to be consulted, much less to decide what is good for us. I am unable to give my support to the measures which the Secretary of State for India has taken."

Gandhi was the only Indian delegate to protest. You could almost feel his pain, his humiliation, when he looked around the table to see if other Indians would support him and instead saw one of his fellow countrymen jump up to denounce him. This was a plump Parsi millionaire industrialist by the name of Sir Maneckji Dadabhoy, handpicked by the Viceroy as a delegate. He protested Gandhi's stand as bordering on "disloyalty," pledged his support to the King-Emperor and—unbelievably!—lauded Viceroy Lord Willingdon for his dictatorial action in forcing the rupee to share the ill fortunes of the falling pound. Gandhi sat and listened to this outburst first in disbelief and at the end in shame.

In this mood he decided to get away from London, the futility of the conference, the sickening sycophancy of some of his fellow Indians. He set out for Lancashire to put his case to the cotton textile millowners and workers. He was not sure what reception he would get. India Office officials warned that it might be hostile and that he might get mobbed by the workers, resentful at being thrown out of work by the Indian Congress boycott.

As it turned out, he *was* mobbed by them, but as an object of their affection and admiration, and, no doubt, of their curiosity. The bluff Lancashire cotton-mill hands, many of them barely surviving with their families on the pittance of the dole, knew a man who was devoting his life to helping the poor when they saw one. They gave him a tumultuous welcome.

I followed Gandhi for three days through the Lancashire cotton-mill country, the gloomy "devastated areas," as the English called them, where thousands of looms, millions of spindles and hundreds of thousands of workers had been idled since the Indian nationalist boycott of their goods became effective. Gandhi was visibly moved as he sat at the window of his second-class compartment on the late train from London to Manchester after evening had fallen and watched mile upon mile of factories, dark and silent, pass by.

"The terrible poverty I have seen here," he told a delegation of textile union workers the next day after he had been taken through the silent looms and spindles of the great Greenfield Weaving Mills of Darwen, and later visited the shabby, unheated, overcrowded tenements where the workers and their families lived like cattle, "has distressed and depressed me—even more so because I realize I have had some share in causing it."

He was going to talk as frankly to the Lancashire cotton workers and owners, he said, as he had to everyone else in England. While stressing his sympathy with their plight and admitting his share of the responsibility for it, he was going to remind them that the major blame rested on the refusal of the British government to free India.

"My distress," he continued, "is relieved, however, by the knowledge that it is the result of a step I had to take as part of my duty toward the largest army of unemployed the world has ever seen—India's starving millions, compared to which British poverty is insignificant.

"Unemployment anywhere is bad, and my life is given toward relieving it. But"—and here he began to play on the theme he exploited throughout his three-day tour of Lancashire—"but I am helpless without the cooperation of Britain and India."

This line of talk struck a responsive chord, especially among the British workers. Gandhi sensed it. At one silent mill in Darwen he had beamed with pleasure at a large notice of greeting plastered on the wall.

We welcome Gandhi in all friendliness because we realize the future of Lancashire and India depends on reconciliation and cooperation.

"You put it as well as I could," Gandhi remarked to his guides. "I agree with you completely. As I told the Round Table Conference in London at the outset: 'What could our two great nations not do together in an equal partnership!'"

His listeners, both workers and employers, seemed surprised that Gandhi appeared to be so much at home in discussing their problems and that he had such a grasp of detail of the cotton manufacturing business. They did not know that Gandhi had spent most of his life since his return to India in 1914, except for his sojourns in British prisons, in Ahmedabad, the center of the cotton textile industry in India, and that he had led the first major strike in India's history on behalf of the Indian textile workers there.

To deputation after deputation, of employers and hands, he slyly threw out the suggestion that Lancashire might regain its former lucrative cotton trade with India, and put back to work half a million men and women, if the British government would grant India independence.

"Lacking that," he said, "the Indian boycott of foreign cloth must continue. But if Britain and India could arrange to work together in a friendly partnership, instead of drifting further apart as now, I would favor importing from Lancashire all the cloth and yarn we cannot produce ourselves."

The next day, at Manchester, in a talk with the millowners, he was more specific. He told them that if India were granted self-rule he would propose a ban on the importation into India of all foreign cloth except that from Lancashire. He urged the industrialists to send that message to their representatives in Parliament.

"You see," Gandhi explained, like the old trader he could be on such occasions, "it would just be a case of friendly business relations between two equal partners. We would not like to discriminate against Japan, the United States and Western Europe. But naturally two happy equal partners like India and Great Britain could not be blamed for making an arrangement to their mutual interests and benefit."

The manufacturers were delighted. They were businessmen and not politicians. This was evident from the remarks of one of them who rose to reply to Gandhi.

"We do not care," he said, "about the political aspects of this question so long as business is resumed and Lancashire rescued from being a cotton graveyard. It would mean everything to us and to our workers."

He estimated that if England could supply the cloth and yarn now being imported into India from Japan, China, America and Western Europe, it would put half a million English men and women back to work. Gandhi humbly agreed.

He was getting along famously with the cotton magnates, and even better with their workers. At one meeting with the latter, a union leader had reminded Gandhi bluntly that part of the problem for Lancashire was that it could not compete against Indian sweated labor, a topic Gandhi had not mentioned.

"We pride ourselves," he said, "on the long struggle by which we gradually obtained a decent standard of living for Lancashire cotton workers. It was considerably lowered by the competition of sweated labor in India and Japan, and now it is ruined by your boycott. We are fighting to keep a decent standard of living for our wives and children, just as your workers will fight someday when you have stopped sweating them. But your boycott makes the battle hopeless."

Gandhi was a little taken back by the references to Indian sweated labor, but he quickly took up the challenge, reminding the English workers that wages which might seem sweated in England were substantial in India, with its much lower cost of living. Substantial, but far from high enough, he smiled, and then told of his leading India's first big strike against the cotton-mill owners in Ahmedabad shortly after the war, at the end of which he won a considerable increase in wages and an improvement in working conditions and hours of labor. He did not, I noted, mention that to win the strike he had had to resort to a fast. It would have been incomprehensible to these British workers. They had scarcely imagined Gandhi as a strike leader. When he revealed it, they burst into applause.

Gandhi was too tactful to mention—to the workers or the employers—a strong impression he had gained after three days in Lancashire. It would have amazed them, I think. But he remarked on it to me the last day in Manchester. He was taken back, he said, by the backwardness of Lancashire's cotton industries.

"I'm no mechanic," he smiled, "but I've seen enough up here in three days to show me that the English are using antiquated machinery. It probably explains their inability to compete with other countries. The machinery in the Bombay and Ahmedabad mills is one hundred percent more efficient."

This man, I thought, will never cease to astound me.

12

In London the Round Table Conference gradually petered out.

The British strategy for avoiding any serious commitment to Indian self-rule was obvious, and it also was obvious that it was working. The game was to keep the Hindus and the Moslems, and the other minorities such as the untouchables, squabbling among themselves so that the government could proclaim that until the Indians themselves agreed on what they wanted it was futile for the government to make any proposals of its own. This proved easier— to Gandhi's humiliation—than even the British had counted on.

For a day or two toward the end of September it looked as though the Hindus and the Moslems, stung by the taunts of the Prime Minister, Ramsay MacDonald, would finally reach an accord. Night after night Gandhi met with the Moslems in the Ritz suite of the Aga Khan, the millionaire leader of a small Indian Mohammedan cult, who was chiefly known in England for his great racing stable. The headlines in the London newspapers the last few days had dealt not with his labors at the conference but with the strike of his jockeys, trainers and grooms. Gandhi indicated that an agreement was near and once again, as in India during the summer, I allowed myself to become unduly optimistic, reporting that the two sides were about to reach an accord.

I should have been more skeptical since I knew that, behind the scenes, the British were doing their best to prevent an understanding between the two great Indian religious groups. My dispatches to that effect were not pleasing to the government, especially the India Office, but one day, on the twenty-eighth, the liberal *News Chronicle* came out to confirm what I had written.

"Powerful influences," it wrote editorially, "are at work in this country which would make the Indian communal difficulties an effective excuse for breaking up the Conference altogether."

The influences became bolder and more public.

On the evening of October 1 there was a strange scene in one of the committee rooms in the House of Commons, where members of both houses, mostly Tory, gathered to convince an invited group of Indian Moslems that their future would best be served in an India still ruled by the British *raj* and not by the Hindus. All the arts of flattery, at which the British ruling class was so good, and to which the loyalist Moslems were so susceptible, were generously employed.

Led by Lord Lloyd and Lord Brentford, the Tory members of Parliament assured their honored guests that they regarded the Moslems as the salt of the earth, or at least of the British Empire. That Empire, they pointed out, contained more followers of the Prophet than any other nation and therefore fully understood their problems and their aspirations, especially in India. If the Moslems of India remained loyal to the Crown, they would be properly rewarded. They were the "fighting race" in India (actually all but a handful of them were from the same racial stock as the Hindus) and would be given an increasingly important part in building up the Indian Army. They would receive a greater role in the central and provincial governments. The British would never let them down, never permit them to be dominated by the Hindus. And so on. It was pretty strong stuff.

The Moslems, led by Sir Mohammed Shafi and Shaukat Ali, were overwhelmed.

"You grant us our Moslem demands in India and we will remain loyal subjects of the King and Emperor," said Ali, in response to all the flattery and promises. As I had begun to suspect the last months in India, Shaukat Ali, who was a striking presence in the committee room with his towering figure, his native garb and rough speech, had strayed far from the days when he served as a right-hand man of Gandhi and went to jail with him for demanding that the British get out of India.

"I want to be a friend of the British," Ali roared, stopping to smile at and almost embrace Lord Lloyd, who, as governor of Bombay, once had jailed him. There was a loud chorus of "Hear! Hear! Splendid! Splendid!" from the Tory members. They must have thought that it didn't take much to split the Moslems from the Hindus and doom Gandhi's chances of getting the Round Table Conference to grant India *anything.*

The love feast between the Tories and the Indian Moslems was too much for one lonely Labor member of Parliament, who sprang up and said: "We've heard the views of two loyalist Moslems. Aren't there any nationalist Moslems here to give us their views?"

Sir Ali Inman, lone representative of the nationalist Moslems, popped up to answer. But Lord Brentford, who was presiding, did not recognize him—perhaps he did not hear or see him—and quickly adjourned the meeting amid loud cheers for the loyalist Moslems, on whom the good Tory members were counting to help save India from the Indians.

When I saw Gandhi for a few moments later that evening he said that "things looked dark," but he had not given up. At his request Prime Minister MacDonald had adjourned for another week the meetings of the Minorities Committee so that Gandhi could make one last effort to get the squabbling Indian groups to agree on something. He had acidly remarked to his fellow countrymen just before the adjournment that they were quarreling among themselves about their share in the spoils—spoils which the British had not yet given them and would never give them until they buried their differences. Gandhi told me he would be continuing his discussions with the Aga Khan and other Moslems at the Ritz. "If I am not optimistic," he smiled, "I am at least hopeful. By the way," he said with a grin, as we parted, "you are invited to a little birthday party tomorrow."

I had already been invited by some of his friends among five hundred English and Indians who had organized a birthday lunch at Westminster Hall. They had wanted to make it a gala occasion, but Gandhi had put his foot down. He told them he would not attend unless they abandoned, among other things, their plan to bake a mammoth birthday cake and serve a varied vegetarian menu. He asked that only fruit be served, and that the charge be only a shilling for the lunch so that the poor could afford to come.

I could not remember for a moment exactly what birthday he would be observing this October 2, 1931. Then it came to me. He would be sixty-two. He might look emaciated to the English but he was actually in the best of health. Not even a damp, cold, foggy English autumn had affected him. He was tired enough. I noticed it as I took my leave. In front of the house I ran into one of his physicians. He was worried about the effects of the Mahatma's unbelievable pace.

"He has averaged only four hours of sleep since arriving in London," the doctor said. "Last night he got home, after a successsion of meetings, at one-thirty. He spun until two-thirty and was up at four, as usual. The night before he was the same. He is keeping five secretaries and a special typist busy. The Scotland Yard men and special police assigned to protect him complain they are already worn out. We keep telling him to slow down. But he pays no attention."

I wondered as I made my way back to the office whether the occasion of another birthday, his sixty-second, had set Gandhi to wondering again as he had wondered out loud to me once in India, about whether he would be spared enough years to complete his self-imposed task of freeing India from the British. The way things were going at the Round Table Conference he would have to live to be as old as Methuselah.

Actually, Gandhi spent his sixty-second birthday, as I wrote in the lead of my dispatch at the end of the day, "fighting all along the line." Underneath the gentle saint was a determined fighter and this seemed to shock many of his English admirers who gathered at the lunch in Westminster Hall to honor him on his birthday.

True, he appeared as pleased as a child when they presented him with an old-fashioned English spinning wheel. And he had grinned from ear to ear when London workmen and their wives poked their heads out the windows of their drab tenements at dawn and wished him happy birthday as he trudged along on his morning walk through the grim streets of the East End.* He stopped several times to acknowledge their greetings, clasping his hands before him, smiling and nodding.

He seemed highly pleased as he returned from his walk to find hundreds of congratulatory telegrams, which had arrived from the four corners of the earth, and to glance at a room full of birthday presents that included everything from gold coins to a pedigreed goat.

But his happiness on this anniversary at such an outpouring of affection did not prevent him from lapsing into a more somber mood and frankly reminding all who listened to him that things were not going well at the London parleys and that he was being forced to conclude that the British government was not serious about granting India independence.

"Usually so humble," I wrote in my dispatch that evening, "Gandhi became almost savage as he addressed the luncheon gathering after the 500 guests had finished their meal of bananas, apples, pears, oranges, and nuts."

*Some of the London newspapers had noted the anniversary.

You could feel the dismay among the 250 or so English well-wishers who apparently had expected that Gandhi, in the spirit of the happy occasion, would eschew politics for the day. On the contrary!

"What you English don't realize," he told them, "is that freedom is our birthright, as it is yours. We are ready to pay any price for it. It is true we do not wish to spill blood in winning it. I believe in non-violence and I insist on practicing it. But I must tell you frankly that if any sacrifice can win our freedom, we will not hesitate to let the Ganges run red with blood to obtain it."

I could not recall the Mahatma ever having spoken before in that bloody vein. It was most unlike him, the very apostle of non-violence, who had so often boasted that nothing could ever bring him to sway from that righteous path. The words, spoken bitingly, which was also out of character, seemed to upset the English in the audience.

The Round Table conference, he went on, was steering for the rocks. Why beat about the bush about that?

"I entertained no illusions when I came here. But the more I stay here, the more I realize how difficult is our task. It has become almost superhuman. And to make matters worse, there is much ignorance among you about India and why we are here."

He had told the members of Parliament that a fortnight before, but his remarks had not been published in the London press. Now they came as a surprise to his English listeners, sympathetic as most of them were to him.

"You have been taught that the sum total of British rule in India is beneficial. Nothing is more false! You cannot escape two facts: first, that under the British, India has become the world's poorest country; and second, that it is denied advantages and decencies to which any free country is entitled.

"What you laud as British rule we loathe as British misrule. England has failed in India!"

A stunned silence greeted his words. These were not the kind of happy birthday remarks so many of the English had obviously anticipated. Gandhi hurried from the luncheon and sat the rest of the afternoon in St. James's Palace arguing with his fellow Indians and beseeching them to compromise their differences. Later he went to the India Office to talk with the Secretary of State, Sir Samuel Hoare. But he was trying to move mountains, both with his own people and the British.

There were times, Gandhi had often told me, when he became sick of politics, and by the end of this birthday, he must have felt that this was one of them. He hurried back to his East End settlement to attend a final birthday party, this one given him by the children of the dock workers who lived in the neighborhood. These were the sort of occasions he liked—among the poor. Once more, as he squatted with the children and talked and joked with them, he was his radiant, beaming self. I felt it was the happiest part of his anniversary day.

The weekend that followed was a nightmare.

Belittled by a mostly hostile London press, which had already begun to hail his downfall, besieged by shouting minorities of Moslems, Sikhs, Christians, Parsis, untouchables, Anglo-Indians, and Europeans, all clamoring for special privileges in a new India, Gandhi, after trying to deal with them all day Saturday, took refuge Sunday in Canterbury, spending most of the Sabbath strolling in the cloistered gardens of the cathedral with the Archbishop and the Dean.

Throughout Saturday and on Sunday morning, before he departed for Canterbury, Gandhi, in a succession of meetings, pleaded with the minorities to submerge their differences until they learned what the British government was granting India, if anything.

"Let us make a united demand to the British government," he proposed, "to discuss its decision on our political demands for self-government, leaving such matters as separate electorates and special representation for minorities to be settled either by an impartial tribunal or by a special convention of Indian leaders, elected by their constituencies."

This was promptly rejected, and no wonder, since, as Gandhi himself had pointed out at an early meeting of the conference, most of the delegates had no constituencies of their own and couldn't have won an election any place in India. They had been selected as delegates by the Viceroy, not by a vote of the people.

Obviously fatigued and disheartened by all the wrangling, Gandhi had warned: "By our internal squabbles we are playing right into the hands of the British. It is a humiliation for all of us Indians."

The warning was to no avail.

The London newspapers, predominately Conservative, now began to express their pleasure at the prospect of the imminent breakup of the Round Table Conference and the deflation of Gandhi, whom they blamed for the failure, as an Indian leader. That Sabbath, while the Mahatma was relaxing with the Archbishop and the Dean of Canterbury in the lovely cathedral gardens, the Sunday newspapers warmed up their attack on him.

J. L. Garvin, editor of the *Observer,* perhaps the most influential publicist in England, wrote that Gandhi's ideas of Indian independence were "a vain dream. If the British position in India is further weakened, there will ensue worse anarchy than in China."

It was a familiar but stale excuse.

"Though Gandhi is a gifted and fascinating agitator [sic]," this noted editor concluded, "his exalted but unconstructive ideology suggests the breaking and not the making of India."

Lord Beaverbrook's conservative *Sunday Express* went right after Gandhi. In a lead editorial entitled "The Failure of Gandhi," it wrote with that condescension and shallowness so characteristic of the British Tories:

> Gandhi is out of his depth in England. He has gained publicity which a film star might envy, but he has been a complete failure in solving Indian problems. Unless he provides a miracle, the Conference will break up in two or three days, and the last remnants of his prestige will disappear.

The esteemed *Sunday Express* was more accurate in its short-term prediction than in its long-term one. Before the week was up the Round Table Conference adjourned—forever, as it turned out.

On the night of Tuesday, October 6, after a last-ditch attempt to obtain a Hindu-Moslem accord during a meeting which had continued with scarcely a break for twenty-four hours, Gandhi, trying to shake off his fatigue, called me in. He had failed—failed on two counts, he said: to solve the communal problem and to wring concessions from the British government.

"The end will come tomorrow," he said quietly. "I seem to have failed."

He had failed, of course, to get what he had come for: independence for India. But he had not really expected to obtain that. The time was not yet ripe.

The British were not about to hand over India to the Indians. He had known that all along. He had worked night and day for a Hindu-Moslem accord. But was it his fault that it had not been reached? Had not the Moslems, flattered and encouraged by the British, made it impossible?

I could not quite understand, I said, why he seemed to blame himself for the breakup of the conference. Was this not an admission that he had been outmaneuvered by the British government, which for several days had been attempting to put the onus on him because of his failure to achieve a Hindu-Moslem settlement?

Certainly the Indians were at fault for their inability to sink their differences so that they could present a common front. But surely the main responsibility for the collapse of the conference lay with the British government. Despite all his pleadings, it had not said one word about how far it would go in granting India self-rule. It had not even mentioned a serious beginning toward such a step.

"You've pointed that out yourself, publicly, a dozen times," I said.

But he was in no mood for discussion. He had reached a point, I felt, of sheer exhaustion. And of frustration.

The end came a day later than Gandhi had predicted—on Thursday, October 8.

"This has been," Gandhi told me that evening, after all was over, "the most humiliating day of my life."

He was humiliated, he made clear, not so much because the British government had offered India nothing, but because of the sorry spectacle his fellow Indians made of themselves on this final day. They seemed determined to prove what the British authorities had said all along: that the Indians were incapable, at this stage, of governing themselves.

I myself had never seen such a spectacle among the Indians. Hindus, Moslems, Sikhs, Christians and untouchables fairly flew at one another's throats. Gandhi himself was not spared. Dr. Bhimrao Ramji Ambedkar, the embittered leader of the untouchables, an able lawyer from Bombay who had received his education at Columbia University in New York, made such a virulent attack on the Mahatma that there were cries of protest from the British and Indian delegates alike. Gandhi sat at his place visibly moved as Dr. Ambedkar heaped insults on him, accusing him of "breach of faith," of "going back on his many promises" and of being "wholly irresponsible with his many false claims."

Gandhi turned his other cheek. "Thank you, sir," he broke in to say.

Then he rose to give a brief report on the failure of the Hindus and the Indian minorities to reach agreement despite weeks of talk.

"I speak," he said, "with deep sorrow and deeper humiliation. But my failure does not mean at all my utter defeat. There is no such word in my vocabulary."

He made one last appeal to his countrymen.

"It is absurd for us to quarrel among ourselves," he said, "before we know what we are going to get from the British government. If we knew definitely that we were going to get what we want, then we would hesitate fifty times before we threw it away in a sinful wrangle. The communal [Hindu-Moslem] solution can be the crown of the national constitution, not its foundation, if only because our differences are hardened by reason of foreign domination. I have no shadow of doubt that the iceberg of communal differences would melt under the warmth of the sun of freedom."

But the communal leaders were no longer heeding him. When they resumed their wrangling, Prime Minister MacDonald intervened. Like a confident schoolmaster lecturing his adolescents, he chided them, including Gandhi, for their quarrels and warned them that the government could not offer them anything until they had first settled their own differences.

His brazen hypocrisy fascinated me. I had been struck with it at Geneva in recent years when he had come there as Prime Minister of a Labor government to lecture the League of Nations about the British love of peace and understanding. As he spoke this day in the great hall of St. James's Palace I recalled what he had written when he had first gone out to India as a brilliant young Labor Party leader to assess the situation at first hand. He had been deeply sympathetic with the aspirations of the Indians to be free. He had changed greatly since then. Now dependent upon the Tories for staying in office, he had become as imperialist and as hypocritical on India as they. He had also become terribly vain.

"You know perfectly well," he told the Indian delegates, "that the British government will not stand in the way of an agreement on communal problems. We have been determined to make the Round Table Conference a success."

He then reminded the Indians of something that everyone, including Gandhi, I fear, had forgotten. The conference, he said, had never been more than a consultative body. How could it offer anything definite, as Gandhi had demanded?

"What did we promise you at the very beginning?" he asked. "Only that we would not make up our minds about the future of India until we consulted you. Do you suggest that in the middle of the consultation we break off and produce proposals?"

Gandhi, in fact, had suggested just that—time after time.

And then, in a moment of frankness, or so it must have seemed to the Indians, MacDonald let slip what had always been the core of the British position—that the road toward Indian self-government would be a long one. But he dressed it up a bit.

"If the government produces its proposals, that is as near its last word as the circumstances will allow. The British government wants to go on. It will take action if you cannot, because we are determined to make such improvements in the government of India as will make it consistent with our idea that it is capable of greater expansion toward liberty."

Stripped of the verbiage, that meant that British arbitrary rule of India would continue indefinitely. "Expansion toward liberty" could take an age. The Prime Minister was tossing the Indians crumbs. He reserved one last crack for Gandhi.

"If the British government forced a constitution on India before a communal accord is reached," he said, turning to smile at the Congress leader, "our friend Mahatma Gandhi would probably at once launch another passive resistance movement."

Gandhi did not match the Prime Minister's smile. He remained silent. He struck me as being too humiliated, too depressed, to utter another word. MacDonald pounded his gavel. The Round Table Conference was over. So were the prospects of the Indians advancing a single step further toward ruling their own country— unless they did it on their own.

Gandhi was gloomy, but not surprised. He was too astute a politician and revolutionary to say, when questioned, what he would do now. I gathered from my farewell talks with him that he had concluded, as had the American revolutionary leaders by 1775, that he could never win independence for India purely by negotiation. He did not say so explicitly—that would have been to give away his hand—but he left no doubt in my mind that when he returned shortly to his native land he would, after assessing the situation with Nehru, Patel, and his other aides in the Congress, resume the struggle. That meant launching another civil-disobedience movement. It meant throwing India once more into turmoil. It meant imprisonment again for him, for his chief aides and for tens of thousands of followers, men and women.

But it was the only course left to him that could further undermine the British hold on his country. Some day—some day before he died—the British would again negotiate, seriously, for their own withdrawal. But only when he made them realize, by his own efforts to arouse the country against them, that they could no longer stay.

That, I gathered, was the gist of his strategy. That was what he would have to do. As it happened, history would bear him out, but he could not know that for sure in the chilly, wet autumn of 1931 when he left England for the last time.

There was an added burden to bear now. The futile wrangling of the Indians at the Round Table Conference had convinced him at last that he would have to contend not only with the British but with great segments of his fellow Indians, the Moslems above all, who did not want the British to quit India before what they conceived to be their rights were secured. I think it was this mistrust of him by so many of his fellow countrymen, which had become much more outspoken in London than it had at home, especially on the part of the Moslems and the untouchables, that hurt his feelings and discouraged him more than anything else that had happened in England. He was used to the taunts of the British, who were his adversaries. But not of the Indians, who, despite his differences with them, he regarded as his brothers.

Before leaving London, I went down to Kingsley Hall, in the East End, to bid farewell to this great man, who towered over all the others I had ever known or reported on, and who already had had such an immense impact on me. He was friendly and warm, at moments almost teasing, as he had often been in India. We laughed a little. He asked me if I were returning to India, and I said probably not—there was so much for an American to report on from Europe, which, beset by mounting unemployment and a slumping economy, seemed to me to be sliding downhill toward chaos, fascism and war.

"You think so?" Gandhi asked. "I have not had time to see that for myself."

He paused, as if to put that down for future thought. Anything which weakened England in Europe would weaken the British in India. He had noted not only privately but publicly, these last weeks in London, Britain's precarious position: the social unrest, the vast and growing unemployment, the stagnant economy, the financial and political crisis, the unbalanced budget, the slipping of the pound, and finally on September 21, three weeks before, its devaluation by more than a quarter as the National government, seized by panic, abandoned the gold standard, which for so long had been the Rock of Gibraltar on which Britain's financial leadership in the world rested. A National government of all parties, which had taken over from a Labor government on August 24, a fortnight before the Round Table Conference convened, to save the pound, was unable to save it.

As the English historian A. J. P. Taylor would later write: this was the end of an age in Britain.* Gandhi, with his political acumen, sensed it. He had been swift to take advantage of England's relative weakness after the Great War. He would not hesitate to take advantage of the rapid further deterioration now.

---

*A. J. P. Taylor: *English History: 1914–1945*, p. 297.

The background of events in London just prior to, and during, the Round Table Conference had been closely followed by Gandhi. Under pressure from the Bank of England and other financial interests, and also from his Chancellor of the Exchequer, Philip Snowden, who though once a left-wing Laborite had now become conservative in fiscal matters, Ramsay MacDonald, on August 24, a fortnight before the Indians assembled in London, had formed a "National government" to succeed his own Labor government. He had remained Prime Minister and retained Snowden, but had given four cabinet posts to the Conservatives (to equal Labor's four) and two to the Liberals. The "Government of Cooperation," as MacDonald called it, had been formed, he announced, for a specific purpose: "To deal with the national emergency." When that purpose had been achieved, he explained, "the political parties will resume their respective positions."

The vast majority of the Labor leaders in the Commons had refused to go along with their Prime Minister and had passed into the opposition, accusing MacDonald, who had

Gandhi had been a little surprised that I was not returning to India, though I realized it was of no real importance to him—it was just that he had become fond of me, or at least used to me.

"If you win independence for India in your lifetime, as you've sworn me you will," I joked, "I'll hurry back to write about it."

"Then perhaps we'll be seeing you soon," he said with a chuckle. Then more seriously: "Heaven knows we need more understanding in the West. That is one of the lessons, as I have told you, I have learned this time in London. You have helped."

"Can I write you, or even cable you, when I don't understand what you're up to back in India?" I asked.

"Certainly. Please do," he smiled. "I'll try to answer you, as I have before—even if I'm in prison."

He proved to be as good as his word. even when he was in prison.

It was the last time I saw Mahatma Gandhi.

been their leader so long, of being "a traitor." Thus the traditional politics of Britain when Gandhi arrived were falling apart.

On September 15, the day Gandhi made his historic speech to the Round Table Conference demanding complete independence for India, the headlines in the London press had been concerned with something else. "Mutiny in the Navy!" they read. This came as a shock to the British people. At Invergordon, the men of the Atlantic Fleet had refused duty to protest against pay cuts in the lower decks.

On September 19 Gandhi, like everyone else, had been surprised at an announcement by the Bank of England that its foreign credits were exhausted. Two days later the government hastily suspended the gold standard and devalued the pound.

On October 7, the day before the Round Table Conference collapsed, Parliament was dissolved and new elections called for October 27. It was obvious to Gandhi and most of the other Indians that for the rest of the month MacDonald and his cabinet members would be entirely preoccupied with getting re-elected. This, Gandhi thought, was the main reason why MacDonald adjourned the conference so hastily. India was quickly forgotten.

The Conservative Party scored an overwhelming victory in the elections, wining 473 seats to 52 for Labor, despite the latter gaining a third of the total vote. The other parties in the coalition won few seats: National Liberals 35, National Labor 13. The National government was maintained but it was now dominated by the Tories.

Gandhi, on his way home, took note of that too. The Tories would cling to British rule in India even more stubbornly than Labor.

I did keep in touch with him, however, by mail and cable, and with events in India by correspondence with other Indian leaders, and by reading the Indian and London newspapers. I cannot leave this Indian story, which constituted so important a chapter in my own journalistic career and in my life, without a summary of what happened after Gandhi left London that late autumn of 1931, though I was no longer an eyewitness.

13

It was one of the most important and exciting developments of the twentieth century, ending as it did just sixteen years later with Gandhi achieving what he had sworn to me he would achieve in his lifetime: political independence for nearly half a billion human beings on this earth. And ending too with his martyrdom, which, I think, was foreordained, or at least inevitable, for so great and saintly a man after such a momentous struggle for the freedom of his fellowmen. It was almost as if Gandhi's tumultuous life was bound to come to such an end and that his martyrdom was a part of that mysterious ordering of things on this earth that ordains that every once in a while a unique character in history be done to death for his beliefs, teachings and accomplishments. So many, not only in India and the rest of Asia but in the West, in England and America, had compared Gandhi in life to Christ. It was fitting that in a martyr's death the comparison held. Both had preached love and non-violence, and had practiced it. Both met a violent end, victims of the hatred of lesser men.

From my post in Vienna, to which I returned from London, I followed through the press and radio the Mahatma's triumphal journey through France, Switzerland and Italy on his leisurely way home. Vast crowds of French, Swiss and Italians gathered at every stopping place to hail him, but I doubt if they got his message. Tirelessly he repeated it, usually in the words he had uttered in his broadcast to America from London.

> The world is sick to death of blood-spilling. It is seeking a way out of its miseries. I flatter myself that India's unique method—non-violence—may show the world the way out from all its violent turmoil.

Perhaps it was too late. In Europe that fall the tensions between nations were increasing, hatred among the peoples was rising in the swell of intolerance and shrieking demagoguery, the storm troopers were taking to the streets to beat up and kill those who disagreed with them, businesses and banks were going under, the ranks of the unemployed were swelling, arms were piling up and there was increasing talk of war—so soon after the last terrible one. No one in depressed Europe knew the way out. Gandhi's way seemed impracticable and at any rate impossible. Violence, as a means of solving problems, was a habit too deeply ingrained in the West to admit of change now.

Gandhi stopped off in Switzerland to see Romain Rolland, who had been one of the first in the West to hail him. With this gifted French writer and pacifist, then at the height of his world fame (he had won the Nobel Prize for literature for his ten-volume novel, *Jean-Christophe*), he talked for hours on the subjects they loved: pacifism, non-violence, God.

"God is not a person," Gandhi told Rolland, who was a non-believer. "God is an eternal principle. That is why I say that Truth is God."

In Rome Gandhi saw Mussolini, saw through him at once, could find nothing to talk about and after ten minutes took his leave. As a deeply religious man, who in India had preached the message of Christ, Gandhi had looked forward to a meeting with the Pope. But His Holiness declined to see him. Nevertheless, the Mahatma insisted on seeing the Vatican, strolling through the wide aisles of St. Peter's, whose grandeur awed him, and spending an hour in the Sistine Chapel, visibly moved by the frescoes of Michelangelo. He stood long gazing at the statue of Christ on the Cross, and wept.

Gandhi arrived home three days after Christmas, landing in Bombay on December 28, 1931. To the vast multitudes which greeted him he readily confessed that his mission to London had failed.

"I have come back empty-handed," he told a huge mass meeting in Bombay. "But I have not compromised the honor of my country."

Despite the good will shown him personally in England, from the King, the Prime Minister and the Archbishop of Canterbury on down, the willingness of His Majesty's government at least to hear him out, and the repeated expression of its desire to ascertain Indian opinion about further steps toward home rule, Gandhi found on alighting on Indian soil that the viceregal government, in his absence, had instituted harsh, repressive measures over much of the country. Bengal, the United Provinces and the North-West Frontier had been placed under virtual martial law. The Viceroy was threatening to crack down on the Congress if Gandhi dared to resume the civil-disobedience movement. Jawaharlal Nehru was hauled off a train on his way to greet Gandhi in Bombay, arrested and incarcerated. Like most weak and mediocre men, Lord Willingdon was trying to show that he could be tough and bold. Britain might be in distress at home, but he would teach the Indians that its rule of India had not slackened.

Gandhi sought in vain to see the Viceroy before deciding on his course of action. The British Prime Minister and his cabinet members had talked to him almost daily. But the British Viceroy in New Delhi declined even to see him. After the courtesies he had received in London, Lord Willingdon's intransigence puzzled him. He appealed again to the Viceroy to receive him for a frank talk, as Lord Irwin had done before. Turned down again, and prodded by the Congress Working Committee to resume the civil-disobedience movement, Gandhi reluctantly agreed. "The government," he said, "has flagrantly broken the Delhi Pact . . . The nation must now respond to its challenge."

The next day, at three o'clock in the morning of January 4, 1932, Gandhi was arrested in Bombay and hauled off to prison. He who but a few weeks before had been the King-Emperor's guest for tea at Buckingham Palace in London was now, once more, His Majesty's guest in Yeravda prison in Poona, a familiar abode for him. Again the government did not risk giving him a trial. He was simply incarcerated, as he had been twenty months before, under an obscure Bombay State law of 1827—when India was still run by the East India Company—which empowered the government "for reasons of State" to imprison any individual it wished without trial for as long as it pleased. Within twenty-four hours all the members of the Congress Working Committee were also arrested and the Congress was outlawed. On the morning Gandhi was arrested, Jawaharlal Nehru was sentenced to two years at hard labor for disobeying a court order not to leave his home city of Allahabad. He had left it to greet Gandhi at Bombay on his return from Europe, but, as we have seen, was arrested before he got there.

Arrested and imprisoned within a week of returning to India, Gandhi had not had time to organize the civil-disobedience movement, as he had two years before. Within two months thirty-five-thousand of the lesser Congress leaders, men and women, had been put behind bars. This time the government gained the upper hand. The movement gradually petered out, but not before Gandhi had aroused the country, and indeed the world, with a strange fast, which almost cost him his life.

When I first heard of it in Vienna I could not believe it. On September 13, 1932, Gandhi from his prison cell in Poona announced that on the twentieth he would begin a "fast unto death" to protest the British government's providing for separate electorates for the untouchables in elections to the provincial legislatures. His announcement amazed everyone, especially his followers, since Gandhi had devoted much of his life to championing the cause of the untouchables, and considered himself to be the real leader of this afflicted class. The government's provision merely guaranteed some representation for the untouchables in the legislatures, where they could voice their demands. Without separate electorates they would have been swamped by the caste Hindus, who for centuries had denied them the most elemental civil and religious rights. I would have expected Gandhi to support this necessary safeguard for his beloved untouchables. Instead, he was going to "fast unto death" to oppose it. This baffled me. It made no sense. From Vienna I sent an urgent cable to Gandhi in Yeravda prison in Poona.

I cannot understand your willfully throwing away your leadership of Indian nationalism by starving to death, thus leaving nationalism to die when it seemed about to achieve self-government. You often said you would die for India, and yet are you not dying now for only one class of Indians and not the entire nation, which you claimed to represent?

The struggle for *Swaraj,* you told me once, is above all religious groups and that as leader of the Congress Party you represented nationalist Hindus, Moslems, Parsis, Christians, and untouchables. Are you deliberately deserting that leadership now for a religious principle which non-Hindus have no right to judge?

Within a few hours a six-hundred-word reply came back from Yeravda prison.

You should know that my politics are derived from my religion. If God has ordained my death by starvation I know that it will set the last seal upon my political leadership. But Indian nationalism will be the stronger for my sacrificial death. I am convinced that real self-government has been advanced by this penance, and if God gives me the strength to see this fast through without mind or body wavering, the advancement will be still greater. Hence every day well passed in equilibrium brings *Swaraj* nearer as it can by no other step. This preparation for death for untouchability is a veritable preparation for death for the whole of India. For me the removal of untouchability is an integral part of *Swaraj*.

Though I had not raised in my cable the question of whether Gandhi could really speak for the untouchables despite his vast labors in their behalf—and there were some in India, led by Dr. Ambedkar, the embittered leader of the pariahs, and elsewhere, who doubted that he could—he devoted a paragraph of his cabled reply to this issue.

Were I not sure that the mass opinion of the depressed classes was behind me, as distinguished from its leaders [this was a slap at Dr. Ambedkar, who had denounced him at the Round Table Conference], I could not have undertaken this fast in the manner I have done. And even among the depressed class leaders, so far as I know, the vast majority are behind me . . . You must not be startled by my presumption of claiming to know the interests of the depressed classes more than its leaders. Though I am not untouchable by birth, for the past fifty years I have been untouchable by choice.*

Gandhi said he was "not surprised" that the world did not understand the reasons for his fast. He could not explain it in full, he said, because "the laws of the jail administration have prohibited correspondence with the outside world." In addition, he explained, "the laws of decorum imposed rigorous restraint in my letter to the British government." I had not realized that he had pulled his

*The Bombay correspondent of *The Times* of London included in his dispatch of September 23 part of the exchange of cables, and it was published in the newspaper the next day. Whether he got it from Gandhi's aides or from the government I never learned.

punches in that letter, in which he had informed the MacDonald government why he was resorting to a "fast unto death."

Gandhi seemed not only a little surprised but also slightly impatient at my raising the question in the second paragraph of my query of his mixing religion with politics. After all, he had often spoken to me at length about it. Perhaps that was why he began by saying that I "should know" that his politics were derived from his religion.

He returned to the subject toward the end of his cablegram, enlarging on the talks we had in India that spring and summer in which he had explained his belief that there is only one real universal religion.

> For me, religion is one in its essence, but it has many branches and if I, in the Hindu branch, fail in my duty to the parent trunk, I am an unworthy follower of that one invisible and visible religion.

Gandhi saw his sacrifice as benefiting the whole world, and aware that his message to me would be widely read in the United States, he made a special appeal for American understanding and support.

> According to this reasoning, my sacrifice promotes the deliverance of humanity from untouchability in every shape or form, and therefore it serves all religious groups.
>
> If, then, America, which has sent me through her known and unknown sympathizers so much sympathy in my distress, now understands the inwardness of this sacrifice, I expect her to mobilize world opinion in favor of this sacrifice. Though apparently conceived to apply to a corner of this world, it is really intended to cover the whole world.

The Mahatma closed his message on a familiar theme, which was the essence of his life and his lifework, as he saw them.

Those who have at all followed my humble career, even superficially, cannot fail to observe that not a single act of my life has been done to the injury of any individual or nation. My nationalism, as my religion, is not exclusive but inclusive, and must be so consistently with the welfare of all life.

I claim no infallibility. I am conscious of having made Himalayan blunders, but I am not conscious of having made them intentionally toward any person or nation, or any life, human or subhuman.

Gandhi's reply reached me in Vienna on the evening of September 23, the fourth day of his fast.* Cabled dispatches from Poona, which I read avidly, said he had been eighty-two hours without food. He was fast losing strength. They told of frantic meetings of Dr. Ambedkar and Hindu leaders with Gandhi, who, to conserve his strength, lay stretched out on an iron cot in the prison yard under the shade of an old mango tree. Their attempt to reach an agreement on the franchise for the untouchables that would satisfy Gandhi, Dr. Ambedkar and the government had now become a race against time. Private and prison doctors who examined the Mahatma on the afternoon of the twenty-third announced that his condition had become "dangerous." Death, they said, was possible any moment. From all over India came telegrams urging the negotiators to reach an accord—to save Gandhi's life.

The next day it was achieved. Gandhi approved it and the negotiators pressed him to end his fast forthwith. To their consternation he posed a condition. He would not end his fast, he told them, until the British government in London approved the settlement. They protested that this might take days and that in the meantime he might die. But with that stubborn will of his, he persisted.

At 4 P.M. on September 26, according to the dispatches, a long telegram arrived for Gandhi from Prime Minister MacDonald

*It was the last important story I would ever file to the *Chicago Tribune*.

informing him of the government's approval. An hour later, in the presence of the doctors and the prison superintendent, Gandhi broke his fast, sipping a glass of orange juice. India—and the British government—breathed a sigh of relief.

Gandhi had been shrewder, as was the case with his Salt March two and a half years before, than even his closest followers, who had opposed the fast, at first realized. In the Poona settlement he got more for the untouchables than the government had provided. They were guaranteed 18 percent of the seats in the provincial legislatures—more than their numbers called for. And yet Gandhi had preserved his principle that there be no separate electorates; he thought they were dangerously divisive and played into the hands of the British, who wanted to keep the Indians divided and quarreling among themselves. By an ingenious method, which had the stamp of Gandhi as a shrewd lawyer, it was stipulated that though all Hindus, including untouchables, would vote in joint electorates, 18 percent of the seats would be "reserved" for the depressed classses regardless of the vote.

Gandhi got more. Hindu temples, even the most orthodox one at the holy city of Benares, were suddenly opened for the first time to the untouchables. Schools, from which they also had been barred, were made available to them. All over the country contributions were being raised among Hindus to further the education of the depressed classes.

It was a notable victory.

Over the next years the British popped Gandhi in and out of prison, releasing him twice when he embarked on twenty-one-day fasts and rearresting him. By 1935, when the Government of India Act was promulgated, he was once more free. But he was not much interested in the new constitution, which granted the provinces a small measure of self-rule. His attention was focused on the center in Delhi, from which India was governed. When he saw that the British had no intention of relinquishing any part of their power there, he decided to withdraw from politics, at least for the moment, bide his time, and devote himself to a task nearer to his heart: working to improve the lot of the hungering poor. Trudging from village to village, unmindful of the heat of the sun or the drenching of the monsoons, he called upon the peasants to take part in what he called his Constructive Program, a sort of rural socialism, a positive side to the essentially negative non-cooperation and civil-disobedience movements he had led for so long. He told the villagers that regardless of politics, even the politics of an independent India, they could in the long run achieve the goal of a decent life only by their own efforts.

I followed this venture from afar, mainly through the pages of Gandhi's weekly *Young India,* in which he reported on his activities. They were extensive. Few outside India, and not many within it, certainly not the British authorities, realized what I myself had learned from my experience with Gandhi: that he had made himself extremely knowledgeable about what was needed to rescue the impoverished peasantry from their primitive life. So it was not surprising to me to read his accounts of how he exhorted the illiterate villagers to educate their children, clean up their filthy streets and backyards, stop defecating in them and build proper latrines, purify their drinking water, do other things to improve sanitation and hygiene and thus their health, learn how to breed cattle and fertilize their fields, take up spinning and weaving to clothe themselves properly and augment their meager earnings, establish co-ops to market their produce and buy what they needed, improve their village life by taking part in the village councils, abolish *purdah* and accord women equal rights, practice toleration of other faiths, do away with untouchability, stop drinking alcohol, and, above all, discover that in themselves and in their cooperative efforts lay their salvation.

The British in Delhi and in London breathed a sigh of relief that Gandhi had withdrawn from politics to devote himself to good works. He would no longer trouble them. Indian nationalists resented Gandhi for abandoning his leadership of the struggle for independence. And both the British and many Indians concluded that Gandhi was through as a political leader. He had shot his bolt, and knew it.

Churchill, the one Englishman of stature who had refused to see Gandhi in London during the Round Table Conference, knew better. In 1935, inveighing against even the modest reforms of the new constitution for India, he cried out: "Gandhi, and all he stands for, must ultimately be grappled with, and finally crushed!" When he became the wartime Prime Minister, Churchill would try to do just that—and fail. He would ultimately triumph over Adolf Hitler, but Mohandas K. Gandhi eventually would triumph over him—and gain "all he stood for."

The coming of the second World War, in 1939, brought Gandhi once more back into politics and the struggle to free India of the British.

As in 1914, the British government simply took India into the war by proclamation without consulting the Indians. Gandhi, preoccupied though he was by his work among the villagers, had seen the war coming. In 1938, revolted by the Nazi persecution of the Jews, he had written that "if there ever could be a justifiable war in the name of and for humanity, war against Germany to prevent the wanton persecution of a whole race would be completely justified.

"But,"—and here was the catch—"I do not believe in any war."

It became painfully obvious to me as I sat in Berlin, the center of the storm, and read the above pronouncement and many others Gandhi wrote in *Young India,* that though he was sympathetic to the Jews and the Western democracies threatened by Hitler, he did not understand the nature of the Nazi totalitarian dictatorship. He had no conception of how brutally far it would go in destroying those it believed stood in the way of its domination of the world. His "advice" to the Jews to practice *Satyagraha,* to the Ethiopians to "allow themselves to be slaughtered by Mussolini's legions," and especially to the English during the worst days of the Blitz, when they were fighting for survival, to let Hitler "take possession of your beautiful island" but not of "your minds and your souls" sounded inane to those actually facing the fascist tyrants.

The men around Gandhi in the Congress, Nehru above all, took a more practical view of the war. They opposed fascist totalitarianism and saw in it, and in the imperialist designs of Japan, a threat to India. They therefore proposed, against Gandhi's strenuous opposition, to offer cooperation in the war effort if Britain granted independence to India. To Churchill, who had taken over as Prime Minister in Britain's darkest moment of the war, this was blackmail, and despite the urging of President Roosevelt, he refused to make the slightest concession to the Indian nationalists.

"I have not," he would say in a famous speech in answer to the criticisms of his intransigence about India, "become the King's First Minister in order to preside at the liquidation of the British Empire."

Only the threat of the Japanese Army to invade and overrun India from Burma softened his view, and in the spring of 1942 he sent Sir Stafford Cripps, a left-wing socialist and a friend of the Congress leaders, with whose aspirations he personally sympathized, to Delhi to make—at last—a serious offer to the Indians. Britain was prepared to grant them immediate representation in the viceregal government and full Dominion status at the war's end in return for India's all-out participation in the war. But, not surprisingly, there was a catch: Indian provinces, princely states and religious minorities could, if they wished, work out a separate settlement with the British.

Gandhi would have none of it. "You are proposing," he told Cripps, "perpetual vivisection of India." The Indian nation would be destroyed. Anyway, Gandhi had no confidence in British promises—they had been made during the first World War, he maintained, and broken. He told Cripps he considered the offer "a postdated check on a failing bank."

Though he had refused for three years to stab the British in the back by relaunching his civil-disobedience movement (he had not helped them in the war, either), his inner voice now told him, he said later, that it was time to resume the struggle with them for independence "now."

On August 8, 1942, he launched a new campaign with the slogan "Quit India!" He demanded the British clear out at once.

"I want freedom immediately," he declared, "this very night—before dawn, if it can be had."

He gave his followers a brief prayer:

"Do or die! We shall either free India or die in the attempt. We shall not live to see the perpetuation of our slavery."

These were strong words for the pacifist, non-violent Mahatma. They aroused the country, and his immediate arrest, along with all the other leaders of the Congress, provoked a storm of violence all over India. Police stations and government buildings were sacked and set on fire, railroad tracks and telegraph lines were cut, British officials were attacked, some wounded and a few killed.

Lord Linlithgow, the new Viceroy, blamed Gandhi for the violence. The Mahatma not only denied it but expressed his shock at such a charge. Letters streamed back and forth between the viceregal palace in Delhi and Gandhi's place of incarceration, which was now the old palace of the Aga Khan, not far from Yeravda prison in Poona, which the British had taken over expressly for him. Gandhi insisted that it was the Viceroy's arrest of him and his outlawing of the Congress that had provoked India into unrest. Lord Linlithgow persisted that the violence was Gandhi's responsibility.

Once again, in February 1943, in his seventy-third year, the Indian leader resorted to a twenty-one-day fast, this time, he said, to ask God's intervention in settling his "misunderstanding" with the Viceroy. Linlithgow retorted that the fast was "political blackmail." By now Prime Minister Winston Churchill was making the major decisions on India. He instructed the Viceroy to let Gandhi starve to death, if he insisted.

Preparations were discreetly made by the British authorities for his death. According to one source,* Brahman priests were hurriedly summoned to Poona to preside at the funeral services, and sandalwood for the funeral pyre was secretly stored in the nearby prison. But the aging leader, sinking a little further each day of his fast, refused to die. He survived, but barely. His health was now in a serious state. Doctors diagnosed malaria, hookworm, amoebic dysentery and acute anemia.

Another blow awaited him. On February 22, 1944, his wife, Kasturbai, who had shared his imprisonment, died in his arms in Poona. Gandhi's sorrow was perhaps deepened by doubts as to whether he had done the right thing in forbidding the doctors to save her life—she was suffering from acute bronchitis—by injections of penicillin, which had been flown by the British to Poona especially for her. Gandhi had convinced himself that the injections would be a violent act, in violation of his belief in non-violence.

His spirits were further depressed, I later learned, by the sudden appearance in prison of his wayward son, Harilal, by now a dissolute derelict in his late fifties, as Mrs. Gandhi lay dying. Harilal was drunk, reeking of whiskey, and Kasturbai, who had often begged her husband to have more compassion for their erring son, was prostrated with grief and shock. The next day she died.

It had been a long marriage, of some sixty years, and to Western eyes a rather strange one. Despite Gandhi's efforts to educate his wife, she had remained illiterate all her life, woefully ignorant of politics, to which her husband had devoted so much of his life, and of the larger world, on which he had made such an impact. I often wondered whether she even faintly comprehended Gandhi's singular way of life, the philosophy and the deeply religious grounds on which it was based. There was no intellectual communication between them, no connection between their minds. The world in

---

* Larry Collins and Dominique Lapierre: *Freedom at Midnight,* p. 75. The authors also recount that a few months later Churchill cabled the Viceroy asking why Gandhi had not died yet.

which Gandhi moved and thought and acted was far beyond her ken, as if it were another planet.

In the dozens of times I had squatted on the floor to talk with him, Kasturbai was often present, but silent. They rarely exchanged a word. Gandhi almost never addressed her, nor she him. His conversations with women took place with Sarojini Naidu, Madeline Slade and many others who had become figures in the civil-disobedience movement and personally and politically close to him. He seemed to me to like the presence of women, loved to talk to them, and did so endlessly. Mrs. Gandhi never took part.

Yet Kasturbai, to me, was a woman of considerable character. Though she realized his greatness, she did not submit meekly to her renowned husband. As Gandhi freely conceded, she spoke her mind about the matters of family life. The marriage had had its stormy periods from the beginning, when as a child bride she would leave him and take refuge with her parents, and it continued to be turbulent, one gathers from Gandhi himself, up to the time when he took his vow of *brahmacharya*—sexual abstinence—at thirty-six, after twenty-three years of marriage and five children, an act I often wondered whether she approved. In his autobiography Gandhi writes frankly, and often with humor, of their differences, at one point recounting how in South Africa, when they were twenty-eight, she tried to leave home after he had threatened to kick her out.

She had objected to his demand that she help him clean the chamber pots of one of his law clerks, who was an untouchable. She had finally forced herself to do it but Gandhi was angered because, he says, she did not do it *cheerfully*.

So I said, raising my voice: 'I will not stand this nonsense in my house!' . . .

She shouted back: 'Keep your house to yourself and let me go!' I forgot myself . . . I caught her by the hand, dragged the helpless woman to the gate . . . and proceeded to open it with the intention of pushing her out. The tears were running down her cheeks . . . and she cried: 'Have you no sense of shame? . . . Where am I to go? . . . Being your wife, you think I must put up with your cuffs and kicks? For Heaven's sake behave yourself, and shut the gate. . . .'

I . . . was really ashamed and shut the gate. If my wife could not leave me, neither could I leave her.

"We have had numerous bickerings," Gandhi wrote in 1925, looking back at his marriage, "but the end has always been peace between us. The wife, with her matchless powers of endurance, has always been the victor . . . We are tried friends . . . Let no one conclude . . . that we are by any means an ideal couple, or that there is a complete identity of ideals between us. . . . It is likely that many of my doings have not her approval even today. We never discuss them . . . Though . . . there is a wide difference between us intellectually, I have always had the feeling that ours is a life of contentment, happinesss and progress." *

Since Gandhi had put an end to a normal marital life in 1906, and Kasturbai had been unable to share in the life of his mind and spirit, as other women had done, some in India wondered what was left between them. Was it what Gandhi said he had felt?

Whatever it was—and the truth about so intimate and difficult a relationship as marriage can seldom become known to others— Gandhi was despondent over his wife's death, and this contributed to the further deterioration of his health.

It began to worry the British in London and Delhi. Except for Churchill, they did not want him to die in a British prison and further inflame the rebellious feelings of the Indian people. After the death of Mrs. Gandhi there were renewed cries in India for the Mahatma's release. Reluctantly, Churchill gave in to the pressures of his cabinet colleagues and the Viceroy and agreed that, for

* Gandhi, op. cit. pp.277–79.

political reasons, it was better for Gandhi to die out of prison than in it. It was becoming difficult enough to keep down the growing unrest in India, now that it was denuded of British troops needed elsewhere in the war.

On May 6, 1944, Gandhi walked out of a British prison for the last time in his life. He had spent almost six and a half years in them—2,089 days in India, 249 days in South Africa.

14

Independence for India came sooner than Gandhi expected, on August 15, 1947. He had achieved it, as he had boasted so often to me, in his lifetime—in his seventy-seventh year. There was not much time left, but it had proved enough.

When freedom came—this thing he had fought for so tenaciously, so skillfully, so long, and which was the crowning glory of his long life—he did not like it. He refused to take part in the ceremonies of national rejoicing that ushered it in. He was heartbroken that independence had been won at the cost of dividing India—the Moslems under the fanatical Jinnah had broken away to form the Islamic nation of Pakistan.

He was utterly crushed by the terrible bloodshed that swept India, just as self-government was won, provoked this time not by the British but by the savage quarrels of his fellow Indians. Fleeing by the millions across the new boundaries, the Moslems from India, the Hindus from Pakistan, a half million of them had been slain in cold blood before they could reach safety. Desperately and with heavy heart, and at the risk of his life, Gandhi had gone among them, into the blood-soaked streets of Calcutta and the lanes of smaller towns and villages, littered with corpses and the debris of burning buildings, and beseeched them to stop the slaughter. He had fasted twice to induce the Hindus and the Moslems to make peace. But, except for temporary truces that were quickly broken, to little avail. All his lifelong teaching and practice of non-violence, which had been so successful in the struggle against the British, had come to naught. The realization that it had failed to keep his fellow Indians from flying at one another's throats the moment they were free from the British shattered him.

At the close of World War II, in 1945, a new Labor government, which had been voted into office by the British people to replace Churchill at the very moment when the indomitable Tory leader had led them to victory over Hitler, decided that Britain could no longer hold on to India. Crippled and nearly bankrupted by the long war, which for a time it had to fight alone, until Russia and the United States were sucked in, Britain no longer had the power or the resources to keep the Indians down.

It took Clement Attlee, the Labor Prime Minister, two years to get the Indians to agree among themselves on how to take over their own country. Both the British government and the Indian leaders were immensely helped by what seemed to be a most unlikely figure: Admiral Lord Louis Mountbatten, a great-grandson of Queen Victoria, the first Empress of India; a cousin of the reigning king, George VI; a relative of Kaiser Wilhelm II, Czar Nicholas II, King Alfonso of Spain and of most of the remaining European monarchs; and son of Prince Louis of Battenberg, who as First Sea Lord had been forced out of that post when the war came in 1914 because of his German background.*

Though Louis Mountbatten turned out to be a brilliant naval officer and during the latter part of the second World War was

*The German name was quickly anglicized to Mountbatten, just as the royal family discarded their family name of Saxe-Coburg-Gotha and adopted the new one of Windsor.

named Supreme Allied Commander Southeast Asia, he had spent most of his social life with members of royalty, English and European (his closest friend had been his cousin, the Duke of Windsor), in whose narrow circles he was popular as a tall, handsome, outgoing, dashing man who loved polo, dancing and partygoing.

He had gloried, as had his cousins in the royal family and his friend, Winston Churchill, in the British Empire, especially in its brightest jewel, India, to which he had first gone as an aide-de-camp to the then Prince of Wales in 1921. There he had the time of his life in a round of parties, dances, parades, polo matches, pigsticking, and the tiger hunts and elephant rides provided by the maharajas. He saw India as Kipling saw it. He loved it.

Now, in the spring of 1947, at the behest of a Socialist Prime Minister and of the Emperor of India, he was going out to India as Viceroy. His long line of predecessors had gone out to India to rule it. He was being sent, as the last British Viceroy, to liberate it.

He brought to his unenviable task certain qualities which some had not suspected: intelligence, tact, patience (though little time was left for him), a sense of the way history was moving so inexorably, and an ability to size up the Indian leaders and to win their confidence. Once he had arrived in Delhi and quickly surveyed the chaotic situation, he determined to accomplish three objectives: honor the date set for handing India to the Indians, make the transfer of power orderly so far as the British were concerned, and salvage one thing for Britain—keep independent India within the British Commonwealth.

As a condition for accepting his job, he had forced the British government to do what it had never been able to bring itself to do: set a definite date for leaving India. On February 18, 1947, Prime Minister Attlee had read a historic declaration to the House of Commons. "His Majesty's Government," it said, "wish to make it clear that it is their definite intention to take the necessary steps to effect the transference of power into responsible Indian hands by a date not later than June 1948."

Once in Delhi, Mountbatten decided to push up that date by nine months. Displaying a mixture of tact and firmness, he quickly knocked Indian heads together. He got along splendidly with Gandhi. Though often baffled by his quirks and contradictions he realized Gandhi's greatness and his hold on the Indian people. Still, when confronted with Gandhi's intransigence, he circled around him to try to reach an understanding with his principal aides. He forged a bond of personal friendship and of mutual respect with Nehru. He established a good relationship with Patel, overcoming Patel's innate suspicion of the British. Jinnah, the embittered, unbending, fanatical Moslem leader, he found more difficult. He tried for weeks to talk Jinnah out of his demand for a Pakistan, but failed to move him.

"Either India will be divided," Jinnah told him, "or it will be destroyed—by the Moslems."

Reluctantly, Mountbatten gave in. He could see no other solution. But he could not persuade Gandhi to go along.

"You'll have to divide my body before you divide India," he warned.

The other leaders of the Congress, chiefly Nehru and Patel, proved more practical. With the bloody strife between Moslems and Hindus threatening to leave India a vast wasteland, they gave in to the new Viceroy's importuning. For the first time in their lives they broke with Gandhi. They wanted to preserve what they could of Gandhi's goal—a free, if divided, India.

For more than a quarter of a century the Congress had never questioned Gandhi's leadership, which had, after all, brought India to the threshold of independence. Now, at last, it had not only been questiond but rejected. The aging leader felt his isolation.

"I find myself alone," he told an aide. "Even Patel and Nehru think I'm wrong . . . They wonder if I have not deteriorated with age. Maybe they are right and I alone am floundering in darkness."

When, at the stroke of midnight on August 14, 1947, Prime Minister Nehru in Delhi proclaimed India independent and the celebrations began throughout the land, Gandhi, in faraway

Calcutta, slept. The next day he spent mostly in prayer. He made no public statement of any kind.

Only on his seventy-eighth birthday, six weeks later, did he give vent to his feelings. He had been, as usual, besieged by birthday greetings, but this time he was also hailed as the man who had liberated his country.

"Where do congratulations come in?" he asked. "Would it not be more appropriate to send condolences? . . . There was a time when whatever I said, the masses followed. Today, mine is a lonely voice."

Yet for half a century it had been the voice that first in South Africa and then in India had aroused the Indians to revolt against the white man's rule. He had, finally, against all the odds and in such an odd manner, won what he had set out to get. If he thought, as he said, that all his labors had come "to an inglorious end," I could not help but feel, as I tried to follow him as best one could from afar, that despite his public statements to the contrary, there must have been, there had to be, deep down, a feeling of pride that he had reached the principal goal of his long and embattled life. He had made his people free.

He had not much longer to live.

The last act in the life of this great man now began. He arrived in Delhi from Calcutta on September 9, 1947, worn out by his efforts, which included another fast, to get the Hindus and the Moslems in Bengal to stop butchering one another. Worn out; and disheartened, saddened and humiliated that all that he had lived and worked for—non-violence, tolerance, love—had obviously failed to take root among his own people.

Delhi, the ancient and modern capital, had not escaped the holocaust. Swollen by tens of thousands of Moslem refugees seeking safety in the city until they could be sent to Pakistan and by even more Sikhs and Hindus, survivors of the trek from the Punjab, where so many of their kind had been done to death by the Moslems, the city had been ravaged as Sikhs and Hindus set out to get revenge. In the week before Gandhi arrived they had slaughtered more than a thousand Moslems in a blaze of savagery such as the old capital had never seen. What little government there was in Delhi, in power less than a month since the British pulled out, was breaking down into chaos. No one, including government officials, dared to go out into the streets. The Indian police, its British officers gone, its Hindu and Moslem replacements suspicious of one another, seemed powerless to stop the massacre.

In Calcutta Gandhi had stayed with the untouchables in the filthy slums. On his arrival in Delhi he had been carried off, protesting, by Patel to the palatial home of G. D. Birla, one of India's wealthiest industrialists and a longtime follower and financial supporter of Gandhi. Patel explained to him that his life would be safer there. Birla House, with its spacious lawns and flower beds, was surrounded by a stone wall to protect it. In addition, the ample lawns within the walls afforded Gandhi a secure space in which to conduct his public evening prayer meetings.

The Mahatma was devastated by what he found in Delhi, the streets clogged with decaying corpses, whole areas burned down, the frightened Mohammedans living in camps and old mosques in fear of instant death. In Calcutta, by imploring both sides to desist from their killing and arson and by staging a fast until they did, he had been able to restore a semblance of peace and order. At first, in Delhi, no one heeded him. The burning hatred, inflamed by hideous atrocities, rapes, mutilation, murder and by a determination to revenge them, seemed beyond quenching.

So once again, and for the last time, on January 13, 1948, Gandhi began a fast, swearing he would not end it until the Moslems and the Hindus in Delhi agreed on a truce. And once again, this peculiar weapon, which he had used so often against the British, worked. Hindu, Sikh and Moslem leaders flocked to Birla House to implore him to end his fast. Day after day, as his condition worsened, they frantically hammered out the agreement Gandhi had demanded. By January 17 the life of the old man was rapidly slipping away. His doctors issued a bulletin saying he could not survive more than two or three days. The communal leaders worked all night on the draft of an agreement. The signed it the next day and Gandhi, coming out of a coma, ended his final fast. It had almost cost him his life. But it brought the end of massacre in Delhi.

There were some Hindus, however, who hoped that Gandhi would die. Fanatical members of the right-wing Hindu Mahasabha and its militant militia, the R.S.S.S. (Rashtriya Swayam Sewak Sangh), they blamed Gandhi for the partition of India and for the ensuing slaughter of Hindus by Moslems. They loathed his toleration for the followers of Allah. They accused him of betraying his own community, the Hindus.

Since he had not died, they decided to kill him. Two fanatical Brahmans from Poona would do it. They struck quickly. On January 20, 1948, two days after the end of his fast, Gandhi felt strong enough to attend evening prayer on the lawn of Birla House. Still too weak to walk, the Mahatma was carried on a chair to the platform from which he conducted the prayers. His voice was too feeble to be heard, even when amplified by a loudspeaker. Dr. Sushila Nayar, his physician and co-worker, bent down to catch his whispers and then she repeated them to the assemblage. Suddenly a bomb went off. Miraculously, no one was hurt. Gandhi calmed the crowd and continued his prayers. The conspirators had bungled their job. But their bungling was nothing compared to that of the Indian police. They caught the young man who had set off the bomb. He named his accomplices. Yet the police dawdled for days in rounding them up.

Ten days later, with the police finally closing in on them, they struck again.

January 30, 1948, was a Friday, the day of the week on which Christ, whom so many thought Gandhi resembled in life, was crucified. After his evening meal of fruit and goat's milk Gandhi left his quarters for his daily prayer meeting. He was now strong enough to walk, but as he traversed the garden he leaned on the arms of two young women aides. He was pleased to note that the police officer assigned since the bombing to stand by his side during the prayers was not there. He had protested his presence. He wanted no police protection at his prayer meetings.

As Gandhi made his way to the prayer platform, the crowd of about five hundred parted to let him through. Many bowed and some fell at his feet. One who bowed as Gandhi approached was a heavyset thirty-nine-year-old Poona Brahman by the name of Nathuram Godse. As he lifted his head he whipped out a black Beretta automatic pistol and fired three shots point-blank at Gandhi. All three bullets penetrated his chest. Crying out *"He Ram!"* ("O God!"), Gandhi collapsed to the ground, dead.

That evening Jawaharlal Nehru, heartbroken, fighting back the tears and a choking of his voice, spoke to the nation on radio. I picked up his words relayed by the BBC in London to New York.

> The light has gone out of our lives and there is darkness everywhere. Our beloved leader, . . . the father of our nation, is no more.*

In the great American metropolis, so far removed in space and in spirit from Gandhi's India, I looked out through my own tears to the wintry East River beyond the windows of my living room and I felt too that the light had gone out of my life. I too felt the darkness.

But not for long. The light that Mahatma Gandhi shed on this

---

*Just as moving to me as Nehru's eloquent words was an editorial in the *Hindustan Standard* sent to me by a friend in India. The editorial page, lined by a black border, had been left blank except for a few lines in the center.

> Gandhiji has been killed by his own people for whose redemption he lived. This second crucifixion in the history of the world has been enacted on a Friday—the same day Jesus was done to death one thousand nine hundred and fifteen years ago. Father, forgive us.

earth was too strong and penetrating to go out with his death. It will shine, I believe, for centuries to come. It will continue to illumine my own life to the end.

Two of my oldest friends and colleagues, Vincent Sheean and Edgar Snow, were standing a few feet away when they heard the fatal shots ring out. They have left memorable accounts of that tragic evening on the lawn of Birla House in New Delhi.

Jimmy Sheean had had a premonition of Gandhi's death. One day early in November 1947, he phoned me in New York and implored me to come over immediately and tell him what I knew of the Mahatma.

"Gandhi is going to die soon," he said when I arrived at his apartment. "I've got to go out to India and see him before he is gone. There is something he alone can teach me about the meaning, purpose and significance of life."

"He taught me a lot," I said.

"I know he did. You've been trying to tell me what it was for the last fifteen years."

"It seemed to bore you," I said. We had been kidding each other since our Paris days in the mid-twenties.

"Never! I just didn't get it. I wasn't ready. Now I think I am. But I have to get it from Gandhi himself."

Jimmy left New York on November 13, but as was his wont, he dawdled in Europe, Egypt and Pakistan, arriving in Delhi only on January 14, 1948, the day after Gandhi began his last fast. He had his first talk with him on January 27, a second the next day and arranged for a third conversation on Friday, the thirtieth, immediately after the prayer meeting. He described these talks and the death of Gandhi in a long dispatch to the *New York Herald-Tribune* and in a book, *Lead, Kindly Light*.

Ed Snow had first come to India from China in 1931. We had met in Simla the summer of that year and it was there that he had had his first meeting with Gandhi. But Ed's great love was China, from which he had just come and would shortly return. I gathered from our talks that summer that after China he found India rather uninteresting. He did not seem much impressed by Gandhi. During the second World War, when we met from time to time in one place or another, he would often criticize the Indian leader for not supporting the British in the war. Even afterward, when the fruits of Allied victory turned to ashes and disillusioned him, Ed would tell me that he still felt out of sympathy for the man I revered. We had many discussions of Gandhi, but I could not budge him from his disbelief.

Back in Delhi at the beginning of 1948, as a roving correspondent for *The Saturday Evening Post,* he had met Gandhi again and experienced a great awakening. Gandhi had "gently rebuked" him, he told me later, for his attacks on him, and then the Mahatma had quickly won his mind and heart. "On my last visit to him, shortly before his death," Ed would write, "I saw him as a giant."

Snow's dispatch to the *Post* on the death of Gandhi (published on March 27, 1948) is one of the classics of American journalism.

What I remember about being at Birla House the night Gandhi was killed [it began] was how much more terrible a moment it was than anyone can describe in words. Men and women did not really grieve . . . for Gandhi, who died almost instantly and who through the window over the low porch could be seen lying with a face serene and peaceful. But each man mourned for something in himself left without a friend, a personal sorrow, as if fate had seized an intimate treasure that one had always assumed would be there . . .

This small man, so full of a large love of men, extended beyond India and beyond time . . . There was a mirror in the Mahatma in which everyone could see the best in himself, and when the mirror broke, it seemed that the thing in oneself might be fled forever.

Gandhi had been murdered not only by one of "his own people," an Indian, but by one of his own religion and culture, a Hindu, and one of the highest caste. Had his assailant been a Moslem, as was first feared, India might well have been torn apart in a wild outburst of slaughter that would have destroyed it in the very first year of its liberation. Shattered as they were by Gandhi's sudden death, the Indian authorities breathed a sigh of relief when they learned the identity of the assassin. They rushed the news to All-India Radio, which had held up an announcement for several minutes. At 6 P.M. an announcer went on the air.

Mahatma Gandhi was assassinated in New Delhi at twenty minutes past five this afternoon. His assassin was a Hindu.

This was Nathuram Godse. He was seized at the scene of the crime, and eight accomplices were arrested within a few days. Their trial, in the Red Fort at Delhi, took nine months. Godse, a fanatical Hindu, a member of the extremist Hindu Mahasabha and the R.S.S.S., defended his action to the last. Gandhi, he told the court, by his support of the Moslems, had betrayed Hinduism. He was responsible for partition, and for the massacre which followed. If allowed to live he would "emasculate" the Hindu community, destroy the Hindu nation. Godse and his closest accomplice, Narayan Apte, were found guilty and sentenced to death, and, despite the appeals of Gandhi's sons and his disciples for clemency, were hanged in the courtyard of the old prison in Ambala, in East Punjab, on November 15, 1949.

Mohammed Ali Jinnah, the only foe Gandhi could not reason with, died on September 11, 1948, of tuberculosis, seven months after the Mahatma, in Karachi, his birthplace and the provisional capital of Pakistan, which by his fanatical, single-minded zeal he had created.

15

To this day, over a stretch of nearly half a century since I first talked with Gandhi in Delhi as a young man on the eve of my twenty-seventh birthday, I have pondered his life, its greatness, its meaning, and its impact on India, on the world and on me.

On the day of his death and often since, I have been reminded of the moving, simple words that Plato used to describe the martyrdom of Socrates and of how apt they were in summing up my own thoughts of Gandhi's end.

> Such was the end of our friend; concerning whom I may truly say, that of all the men of his time whom I have known, he was the wisest and justest and best.

Gandhi was that, and more than that, to me. Yet it is difficult, if not impossible, at least for me, to sum him up, his mind and personality and soul, from which he drew such inner strength and purity, difficult to understand or reconcile the strange contradictions of his life and teachings, to grasp the nature and sources of his genius. In the face of the mystery of genius perhaps all that one can say is that he witnessed it; it is a phenomenon beyond analysis.

Even Jawaharlal Nehru, perhaps the closest of all men to Gandhi, though of vastly different mold and outlook, felt this. No man, he concluded, could ever write a "real life of Gandhi unless he was as big as Gandhi." The best one could do, he thought, if one had known the Mahatma, was to set down his impressions.

There were the contradictions in the man which often baffled one, and sometimes they were disturbing to all who revered him, as when in the last years of his life, when he was in his late seventies, he took pretty young women to bed with him, explaining to his followers, who fought their skepticism because they wanted to believe, that it was not only for bodily warmth against the chill of the winter nights, but to test his ability to avoid temptation and to adhere to his vow of chastity, which he had taken when he was thirty-six, after twenty-three years of marriage and five children, and which he had insisted upon from some of his closest followers, even from those happily married. This strange episode must now be briefly recounted. Not until a great deal of evidence was in could I believe it.

True, sitting around in Gandhi's quarters in Delhi that winter and early spring of 1931, I had felt a strong sexuality in him. He had a sensual mouth, which the full, slightly protruding lower lip seemed to emphasize. In the very first meeting with Gandhi, as I have noted, I thought I detected a special empathy between him and Madeleine Slade. Kasturbai, Gandhi's wife, toothless but indomitable, seemed to feel it too. She would sit silently at one side observing them, as Miss Slade (Mirabai) ministered to her husband's needs, bringing in his lunch, brushing the flies off his face, occasionally taking dictation when his two secretaries were otherwise occupied, and often engaging him in conversation which, being in English, the wife could not understand. As she watched them, a strange sort of fascination would come over Kasturbai's strong, expressive face and then, sometimes, turn to an expression of displeasure—or so I thought—which seemed to say: "What does he see in her?" Tall, gaunt, with a pasty complexion, shaved head and severe features, Mirabai was not beautiful.*

But even aside from Mirabai, often when she was not present, I felt a certain sexual force emanating from Gandhi that pervaded the room. I was more surprised than I should have been, since he had written frankly about his problems with sex in his autobiography and in subsequent articles in *Young India*. In his search for truth, in his determination not to hide his shortcomings, he revealed that despite his vow of *brahmacharya*, his struggle to remain sexually pure had been "like walking on the sword's edge" and had lasted the rest of his life.

In the very opening pages of his autobiography he had written with brutal frankness about his early lusts and of one instance in particular that remained traumatic in his memory to the end of his life. This happened in 1885, after three years of marriage, when Gandhi and his wife were sixteen. She was, he writes, expecting a baby. His father, to whom he was very devoted, was dying, and he was spending his evenings at his bedside caring for him. But his thoughts were elsewhere.

Every night [Gandhi writes] whilst my hands were busy massaging my father's legs, my mind was hovering about the bed-room—and that too at a time when religion, medical science and commonsense alike forbade sexual intercourse. I was always glad to be relieved from my duty, and went straight to the bed-room . . .

*I could not help but note that Mirabai sometimes irritated Gandhi, not, so far as I could see, by what she did or said but by her manner and personality. They could be grating. She could not relax, as Gandhi did, and she tended to be a bit overbearing with the women around Gandhi. Occasionally he would turn on her rather sharply and more than once he had sent her away, apparently for the sake of his own peace of mind. Yet, a strong attachment remained. She haunted his dreams, he would write to her, and he felt that she "squandered" her love on him. To Louis Fischer, as he noted in his excellent biography of Gandhi, "Her bond with him was one of the remarkable platonic associations of our age. He often said to her, 'When this body is no more there will not be separation, but I shall be nearer to you. The body is a hindrance.'"—Louis Fischer: *The Life of Mahatma Gandhi*, p. 440.

Then, Gandhi recounts, "the dreadful night came."

It was 10-30 or 11 p.m. I was giving the massage. My uncle offered to relieve me. I was glad and went straight to the bed-room. My wife, poor thing, was fast asleep. . . . I woke her up.

Five or six minutes later, there was a knock on the door. A servant told young Gandhi his father was dead.

I felt deeply ashamed and miserable. I ran to my father's room. I saw that, if animal passion had not blinded me, I should have been spared the torture of separation from my father during his last moments. . . . He would have died in my arms.

The shame . . . of my carnal desire even at the critical hour of my father's death . . . is a blot I have never been able to efface or forget, . . . my devotion to my parents . . . was weighed and found unpardonably wanting because my mind was at the same moment in the grip of lust. . . . It took me long to get free from the shackles of lust, and I had to pass through many ordeals before I could overcome it.*

By his own account it took him twenty-one more years to get free. After the birth of his fifth child, he began to think of trying to achieve sexual abstinence. His "main object," he admits, "was to escape having more children." I often wondered, though I did not dare to say so when we discussed this chapter in his life, whether there was not an even more important reason: that he had had such a passionate sex life with his wife since they were thirteen that by 1906, when they were thirty-six, he was satiated with it. At any rate, he says,

We began to sleep in separate beds. I decided to retire to bed only

*Gandhi, op. cit. pp. 29–31.

after the day's work had left me completely exhausted. All these efforts did not seem to bear much fruit . . .*

He struggled on with the problem for five years. In 1906, while still in South Africa, he says he "took the plunge—the vow to observe *brahmacharya* for life." He had not, he admits, consulted his wife about it. However, he says, "she had no objection." The "elimination of carnal relationship with one's wife," Gandhi writes, "seemed then a strange thing." Still, it brought him, he adds, "pleasure and wonderment."

But "it was not an easy thing," he relates, looking back on it all twenty years later when he was fifty-six and writing his autobiography. He says he sees "every moment the necessity for eternal vigilance," lest he fall from the straight and narrow path.

He cannot always keep his thoughts pure, as *brahmacharya* calls for, and in one instance he makes a strange confession to the readers of *Young India* and of its Gujarati edition, *Harijan,* in the issue of December 26, 1936, when he was sixty-seven. During a recent night in Bombay he had dreamt of a woman, experienced an erection, and, according to his official biographer, a seminal emission. It horrified him.

My darkest hour was when I was in Bombay a few months ago. It was the hour of my temptation. Whilst I was asleep I suddenly felt as though I wanted to see a woman. Well, a man who had tried to rise superior to the instinct for nearly forty years was bound to be intensely pained when he had this frightful experience. I ultimately conquered the feeling, but I was face to face with the blackest moment of my life and if I had succumbed to it, it would have been my absolute undoing.

The chilling winter of 1946–47 in northern India appears to

*Gandhi, op. cit. p. 206.

have been the winter of Gandhi's discontent. At seventy-seven he had reached the worst crisis of his life—personal and political. He felt terribly alone. His wife, his lifelong companion, had died two years before in the prison they shared. His closest followers in the Congress, Nehru and Patel above all, were breaking away from him and agreeing with the British to accept a division of India. Beyond independence, the goal for which he had striven all his life, a unified nation in which the Hindus and the Moslems would live in brotherhood, seemed to have slipped out of his grasp. The very foundation of his life and teaching, non-violence, had been shattered by his fellow countrymen, as Hindus and Moslems from one end of the country to the other became involved in a frightful fratricide of murder, rape, mutilation and burning.

After achieving at least a truce in the great city of Calcutta by his fast and his exhortations, Gandhi had set out on foot to the district of Noakhali, a swampy region in East Bengal (now Bangladesh) formed by the Ganges and Brahmaputra rivers, where the Moslem majority had turned on the minority Hindus and begun to butcher them, pillage and burn their villages, and violate the women who survived the killing. It was while he was tramping barefoot through the marshes of Noakhali, at great risk to his life, to try to convince the Mohammedans to stop their slaughter and induce the Hindus to return to their sacked villages, that word leaked out of Gandhi's peculiar practice of having attractive young women share his bed. The explanation at first by Gandhi and by his youthful women associates was that in the cold of a winter night he would take to shivering and that he had asked them to lie with him in order to receive their bodily warmth. But on Gandhi's own word it came out that there was more to it than that. With that utter frankness which he had observed all his life he admitted publicly that he had also slept with the young women, often naked, in order to test his ability to keep his vow of *brahmacharya* and not succumb to temptation.

In the chill, damp Noakhali that winter, Gandhi's orphaned nineteen-year-old grandniece, Manu Gandhi, who had grown up in the Mahatma's household, where she was treated as a daughter, was the principal sharer of his bed. But other beautiful young women had preceded her. When the storm of criticism for his behavior broke, Gandhi took the occasion of a prayer meeting in Noakhali to reveal that his sleeping with Manu was "nothing new to me." He had been doing it for years, he said, with several young women. He had kept it a secret, he explained, because he believed the public would not understand, but he now saw that in doing so he had been untruthful and in error—a terrible blight on one who had devoted his life to seeking the truth and who had sought purity in *brahmacharya*. He denied, however, any wrongdoing with the young women involved. He resented, he said, the "whispers and innuendoes" about him. He charged one critic with "unwarranted assumptions" and added: "I do hope you will acquit me of having any lustful designs upon women or girls who have been naked with me." This critic was Nirmal Kumar Bose, a forty-year-old teacher at the University of Calcutta, who had taken a leave from his post to accompany Gandhi through Noakhali as his Bengali interpreter and guide. Bose's book about the experience, *My Days with Gandhi,* became the principal firsthand source for this episode in Gandhi's life. Erik H. Erikson, while he was doing his research in India on Gandhi, and Ved Mehta, during an identical mission, both met Bose and found him reliable. Erikson thought some of his perceptions about Gandhi's conduct were "brilliant." Mehta, in his book *Mahatma Gandhi and His Apostles,* parts of which were published in *The New Yorker* in the spring of 1976, quotes extensively from a long talk he had with Bose on the subject, and then adds a great deal of new information he obtained by looking up and talking with two other women who, beside Manu, shared Gandhi's bed and were willing to talk of it.

Bose was a great admirer of the Mahatma but, disillusioned, finally left him. He could not agree that a *brahmachari* had constantly to test his vows by taking attractive young women to bed with him. He told Gandhi that he was exploiting the women. He was leaving a mark of injury on each of them. Even after Bose left camp and returned to Calcutta the argument between the two men continued, by correspondence.

Gandhi would not agree that a *brahmachari* must not "touch a woman. What I do today," he said, "is nothing new for me."

And he proceeded to give a definition of the ancient vow, which shocked many in India, even among his own followers.

"My meaning of *brahmacharya* is this: 'One . . . who, by constant attendance upon God, has become . . . capable of lying naked with naked women, however beautiful they may be, without being in any manner whatsoever sexually excited.'"

This seemed scandalous to the orthodox and even to some who weren't. If a godly man was "capable" of such a feat, they contended, what was gained in trying it? If he was not "capable," he had no business fooling around with such temptation.

Mehta sought out two other women who were objects of Gandhi's experiment, and got them to talk about it. Neither was reticent about her part, nor did they think there was anything wrong in it.

"He [Gandhi] first asked me to sleep next to him when I was sixteen," Abha Gandhi, wife of Gandhi's grandnephew Kanu, told Mehta. Abha, like Manu, was one of Gandhi's favorites. It was on them that the Mahatma leaned as he walked to his death in the garden at Delhi.

"But two years later, in Noakhali," Abha said, "I began sleeping next to him regularly." As the experiment went on, she said, the old man asked her to take her clothes off.

"Didn't your husband mind your sleeping with Gandhi?" Mehta asked.

"He did mind," she said. He offered himself to keep Gandhi warm at night. Gandhi turned him down.

"I think he said he wanted me as much for the *brahmacharya* experiments as for the warmth. He said our sleeping together was a way of testing that he was as pure in mind as he was in body."

"What did Kanu say?"

"What could he say?"

Dr. Sushila Nayar, Gandhi's personal physician, told the interviewer a similar story.

"There was nothing special about sleeping next to Bapu [Gandhi]," she said. "But before Manu came into the picture I used to sleep with him, just as I would with my mother."

At first, she said, there was no question of it being an experiment in *brahmacharya*.

"It was just part of the nature cure. Later on, when people started asking questions about his physical contact with women—with Manu, with Abha, with me—the idea of *brahmacharya* experiments was developed."

The good doctor, though a fanatical Gandhi-ite, seemed skeptical of the Mahatma's pious explanation.

Jawaharlal Nehru found Gandhi's attitude toward sex, especially his insistence on abstinence between man and wife, "unnatural and shocking."

> . . .I think Gandhiji is absolutely wrong in this matter. His advice . . . as a general policy . . . can only lead to frustration, inhibition, neurosis, and all manner of physical and nervous ills. . . . I do not know why he is so obsessed by this problem of sex, important as it is. . . . he takes up an extreme position which seems to me most abnormal and unnatural.*

Two or three times during my conversations with Gandhi our talks drifted to the problems of sex. His views seemed to me outlandish, particularly those that a man and wife should live as brother and sister, that intercourse was a sin if indulged in for pleasure, and that sexual attraction between men and women was "unnatural." I could understand Gandhi's search for *brahmacharya*. Many a good Hindu had taken that course in order to free himself from the demands of the body and to purify his mind and spirit. But I could not understand, I told him, his requiring abstinence

*Nehru, op. cit. pp. 316–17.

from so many young married couples in his entourage. I thought it was wrong. Arbitrary. Harmful. If they wanted to live as brother and sister, let them do it purely on their own, as he had done.

Probably we shall never know the whole truth about Gandhi's "experiments" with lying naked with naked women in the evening of his life, which he regarded as a test for his sexual purity. But on the basis of what has been revealed, one is left wondering whether such experiments were necessary. If Gandhi got the shivers on wintry nights, why not reach for an extra blanket instead of a girl? If at seventy-seven or seventy-eight, he still had doubts about his ability to resist sexual temptation, why take the chance? Why go out of your way to let the Devil tempt you? And why risk possible harm to these young women, who were completely under his sway? True, it was a virtue in Gandhi to publicly admit what other men hide. But this strange chapter in the evening of his life is nevertheless confusing and a little chilling to one, at least, who was touched by this man's nobility.

Still, Mahatma Gandhi remains to me much as he did that year in India and London. Not all who came in contact with him saw him as I did: a humble seeker of the truth, who, like Christ, chose to live among the poor and work for them, and who practiced what he preached, and who even in the quicksands of politics was ruthlessly honest.

Not all in India regarded him as a saint. Lord Wavell, the next-to-last Viceroy in India (1943–47), who always struck me as unusually intelligent and sensitive for a military man, came to loathe Gandhi, whom he characterized as a "malevolent old politician . . . Shrewd, obstinate, domineering, double-tongued" with "little true saintliness in him." And as we have seen, Jinnah, who in the end became Gandhi's most embittered opponent in India, thought Gandhi "a cunning fox . . . a Hindu revivalist."

History, I believe, will take a different view, the one expressed by Einstein and Mountbatten in the quotations that head this book, by those, Nehru above all, who knew him best, and by the testimony, such as it is, I have offered in these pages.

*   *   *

So many myths have grown up around Gandhi since his death, as inevitably happens to a towering figure who is martyred, as happened to Christ, that it may have been of worth to try to set him down as he was, or at least as he seemed to be, in the flesh, to those his genius and example touched firsthand—before mythology has completely taken him over.

Gandhi was my greatest teacher, not only by what he said and wrote and did, but by the example he set. Granted that I was a poor student, what did he teach me?

I suppose the greatest single thing was to seek the Truth, to shun hypocrisy and falseness and glibness, to try to be truthful to oneself as well as to others, to be skeptical of the value of most of life's prizes, especially the material ones, to cultivate an inner strength, to be tolerant of others, of their acts and beliefs, however much they jarred you, but not tolerant of your own faults. And yet to stick to your beliefs and values when you thought they were right, never selling them out in exchange for personal gain or out of cowardice, yet seeking to let them grow and daring to change them in the light of experience and of whatever wisdom came your way.

There was much else Gandhi taught me: the value of contemplation and how to achieve it in the midst of the pressures and distractions of life in the twentieth century. Also: the necessity to discipline your mind and body and to keep your greeds and your lusts and your selfishness and your worldly ambitions in check; the obligation to love, to forgive and not to hate; to eschew violence and to understand the power of non-violence, grasping that the latter often demands more courage than the former.

Gandhi also taught me that the practice of what he called "comparative religion" was vastly more rewarding than adhering dogmatically to any one faith, either to his Hinduism or my Christianity, since he had found great truths and splendid poetry in all the principal religions. All were imperfect, he thought. We should lump them together, as he had tried to do, and take the best from each. That my own effort was not very successful was not his fault. Perhaps my reaction to a rather narrow Presbyterian upbringing dulled my capacity to be very religious. All the religions had too many myths that priests and worshipers took too literally, they had all been corrupted by the handiwork of men, some of them charlatans, and by temples and churches, for me to have the faith to base my life on them. But I owe it to Gandhi that he opened my mind and spirit to the beauty, the wisdom, and especially to the poetry and philosophy of the Hindu and Buddhist scripts, and to a lesser extent to those of the Koran, and even to a deeper understanding of Christianity, about which he often talked to me.

After that experience I could never be a true Christian, believing that salvation was reserved for those of that faith alone. If there were a Heaven, it would be open to Hindus, Buddhists, Moslems and others, who far outnumbered Christians.* Nor could I any longer believe that the Christian God was the one and only one, as I had been taught in my youth. There were others, for other faiths, just as legitimate.

Gandhi often talked to me about God, who for him was nothing more than Truth. "There is no other God than Truth," he would say, repeating what he had often written. "I worship God as Truth only, I have not yet found Him." He meant, I gathered, that he had not yet found—and would never find—Absolute Truth, which he equated with God.

Gandhi's conception of religion, as of God, transcending all faiths as it did, helped to liberate me from much of my own skepticism about it.

"What is religion," I would ask, "if not simply worship of whatever God you happened to be brought up to believe in?"

"It's more than that," he answered once. "To me, in its largest sense, religion means self-realization or knowledge of self."

*Or, as Gandhi put it once: "I do not believe that in the other world there are either Hindus, Christians, or Moslems."

If that was what it was—and I had never before heard it put that way—I could readily subscribe to it myself.

Though Gandhi got his principal religious inspiration from the Hindu *Bhagavad Gita,* on whose poetic teachings, he said, he tried to base the conduct of his life, he was strongly attracted to Christianity. At nearly every prayer meeting of his I attended, he included "Lead, Kindly Light" among the hymns to be sung. He loved it.

Gandhi, as I have mentioned, took a dim view of the Old Testament. He was offended by all the violence, the vindictiveness, the lust for revenge and punishment, the "eye for an eye" of the Old Testament fathers and sometimes, it seemed to him, of the God they worshiped. But the New Testament he loved. "Especially the Sermon on the Mount," he would say. "It goes straight to my heart. Like the *Gita!*" And he would sing out the words "'. . . whosoever shall smite thee on thy right cheek, turn to him the other also.'

"That's what I've been trying to do, and to induce others to do, all my life," he would say. "It is the basis of my creed of non-violence."

But however much he revered Jesus Christ and his teachings, he had a certain skepticism of Christianity's celebration of him as the Son of God. He was surprised but pleased when I told him that Thomas Jefferson, in a famous essay that had not gone down well with some of our pious Christians, had shown a similar skepticism. We often discussed it, and he would reiterate, more or less, what he had set down in his autobiography when he told of the efforts of his Christian friends in South Africa to convert him to Christ.

It was more than I could believe that Jesus was the only incarnate son of God, and that only he who believed in him would have everlasting life. If God could have sons, all of us were His sons. If Jesus was like God, or God Himself, then all men were like God and could be God Himself. My reason was not ready to believe literally that Jesus by his death and by his blood redeemed the sins of the world. . . .

I could accept Jesus as a martyr, an embodiment of sacrifice, and a divine teacher, but not as the most perfect man ever born. His death on the Cross was a great example to the world, but that there was anything like a mysterious or miraculous virtue in it my heart could not accept. . . . Philosophically there was nothing extraordinary in Christian principles. From the point of view of sacrifice, it seemed to me that the Hindus greatly surpassed the Christians. It was impossible for me to regard Christianity as a perfect religion or the greatest of all religions.

Thus if I could not accept Christianity either as a perfect, or the greatest religion, neither was I then convinced of Hinduism being such. Hindu defects were pressingly visible to me.*

So though Gandhi remained a devout, if unorthodox, Hindu, he reached out all his life for the Truths of other religions and made them his own, unceasingly preaching tolerance of all faiths. For this he was hated and despised by the rigidly orthodox Hindus of the Hindu Mahasabha, one of whose fanatical Brahman members, as we have seen, killed him for deserting the true faith.

I never knew a more deeply religious man nor a subtler politician, but I was puzzled by Gandhi's insistence on mixing religion and politics. If anything about me irritated this saintly man it was because I questioned this mixture. I thought religion and politics should be kept separate, as the Founding Fathers of our American Republic had had the wisdom to do. Indeed, I ventured to argue that it was Gandhi's inculcating so much Hindu religion in his Indian politics that had kept the majority of Moslems out of his nationalist movement. He would gently rebuke me and contend, as he had in the next-to-last page of his autobiography when he summed up the purpose of his life, that "those who say

*Gandhi, op. cit. pp. 136–37.

that religion has nothing to do with politics do not know what religion means."

There was a little of that rebuke, still, in the cable he sent me in 1932 during his fast in Yeravda prison. "You should know," he began, "that my politics are derived from my religion"—as if to say: "*You*, of all people, should know, since I imparted my views on the subject to you often and at length."

Once in Delhi, while we were again discussing the problem, he rather impatiently—or perhaps it was despairingly—referred me to a piece he had written on the matter in *Young India* entitled "Neither a Saint Nor a Politician."

> A critic tries to see in me a politician, whereas he expected me to be a saint.

After disavowing any pretensions to sainthood, Gandhi continues:

> But though by disclaiming sainthood I disappoint the critic's expectations, I would have him give up his regrets by answering him that the politician in me has never dominated a single decision of mine, and if I seem to take part in politics, it is only because politics encircle us today like the coil of a snake from which one cannot get out, no matter how much one tries . . . Quite selfishly, as I wish to live in peace in the midst of a bellowing howling around me, I have been experimenting with myself and my friends by introducing religion into politics.

He did it all his life. It seemed to many a mistake. But I believe now it was the only way he could arouse the masses, at least the Hindu masses of India, which formed the great majority. They were too ignorant, too downtrodden, too devout in their religion to be awakened by a mere politician. But millenniums of adhering through thick and thin to Hinduism and its way of life had prepared them to follow a great religious leader, especially a saintly one who lived among them in their poverty and rags as one of them. Once again Gandhi had sensed what no other politician, not even Nehru, had faintly grasped. The British never understood it either. But they resented it. Mixing religion with politics was not playing cricket.

I count the days with Gandhi the most fruitful of my life. No other experience was as inspiring and as meaningful and as lasting. No other so shook me out of the rut of banal existence and opened my ordinary mind and spirit, rooted in the materialist, capitalist West as they were, to some conception of the meaning of life on this perplexing earth. No other so sustained me through the upheavals and vicissitudes that I lived through in the years after I left India.

For just ahead, when I returned to my beat in Europe, lay the inexplicable faltering and decline of the Western democracies, the rise of Hitler and the flowering of barbaric Nazi Germany in my years in Berlin, the ordeal of the Second World War, which the Nazi dictator launched in 1939 and nearly won, his cold-blooded extermination of six million Jews in the ovens of the extermination camps, which he accomplished with the willing help of so many Germans; and then, after the war, at home in America the mindlessness of the McCarthy witch-hunting time, in which so many god-fearing Americans participated, as they did in the lies that afflicted us with the war in Vietnam and the six years of Nixon, elected the second time, in 1972, by such an overwhelming majority of our good citizens—all this intertwined for forty years with the ups and downs of my personal and professional life.

What I had got from Gandhi helped me to survive. It showed the way to the development of an inner life, which over that considerable time became ingrained enough, and strong and sufficient enough, to ward off all of the assaults from the outside.

I have tried to put down, however inadequately, what I got from him. The whole wide world got a lot from him too. His impact on it may turn out to be as great and as lasting as that of Christ and

Buddha, as many of us who crossed his path, including the last British Viceroy of India, believe.

The example of his life, like theirs, his search for Truth, as they sought Truth, his humility, his selflessness, which was akin to theirs, his granite integrity, and what he taught and practiced and accomplished were bound to leave an indelible imprint on this earth. *Satyagraha,* his supreme achievement, taught us all that there was a greater power in life than force, which seemed to have ruled the planet since men first sprouted on it. That power lay in the spirit, in Truth and love, in non-violent action.

For those of us who glimpsed, however briefly, Gandhi's use of it, who had the luck, for however short a time, to be in his radiant presence and to feel his greatness—and not many of us are still alive, as I write—it was an experience that enriched and deepened our lives as no other did.

I am grateful that fate took me to him.

Index

Women
  in civil-disobedience movement, 16, 35-36, 42, 43, 81
  equal rights for, 131
  treatment of, 210
Working Committee. *See* Indian National Congress, Working Committee

World War I, 71
World War II, 211, 244

Yeravda prison, 15, 204, 213, 243
Young India, 24, 83, 84, 117, 144, 153, 210, 211, 233, 243
Youth, Gandhi's appeal to, 68-69